Carnegie Commission on Higher Education
Sponsored Research Studies

EDUCATION FOR THE PROFESSIONS OF
MEDICINE, LAW, THEOLOGY, AND SOCIAL
WELFARE
*Everett C. Hughes, Barrie Thorne, Agostino
DeBaggis, Arnold Gurin, and David Williams*

THE FUTURE OF HIGHER EDUCATION:
SOME SPECULATIONS AND SUGGESTIONS
Alexander M. Mood

CONTENT AND CONTEXT:
ESSAYS ON COLLEGE EDUCATION
Carl Kaysen (ed.)

THE RISE OF THE ARTS ON THE AMERICAN
CAMPUS
Jack Morrison

THE UNIVERSITY AND THE CITY:
EIGHT CASES OF INVOLVEMENT
*George Nash, Dan Waldorf, and Robert E.
Price*

THE BEGINNING OF THE FUTURE:
A HISTORICAL APPROACH TO GRADUATE
EDUCATION IN THE ARTS AND SCIENCES
Richard J. Storr

ACADEMIC TRANSFORMATION:
SEVENTEEN INSTITUTIONS UNDER PRESSURE
David Riesman and Verne A. Stadtman (eds.)

THE UNIVERSITY AS AN ORGANIZATION
James A. Perkins (ed.)

NEW DIRECTIONS IN LEGAL EDUCATION
*Herbert L. Packer and Thomas Ehrlich
abridged and unabridged editions*

WHERE COLLEGES ARE AND WHO ATTENDS:
EFFECTS OF ACCESSIBILITY ON COLLEGE
ATTENDANCE
*C. Arnold Anderson, Mary Jean Bowman, and
Vincent Tinto*

THE EMERGING TECHNOLOGY:
INSTRUCTIONAL USE OF THE COMPUTER IN
HIGHER EDUCATION
Roger Levien

A STATISTICAL PORTRAIT OF HIGHER
EDUCATION
Seymour E. Harris

THE HOME OF SCIENCE:
THE ROLE OF THE UNIVERSITY
Dael Wolfle

EDUCATION AND EVANGELISM:
A PROFILE OF PROTESTANT COLLEGES
C. Robert Pace

PROFESSIONAL EDUCATION:
SOME NEW DIRECTIONS
Edgar H. Schein

THE NONPROFIT RESEARCH INSTITUTE:
ITS ORIGIN, OPERATION, PROBLEMS, AND
PROSPECTS
Harold Orlans

THE INVISIBLE COLLEGES:
A PROFILE OF SMALL, PRIVATE COLLEGES
WITH LIMITED RESOURCES
Alexander W. Astin and Calvin B. T. Lee

A DEGREE AND WHAT ELSE?:
CORRELATES AND CONSEQUENCES OF A
COLLEGE EDUCATION
*Stephen B. Withey, Jo Anne Coble, Gerald
Gurin, John P. Robinson, Burkhard Strumpel,
Elizabeth Keogh Taylor, and Arthur C. Wolfe*

THE MULTICAMPUS UNIVERSITY:
A STUDY OF ACADEMIC GOVERNANCE
Eugene C. Lee and Frank M. Bowen

INSTITUTIONS IN TRANSITION:
A PROFILE OF CHANGE IN HIGHER
EDUCATION
(INCORPORATING THE 1970 STATISTICAL
REPORT)
Harold L. Hodgkinson

EFFICIENCY IN LIBERAL EDUCATION:
A STUDY OF COMPARATIVE INSTRUCTIONAL
COSTS FOR DIFFERENT WAYS OF ORGANIZ-
ING TEACHING-LEARNING IN A LIBERAL ARTS
COLLEGE
Howard R. Bowen and Gordon K. Douglass

CREDIT FOR COLLEGE:
PUBLIC POLICY FOR STUDENT LOANS
Robert W. Hartman

MODELS AND MAVERICKS:
A PROFILE OF PRIVATE LIBERAL ARTS
COLLEGES
Morris T. Keeton

BETWEEN TWO WORLDS:
A PROFILE OF NEGRO HIGHER EDUCATION
Frank Bowles and Frank A. DeCosta

BREAKING THE ACCESS BARRIERS:
A PROFILE OF TWO-YEAR COLLEGES
Leland L. Medsker and Dale Tillery

ANY PERSON, ANY STUDY:
AN ESSAY ON HIGHER EDUCATION IN THE
UNITED STATES
Eric Ashby

THE NEW DEPRESSION IN HIGHER
EDUCATION:
A STUDY OF FINANCIAL CONDITIONS AT 41
COLLEGES AND UNIVERSITIES
Earl F. Cheit

FINANCING MEDICAL EDUCATION:
AN ANALYSIS OF ALTERNATIVE POLICIES
AND MECHANISMS
Rashi Fein and Gerald I. Weber

HIGHER EDUCATION IN NINE COUNTRIES:
A COMPARATIVE STUDY OF COLLEGES AND
UNIVERSITIES ABROAD
*Barbara B. Burn, Philip G. Altbach, Clark Kerr,
and James A. Perkins*

BRIDGES TO UNDERSTANDING:
INTERNATIONAL PROGRAMS OF AMERICAN
COLLEGES AND UNIVERSITIES
Irwin T. Sanders and Jennifer C. Ward

GRADUATE AND PROFESSIONAL EDUCATION,
1980:
A SURVEY OF INSTITUTIONAL PLANS
Lewis B. Mayhew

THE AMERICAN COLLEGE AND AMERICAN
CULTURE:
SOCIALIZATION AS A FUNCTION OF HIGHER
EDUCATION
Oscar Handlin and Mary F. Handlin

RECENT ALUMNI AND HIGHER EDUCATION:
A SURVEY OF COLLEGE GRADUATES
Joe L. Spaeth and Andrew M. Greeley

CHANGE IN EDUCATIONAL POLICY:
SELF-STUDIES IN SELECTED COLLEGES AND
UNIVERSITIES
Dwight R. Ladd

STATE OFFICIALS AND HIGHER EDUCATION:
A SURVEY OF THE OPINIONS AND
EXPECTATIONS OF POLICY MAKERS IN NINE
STATES
Heinz Eulau and Harold Quinley

ACADEMIC DEGREE STRUCTURES:
INNOVATIVE APPROACHES
PRINCIPLES OF REFORM IN DEGREE
STRUCTURES IN THE UNITED STATES
Stephen H. Spurr

COLLEGES OF THE FORGOTTEN AMERICANS:
A PROFILE OF STATE COLLEGES AND
REGIONAL UNIVERSITIES
E. Alden Dunham

FROM BACKWATER TO MAINSTREAM:
A PROFILE OF CATHOLIC HIGHER
EDUCATION
Andrew M. Greeley

THE ECONOMICS OF THE MAJOR PRIVATE
UNIVERSITIES
William G. Bowen
*(Out of print, but available from University
Microfilms.)*

THE FINANCE OF HIGHER EDUCATION
Howard R. Bowen
*(Out of print, but available from University
Microfilms.)*

ALTERNATIVE METHODS OF FEDERAL
FUNDING FOR HIGHER EDUCATION
Ron Wolk
*(Out of print, but available from University
Microfilms.)*

INVENTORY OF CURRENT RESEARCH ON
HIGHER EDUCATION 1968
Dale M. Heckman and Warren Bryan Martin
*(Out of print, but available from University
Microfilms.)*

*The following technical reports are available from the Carnegie Commission on Higher Education, 2150
Shattuck Avenue, Berkeley, California 94704.*

RESOURCE USE IN HIGHER EDUCATION:
TRENDS IN OUTPUT AND INPUTS, 1930–1967
June O'Neill

TRENDS AND PROJECTIONS OF PHYSICIANS
IN THE UNITED STATES 1967–2002
Mark S. Blumberg

MAY 1970:
THE CAMPUS AFTERMATH OF CAMBODIA
AND KENT STATE
Richard E. Peterson and John A. Bilorusky

MENTAL ABILITY AND HIGHER EDUCATIONAL
ATTAINMENT IN THE 20TH CENTURY
Paul Taubman and Terence Wales

AMERICAN COLLEGE AND UNIVERSITY
ENROLLMENT TRENDS IN 1971
Richard E. Peterson

PAPERS ON EFFICIENCY IN THE
MANAGEMENT OF HIGHER EDUCATION
*Alexander M. Mood, Colin Bell,
Lawrence Bogard, Helen Brownlee,
and Joseph McCloskey*

AN INVENTORY OF ACADEMIC INNOVATION
AND REFORM
Ann Heiss

ESTIMATING THE RETURNS TO EDUCATION:
A DISAGGREGATED APPROACH
Richard S. Eckaus

SOURCES OF FUNDS TO COLLEGES AND
UNIVERSITIES
June O'Neill

NEW DEPRESSION IN HIGHER
EDUCATION—TWO YEARS LATER
Earl F. Cheit

*The following reprints are available from the Carnegie Commission on Higher Education, 2150 Shattuck
Avenue, Berkeley, California 94704.*

ACCELERATED PROGRAMS OF MEDICAL EDUCATION, *by Mark S. Blumberg, reprinted from*
JOURNAL OF MEDICAL EDUCATION, *vol. 46, no. 8, August 1971.**

SCIENTIFIC MANPOWER FOR 1970–1985, *by Allan M. Cartter, reprinted from* SCIENCE, *vol.
172, no. 3979, pp. 132–140, April 9, 1971.*

A NEW METHOD OF MEASURING STATES' HIGHER EDUCATION BURDEN, *by Neil Timm, reprinted
from* THE JOURNAL OF HIGHER EDUCATION, *vol. 42, no. 1, pp. 27–33, January 1971.**

REGENT WATCHING, *by Earl F. Cheit, reprinted from* AGB REPORTS, *vol. 13, no. 6, pp. 4–13,
March 1971.*

COLLEGE GENERATIONS—FROM THE 1930s TO THE 1960s *by Seymour M. Lipset and Everett
C. Ladd, Jr., reprinted from* THE PUBLIC INTEREST, *no. 25, Summer 1971.*

AMERICAN SOCIAL SCIENTISTS AND THE GROWTH OF CAMPUS POLITICAL ACTIVISM IN THE
1960s, *by Everett C. Ladd, Jr., and Seymour M. Lipset, reprinted from* SOCIAL SCIENCES
INFORMATION, *vol. 10, no. 2, April 1971.*

THE POLITICS OF AMERICAN POLITICAL SCIENTISTS, by Everett C. Ladd, Jr., and Seymour M. Lipset, reprinted from PS, vol. 4, no. 2, Spring 1971.*

THE DIVIDED PROFESSORIATE, by Seymour M. Lipset and Everett C. Ladd, Jr., reprinted from CHANGE, vol. 3, no. 3, pp. 54–60, May 1971.*

JEWISH ACADEMICS IN THE UNITED STATES: THEIR ACHIEVEMENTS, CULTURE AND POLITICS, by Seymour M. Lipset and Everett C. Ladd, Jr., reprinted from AMERICAN JEWISH YEAR BOOK, 1971.

THE UNHOLY ALLIANCE AGAINST THE CAMPUS, by Kenneth Keniston and Michael Lerner, reprinted from NEW YORK TIMES MAGAZINE, November 8, 1970 .

PRECARIOUS PROFESSORS: NEW PATTERNS OF REPRESENTATION, by Joseph W. Garbarino, reprinted from INDUSTRIAL RELATIONS, vol. 10, no. 1, February 1971.*

. . . AND WHAT PROFESSORS THINK: ABOUT STUDENT PROTEST AND MANNERS, MORALS, POLITICS, AND CHAOS ON THE CAMPUS, by Seymour Martin Lipset and Everett C. Ladd, Jr., reprinted from PSYCHOLOGY TODAY, November 1970.*

DEMAND AND SUPPLY IN U.S. HIGHER EDUCATION: A PROGRESS REPORT, by Roy Radner and Leonard S. Miller, reprinted from AMERICAN ECONOMIC REVIEW, May 1970.*

RESOURCES FOR HIGHER EDUCATION: AN ECONOMIST'S VIEW, by Theodore W. Schultz, reprinted from JOURNAL OF POLITICAL ECONOMY, vol. 76, no. 3, University of Chicago, May/June 1968.*

INDUSTRIAL RELATIONS AND UNIVERSITY RELATIONS, by Clark Kerr, reprinted from PROCEEDINGS OF THE 21ST ANNUAL WINTER MEETING OF THE INDUSTRIAL RELATIONS RESEARCH ASSOCIATION, pp. 15–25.*

NEW CHALLENGES TO THE COLLEGE AND UNIVERSITY, by Clark Kerr, reprinted from Kermit Gordon (ed.), AGENDA FOR THE NATION, The Brookings Institution, Washington, D.C., 1968.*

PRESIDENTIAL DISCONTENT, by Clark Kerr, reprinted from David C. Nichols (ed.), PERSPECTIVES ON CAMPUS TENSIONS: PAPERS PREPARED FOR THE SPECIAL COMMITTEE ON CAMPUS TENSIONS, American Council on Education, Washington, D.C., September 1970.*

STUDENT PROTEST—AN INSTITUTIONAL AND NATIONAL PROFILE, by Harold Hodgkinson, reprinted from THE RECORD, vol. 71, no. 4, May 1970.*

WHAT'S BUGGING THE STUDENTS?, by Kenneth Keniston, reprinted from EDUCATIONAL RECORD, American Council on Education, Washington, D.C., Spring 1970.*

THE POLITICS OF ACADEMIA, by Seymour Martin Lipset, reprinted from David C. Nichols (ed.), PERSPECTIVES ON CAMPUS TENSIONS: PAPERS PREPARED FOR THE SPECIAL COMMITTEE ON CAMPUS TENSIONS, American Council on Education, Washington, D.C., September 1970.*

INTERNATIONAL PROGRAMS OF U.S. COLLEGES AND UNIVERSITIES: PRIORITIES FOR THE SEVEN-TIES, *by James A. Perkins, reprinted by permission of the International Council for Educational Development, Occasional Paper no. 1, July 1971.*

FACULTY UNIONISM: FROM THEORY TO PRACTICE, *by Joseph W. Garbarino, reprinted from* INDUSTRIAL RELATIONS, *vol. 11, no. 1, pp. 1–17, February 1972.*

MORE FOR LESS: HIGHER EDUCATION'S NEW PRIORITY, *by Virginia B. Smith, reprinted from* UNIVERSAL HIGHER EDUCATION: COSTS AND BENEFITS, *American Council on Education, Washington, D.C., 1971.*

ACADEMIA AND POLITICS IN AMERICA, *by Seymour M. Lipset, reprinted from Thomas J. Nossiter (ed.),* IMAGINATION AND PRECISION IN THE SOCIAL SCIENCES, *pp. 211–289, Faber and Faber, London, 1972.*

POLITICS OF ACADEMIC NATURAL SCIENTISTS AND ENGINEERS, *by Everett C. Ladd, Jr., and Seymour M. Lipset, reprinted from* SCIENCE, *vol. 176, no. 4039, pp. 1091–1100, June 9, 1972.*

THE INTELLECTUAL AS CRITIC AND REBEL: WITH SPECIAL REFERENCE TO THE UNITED STATES AND THE SOVIET UNION, *by Seymour M. Lipset and Richard B. Dobson, reprinted from* DAEDALUS, *vol. 101, no. 3, pp. 137–198, Summer 1972.*

COMING OF MIDDLE AGE IN HIGHER EDUCATION, *by Earl F. Cheit, address delivered to American Association of State Colleges and Universities and National Association of State Universities and Land-Grant Colleges, Washington, D.C., Nov. 13, 1972.*

THE NATURE AND ORIGINS OF THE CARNEGIE COMMISSION ON HIGHER EDUCATION, by Alan Pifer, *reprinted by permission of The Carnegie Foundation for the Advancement of Teaching, speech delivered to the Pennsylvania Association of Colleges and Universities, Oct. 16, 1972.*

THE DISTRIBUTION OF ACADEMIC TENURE IN AMERICAN HIGHER EDUCATION, *by Martin Trow, reprinted from* THE TENURE DEBATE, *Bardwell Smith (ed.), Jossey-Bass, San Francisco, 1972.*

THE POLITICS OF AMERICAN SOCIOLOGISTS, *by Seymour M. Lipset, and Everett C. Ladd, Jr., reprinted from* THE AMERICAN JOURNAL OF SOCIOLOGY, *vol. 78, no. 1, July 1972.*

*The Commission's stock of this reprint has been exhausted.

Education for the
Professions of
Medicine, Law,
Theology,
and Social Welfare

Education for the Professions of Medicine, Law, Theology, and Social Welfare

Chapters on Medicine, Law, and Theology by

Everett C. Hughes
Professor of Sociology,
Boston College

Barrie Thorne
Assistant Professor of Sociology,
Michigan State University

Agostino M. DeBaggis
Associate Director for Community Services,
West-Ros-Park Mental Health Center,
Hyde Park, Massachusetts

and a chapter on Social Welfare by

Arnold Gurin
Dean,
The Florence Heller Graduate School
for Advanced Studies in Social Welfare,
Brandeis University

David Williams
Social Work Consultant,
Office of Research and Planning,
University of Maine

A Report Prepared for
The Carnegie Commission on Higher Education

MC GRAW-HILL BOOK COMPANY

New York   St. Louis   San Francisco   Düsseldorf
London   Sydney   Toronto   Mexico   Panama
Johannesburg   Kuala Lumpur   Montreal
New Delhi   Rio de Janeiro   Singapore

The Carnegie Commission on Higher Education,
2150 Shattuck Avenue, Berkeley, California 94704,
has sponsored preparation of this profile as a
part of a continuing effort to obtain and present
significant information for public discussion.
The views expressed are those of the authors.

EDUCATION FOR THE PROFESSIONS OF MEDICINE,
LAW, THEOLOGY, AND SOCIAL WELFARE

Library of Congress Cataloging in Publication Data
Main entry under title.

Education for the professions of medicine, law, theology,
and social welfare.

"A report prepared for the Carnegie Commission on
Higher Education."
1. Professional education—History.   I.   Hughes,
Everett Cherrington, date   II.   Carnegie
Commission on Higher Education.
LC1059.E38   378'.01'3   73-6591
ISBN 0-07-010065-9

1 2 3 4 5 6 7 8 9 M A M M 7 9 8 7 6 5 4 3

Contents

Foreword

In recent decades, the increase in the numbers of professionals as a proportion of the labor force has exceeded that of all other categories except that of clerical workers. And more and more students expect professional education to prepare them for their life work. Because of this growth of professional education, this study by Everett Hughes and his colleagues is both timely and of great importance. They trace the history of the ancient professions of medicine, law, and theology, and the newer profession of social work, as they each have struggled with competing occupations and crafts, as they each have secured greater legitimacy for themselves in the university, and as they each have sought to define professional territories and bring about uniformity in practice and among practitioners. These trends set the stage for the expansion of professional education and for the diversification of its mission to meet the needs of new and changing clienteles. These thorough and balanced essays provide a useful and greatly needed introduction to the complex and highly relevant issues facing professional education in the 1970s.

The Carnegie Commission appreciates the thoughtful and thorough-going analysis that Everett Hughes, in his characteristic way, has provided. Few, if any, persons have studied the professions in American society longer, and in more depth and with more insight than Everett Hughes. He and his colleagues have rendered a highly valuable service in illuminating this important aspect of higher education and of American life.

Clark Kerr

Chairman
Carnegie Commission
on Higher Education

March 1973

Preface

Four colleagues and I have produced profiles of education for four professions, at the request of Clark Kerr, chairman of the Carnegie Commission on Higher Education. The original request was that we look at education for the ancient professions of medicine, law, and theology. Later we were asked to do profiles of some modern professions; we accepted the assignment for one — social welfare. The profiles appear as the chapters of this volume, each devoted to one of the professions.

A profile is the form of some object as seen from a certain position or perspective against the light. This is a good metaphor for what we did. Two colleagues, Barrie Thorne and Agostino DeBaggis, joined me at the beginning. The three of us met regularly for some time to prepare a guide to what we considered to be the problems which would turn up in studying these professions, and indeed, any profession. We also started at once to gather material, through visits to professional schools, interviews, and reading. Our outline turned out to be equally applicable to our three professions. Later, when we asked Dean Arnold Gurin to undertake a study of education for professional social welfare work, the outline seemed to suit this as well. We believe that while we have attended to the peculiarities of education for each of these professions as they occur now, we have done it in rather a generic way.

Any human enterprise meets certain contingencies in the course of its operation. These contingencies are combinations of circumstances. All enterprises which educate people for professions meet characteristic contingencies. All require candidates to make a crucial decision to enter training and attempt to have them continue and complete it. Sometimes a profession is flooded with applicants; sometimes applicants are scarce, as for theology just now. A profession cultivates certain beliefs and sentiments about the human or natural phenomena that its members try to manage in the course of their work. If the public, or the profession, or both, lose their faith—in science, in God, in the Creed, in the rights of man—problems follow for the profession and its educational establishment. The public "buys" professional education and professional services, making choices in sometimes very indirect ways. A new invention may make or destroy a profession, or a specialty within it; at least, it may make a whole generation obsolete before its time. We have not tried to make a thorough and systematic layout of all the contingencies—combinations of circumstances—that may arise in education for our four professions; but perhaps our way of approaching and describing what we have seen will help open the minds of students of our educational systems to this way of looking at professional education.

One may ask what skills we brought to our task. Together with my students, I have studied a number of professions and of occupations seeking professional standing. We looked at them with a sociological eye, working out a set of dimensions for comparing them. A first principle of such study is to respect all occupations but to bow down to none. One learns that something that happens in one of them probably occurs in some measure and in some form in most or all.

Barrie Thorne, my full-time colleague throughout the study, came to it directly from work for her degree in sociology. She has been an ardent participant in various social movements of young people who do not like the war, the draft, and other things related to them. In the course of the study she turned the corner from under 30. A keen social observer, she devoted two full years to the study of education in medicine and law. She covered many states, many schools, and met people of all ranks and of all opinions. She knows the movements and conflicts in legal and medical education well. It is not her intention to continue the study of professions, but rather to study social change and collective behavior in general.

Agostino DeBaggis brought to the study some inside knowledge of theological education and a background of sociological study. He and I together wrote the theology chapter. It is theology the profession, not Thomas Aquinas' "queen of the sciences," that we have written about.

Arnold Gurin and David Williams, who did the chapter on social welfare, are in a different position from the rest of us. Gurin is dean of the Florence Heller Graduate School for Advanced Studies in Social Welfare at Brandeis University. He has had long experience as a teacher, as a planner of social work curricula, and as a writer on social work education. He engaged David Williams, also a social work educator, to go to the field and gather data on current problems and trends. They saw our general outline, but proceeded on their own lines. Those lines fit very well with those of the outline; they wrote with inside knowledge but with a certain detachment.

A large number of people gave us time, interest, facts, and ideas. We thank them most heartily. A number of authors, editors, and publishers have given us permission to reprint brief selections which are relevant. We thank them also.

Shirley Urban has managed us, the documents, and the typewriter most efficiently. Bertha Shelkan has seen the manuscript through the long process of editing and proofreading. Blessings be upon them. Howard London, a younger colleague, with the eye but not the degree, has helped greatly.

Everett C. Hughes

*Education for the
Professions of
Medicine, Law,
Theology,
and Social Welfare*

1. *Introduction*

by Everett C. Hughes

Profession has for some centuries designated "the occupation which one professes to be skilled in and to follow," and specifically "the three learned professions of divinity, law and medicine" (*Shorter Oxford English Dictionary,* 1936, p. 1593). These three professions were learned in the Christian universities of Europe from the Middle Ages on. In fact, the universities were schools where young men learned to profess Christian learning and to apply it in these three fields.

The road into the closed and sacred precincts of these three ancient professions, and the newer and not-so-closed domain of professional social welfare work, now leads by way of the American four-year college into and through special schools attached to universities. This particular sequence of study, and the present length (four years of college plus some years of professional school), is, however, a product of recent decades even in the ancient professions; it is already being modified. Of newer professions — and there are many — social welfare work has been one of the more successful in its effort to require its aspirants to go to college for four years and to obtain a bachelor of arts degree before being admitted to professional study. It is the modern professional form of activities that were long included in the duties of the leaders of Christian (and Jewish) communities.

In the chapters that follow we consider the current problems of the three ancient professions and of one of the newer ones. The problems are those of a major feature of higher education — its place in preparing people for the professions. Professions, be it noted, may be learned (with that prestigious pronounced last syllable), but they are also practiced. The relation of practice to other aspects of learning is a perennial problem. That it is a major problem is clear if one notes that probably more than half of the present cohort of young Americans will go to school after high school, and that they will expect that schooling to prepare them—female and male, rich and poor—to enter the labor force (Harris, 1972, pp. 411–423). They expect higher schooling to give them a profession in the broad sense of an occupation they can profess and follow; an increasing proportion expect to continue in school until they are qualified for a profession in the narrower sense common in English speaking countries, the sense used by the U.S. Census and the Department of Labor. By 1969, 14 percent of employed Americans worked at professions. As a proportion of the labor force their increase in recent decades has been greater than any other category, except the general class of clerical workers (Wolfbein, 1971, p. 46).

All occupations which are called professions in English are entered in the same way—by a long period of formal schooling. The number of years of schooling varies, but the sequence is fixed: high school (standard four years), college (varying from none to four years), professional study (varying from one to four years). During or after completing the standard sequence required for admission to the profession, the candidate may be required or may choose to engage in supervised practice; he may also study for specialized work and for certification as a specialist. This is the fixed order of American professional education; the length of the stages varies.

Medicine has set and, with few exceptions, maintains the standard of four years of college followed by four years of professional study and at least one year of supervised practice, called internship. Law and theology make seven years after high school (four of college, plus three of professional school) the respectable, accredited minimum. Social work has striven to make it six, but has had to make concessions to candidates and to schools that do not meet the standard.

It is part of the American ideology that the longer one has to go to school for a profession, the higher that profession's standing. Medicine takes highest honors, and with it, the highest median income of its practitioners. In law the sky is the limit; the bottom is a morass. Theology of the accredited sort gives prestige, but not necessarily a secure or high income. Divinity, once the queen of the professions, is in a parlous state. The more respectable, accredited schools are having to merge to survive, and the leading denominations—including the Roman Catholic—are losing many of their clergy and are not attracting as many seminarians as once they did. Some of the so-called Bible sects, which look upon accredited theology with disdain, are founding unaccredited schools. In this country of separation of church and state, anyone may start a school of religion provided that he can find followers. The graduates need no license to practice except the right to marry couples who have themselves received license from a state to be married.

The length and, in large part, the quality of professional education in the United States are determined, not by law, but by voluntary professional associations, specialty bodies, and associations of professional schools. The movement for accreditation has been generally led by people devoted to the raising of standards of education and practice, although there is often some orthodoxy and rigidity in their programs. The success of the movement varies by profession. There are no unaccredited schools of medicine, but there are schools for practitioners who reject the accepted theories of disease and treatment. Most law schools are accredited, but some are not; these latter are usually not connected with a university, but they flourish. Their graduates must pass state bar examinations and be certified as of good character to be admitted to the bar. The older Protestant denominations support seminaries which are usually accredited; nowadays some Catholic seminaries have sought accreditation by an association in which Catholics are a minority. But one can "practice religion," including the ancient practice of faith healing, without any accredited schooling. Social workers have a fairly successful system of accrediting graduate schools leading to the degree of master of social work, but their attempts to require all social workers to hold this degree have never been close to success. Lately, people with bachelor's degrees have been admitted to their professional association; on the other hand, a number of universities have developed programs leading to the Ph.D. in social work. At that level, social work consists of teaching, administration, research, and policy making.

Thus, while the standard education for this group of professions is the bachelor's degree plus some years of professional school, it has not been completely realized in any profession quite so completely as in medicine. And, indeed, it has no sooner been achieved in medicine and nearly so in other professions than it is being attacked. The nature of the attack will be elaborated in the later chapters.

DISTRIBUTION OF PROFESSIONAL SERVICES The professions deliver advice and other services to individuals or to social bodies. Their services are paid for by fees from individuals or social bodies, by gifts and tithes, by larger philanthropic grants from social agencies and foundations, and by taxes levied on some individuals and businesses. Some professionals get all their income from fees for which they bill their clients. Others have mixed incomes derived from fees and salary or support from an organization; some have only fixed salary or support. The means of support of professions affects the distribution of their services. That distribution is considered by the professions a matter over which they have or should have control; they claim it as part of their mandate. Control over distribution, however, is shared by other bodies that are involved in paying for the services or that consider that their own mandate is in question.

The simplest fee-paying system in the past has been that of medicine and law. The fee was, in theory and often in fact, paid for by the person or social body that received the service or that was in some way responsible for the person who received it. The parent pays for medical or legal services for his dependent child. There are other more complicated situations. Some clients who pay fees have more money than others. This allows the professional, if he sets his own fee, to charge some clients more than others for a given service. In medicine, there has been an idea that the physician could be the great equalizer; he could give services as needed, and charge some more and others less or nothing. But there are not enough rich people to make this an effective way to get medical services to all the poor or those made poor by medical disaster. And physicians do not all have their random share of either rich or poor clients.

There was a time when what the medical profession could do for people was much more limited than now. What they did do was done with little equipment. The bonesetter, the bloodletter, the midwife, and the apothecary did their work without permission of the physician. Most people got little service from physicians and expected little. Now the profession's monopoly or control covers these formerly independent branches of work and many new ones. The equipment is massive and expensive and is paid for by taxes and philanthropy. Physicians can do much more than in the past, but only with the expensive equipment and with the help of what are called the "allied health professions." The public of all classes has come to expect much more medical service than in the past without regard to an individual's or family's ability to pay. The manner and amount of payment have become matters of public discussion. Medical students join in the discussion, not always agreeing with their elders in the profession. Neither the elders nor the young apparently attempt to analyze all the social and economic consequences of a great change in both distribution and the total amount of health service.

In law, services are paid for by fees. The amount and kinds of legal services wanted vary greatly by social class. Property is a legal phenomenon; it is the great affair of the legal profession. Exchanges, risks, and susceptibility to arrest and prosecution all give rise to demand for legal services. Those with the least property and income appear to be most susceptible to arrest, to prosecution, and to loss of what little property they have precarious title to; they also are least able to pay for legal advice or defense. Some students of law are proposing devices to bring about more equitable distribution of legal service.

Religious services are not distributed by fee for service, but by individual payment for support of a collectivity. Presumably anyone may attend the church with the best preaching and the most impressive music and liturgy; but local parishes and congregations are as socially stratified as the areas in which their congregations live. The church a person attends and the pew a person sits in may be determined by sex, race, or manner of dress. But no government authority is likely to intervene either to break or to enforce custom except in the Army, prisons, and mental hospitals. Social workers distribute services that are paid for by a third party: by the "giving public" and by taxpayers. It is the special business of the social worker to invent and administer devices for more equitable distribution of many kinds of service, and even of goods and housing. We should keep it in mind that the educational system itself, of which professional schools are part, is a device to distribute services.

All professional services, including education, are paid for by fees levied upon the recipient of the services or someone on his behalf, by philanthropy, or by taxes. The proportion from each of these sources varies from service to service and from time to time. The fees have been increasing greatly, but they have been decreasing as a proportion of the total cost of some services. It is still true that the professionals of highest income collect fees. Salaries or other fixed payments have been increasing as a proportion of the total cost; and payments from taxes are increasing as a proportion within that proportion. This is true of three of our four professions. Only religion gets no direct public support.

The students of the various professional schools have joined the discussion about payment. A particular point on which they enter is that of the distribution of the profession's services, which is obviously connected with the manner of payment. This in turn involves cost of the schooling itself, which cannot be considered without taking into account the length in years of schooling and its cost per year and as a whole. The cost is a factor in choice of those admitted to study. Cost as well as other factors affects the proportions of the two sexes, the races, the ethnic groups, and the social classes that enter and complete training.

**SPECIALIZA-
TION AND
STRATIFICA-
TION**
The length of schooling is itself a cost, since the longer it lasts, the later the individual becomes a self-supporting member of his profession. Since old age comes on at a rather fixed age, late entry means a shorter career. In medicine it is expected that the schooling will not be interrupted. Parents, loans, and working wives (or husbands) carry the student through. In the other professions there are more intervals of work and of income earned in various ways. In any case, the very long schooling is a substitute for apprenticeship, in which the learner does the supporting work, the fetching and carrying, the menial tasks that permit the full members of the profession to make diagnoses, decide courses of action, and carry out crucial procedures. The apprentice becomes a colleague later. He then passes on the lesser tasks to his apprentices, who will doubt whether the assignment is always in fact done as a learning device and will wonder whether the learning might not have been done with more dispatch. He may suspect that he is being exploited as cheap labor.

No profession can be practiced without an underpinning of auxiliary activities. Writs must be served and witnesses notified and sometimes hauled into court. The sick are often incontinent; they must be kept clean, fed, comforted, and even controlled in straitjackets. The deceased must be removed quickly from among the living and their remains disposed of. Some of these tasks make pariahs of the people who do them. There are no proud professional courses and proud university degrees for those who serve a summons, post bail bonds, or embalm the human body. The people who do these things, in effect, put themselves beyond the pale. These are the people who use the service entrance.

But most of the underpinning activities are public and honorable full-time occupations in which a person may have a career, although he is not on the road to the highest level, that of the master profession of whatever system he works in. Nursing, an ancient activity, was long performed mainly within the family or by religious sisters. It has become so professional that a woman may nurse strange men.

Nurses exert great authority and perform services requiring higher education. But nursing is not part of an apprenticeship to the medical profession. Many newer supporting activities have grown up as a result of developments in the medical sciences, technology, and organization. Things that doctors once did, if they were done, are done by nurses or by technicians of various kinds. Some of these activities are part of what the medical student must learn, but he must under no circumstances learn them in the same classroom as technicians or nurses. He must learn them only in the company of his future colleagues. A one-time apprentice activity may become the main activity of a new auxiliary occupation, sometimes called paraprofessional.

Medicine is thus extended laterally and somewhat upward in specialized branches whose practitioners remain formally peers of each other. The educational system is elaborated to prepare people for these new specialties. But it is also extended downward by increased reliance of the master profession on paraprofessionals, nonprofessional helpers, and half-hidden pariahs. Medicine is perhaps the most elaborate of all the work systems in which the central role is played by a proud profession; its educational system is correspondingly elaborate and stratified. Law is not much less specialized and stratified, but the division of labor and of learning is less clearly articulated. In divinity and social work there are also specialists and auxiliary helpers of many kinds and degrees, again not so clearly and publicly institutionalized.

A recent development downward in higher education is the not-so-high community college where nurses, social workers, dental assistants, and other professional auxiliaries receive their credentials in two years. Although the students may come straight from high school, many come later, after marriage, military, or other episodes. They become qualified to work only at a certain lower level in the appropriate work system. Their community college work is not considered a step toward higher study and toward complete professional standing. They are bound in a rigid hierarchy.

Religion and law do not yet use the community college for training auxiliary help. But they, too, appear to be moving toward a new hierarchical system. The office of deacon in the Roman Catholic Church was once a permanent order; it later became a step in the career of all priests. Now short of help, the Catholic church is again recruiting men to be ordained as permanent deacons. Their training will be shorter; they will not study for full orders. In the law, there is talk of shorter courses for some kinds of law and of developing a system of paralegal workers. Their function might be to offer new kinds of legal service to the poor and disadvantaged, who never see lawyers unless they are in trouble.

Our labor force is becoming professional in a degree never known in history; the process is being advanced by creating structures of less than fully professional occupations to whom the master professional may delegate many auxiliary tasks. Many parts of the essential activity of a profession may be delegated to a middle-level occupation. This does not necessarily free the full professionals to devote themselves to their core activity, for the elaborate work system which they create to serve them and their publics must be administered and financed. In the middle-level professions (nursing, social work) the administrators, policy makers, and teachers are the elite; they usually have longer training and higher degrees.

Thus around each leading profession there is developed an elaborate work system, with an ever-changing division of labor. The educational system changes to provide the kinds of training which the new kind of labor force demands.

At the same time, specialization within the profession requires more narrow and advanced training. Specialties may be learned informally in the institutions where the professionals work or in an extension of the system of higher education. Some of the training for specialties brings the professional back to study in graduate school. The physician may want to become an experimental biochemist. The theologian may find his colleagues among comparative linguists, archaeologists, historians, or psychiatrists. The lawyer may study economics. The social worker may become a student of social organization and administration. Thus specialization leads not always to isolation from other kinds of study, but back into the mainstream of science and scholarship. This creates a new set of relationships of professional schools with the rest of the university. For the academically specialized man may become somewhat marginal to the practicing profession; yet he is often the teacher of the young people entering the profession. In all our professions there arises the question of the role of the specialist in professional education and of the point at which specialized training should come.

MEDICINE, LAW, THEOLOGY, AND SOCIAL WORK IN THE UNIVERSITY The oldest and usually leading public university of a state is almost certain to have a medical school and a law school. Older leading private universities may also have a theological school or complex of them attached in some way. If the university, public or private, has an undergraduate college and a graduate school of arts and sciences of national reputation, its law and medical schools are likely to have similar reputations. If affiliated with a university of wide renown, the theological school will be of broad scholarship and ecumenical in spirit. Its students and staff will be of several denominations. The Catholic diocesan seminary is generally not part of a university, although such orders as the Society of Jesus affiliate their seminaries to their own universities. The fundamentalist, or Bible, denominations keep their candidates for religious work away from the seminaries of the leading universities. It does not seem likely at present that theological schools will wax in importance to the universities of which they are part. The more liberal ones seek to survive by merging across lines that until lately could be crossed only by conversion. One may ask what that portends for the future of theology as a subject of study and as the basis of a profession. People will keep on being born, marrying, getting into trouble, sinning, feeling guilt, and dying. They will want to be helped over these crises in some way. Whether all these matters will be dealt with by one profession is perhaps open to question. Much depends upon social movements and belief about the nature and causes of human conduct and problems. The division of labor between theologically trained people and other professions has changed and will continue to change. The monopoly of the clergy is not secure, nor is it certain how great will be the demand for their services.

Schools of social work are not so central a part of the university complex as these other schools. But training for social administration and policy making will certainly increase in importance, since we are a society which requires a great deal of administration and many decisions on collective policy. Thus, education for all four of our professions is a major activity of American higher education. The relationships of education for these professions to each other and to the rest of the system are changing and will change. In our studies it will be seen what kinds of changes are sought and seem to be under way. They are changes not only in the professional schools, but also in the institutions in which professional work is done.

Much of the learning of how work is done takes place while doing the work. Every professional school has frontiers, generally ill-defined, with a number of institutions in which their graduates serve: with universities, with government agencies, with the public, and with institutions that feel themselves legitimately involved in the professional services.

Professional schools, like other institutions, want support from society but prefer not to have outside voices interfering in their internal affairs. A profession claims a broad mandate to define what ails its clients and the public with respect to some problems and actions. For instance, priests, lawyers, physicians, and social workers all claim a voice on abortion. Although professions do not accept with much grace interference of other professions in their preserve, they do generally manage to compose their boundary fights in a live-and-let-live spirit. They also defend their territory against interference by laymen and lay agencies. Inside the professional school the teachers do not easily yield authority to their students, who will one day become their colleagues. Perhaps that is a special reason for resisting their claims. Patients, or clients, who complain come and go. Professional students who make demands presage dissension in the professional brotherhood itself in the near future, unless they are brought into line before they are on their own. At present, professional schools have to deal with the lifting up of voices from many directions. Perhaps the most insistent is that of the students themselves, sometimes joined by the voice of the younger full members of the profession.

ACCESS TO PROFESSIONAL STUDY AND SERVICES Many, perhaps even a majority, of students in the medical and law schools we have studied want to go through the conventional courses and take up conventional careers. Students of theology vary in their aspirations according to denomination; no doubt some want to be regular pastors to middle-class people. It is not certain that their teachers want to train them for that. Whatever the proportions who want change, there are some students who question almost every aspect of the very professions they have decided to enter.

One of the things questioned is the selection of candidates for professional study. Professionals have always been strongly and rather effectively in favor of selecting their own future colleagues. Those served by professions sometimes succeed in choosing the particular persons who will serve them. With respect to a profession, one might define a minority as some category of persons not well represented in it or by it. Voices are being raised in support of increasing the number and proportion of members of various social groups admitted to professional schools: racial and ethnic minorities, women, and the classes of low income and little education. Students in some law and medical schools have raised some uproar on this point, although in the past, professional students have been thought of as favoring keeping their ranks closed. Theology has always kept women at the paraprofessional level, as nuns, teachers, welfare workers, and nurses. The established churches show little sign of admitting them to the central roles of authority or of the cult, although there is some movement in favor of ordaining them to the full ministry. In black American religious movements, women have sometimes taken the lead. In spite of its doctrine of universal brotherhood, Christianity is organized on lines of sex, race, ethnic group, and nationality. As a latecomer among the professions and as one interested in the poorer people of this country, social work is ethnically quite mixed and is perhaps more open to minorities than are the older professions, except for theology. Any ethnic group may have its own Protestant churches with clergy to match. Women and the ethnic minorities remain minorities in the professional schools we have studied in spite of efforts to open the schools more widely.

As we have indicated, each profession works in conjunction with a variety of paraprofessions and nonprofessions; nonprofessionals are often unionized and do battle for higher wages and a better place in the delivery systems of professional services. Yet the disparity of income between the professionals and the helpers is probably increasing. The more social-minded of the professional students are aware of this disparity of income and status. Yet when they join in meetings or actions with other students, the medical students still tend to dominate and to condescend. The paraprofessionals-to-be are not quite peers although they voice common concerns.

Students complain strongly that the services of the professions are not distributed according to need as perceived by many of the people to be served, nor as discovered by surveys of the needs and problems of people, and especially of poor people and certain minorities. Services are distributed according to the effective demand of those who can pay or who can in some manner avail themselves of the best professional services. We do have a great complex of institutions designed to modify strict market distribution of many services. Yet the most successful member of a privately practiced profession is he who, following a specialty of high prestige, has the most favored clientele. Such a professional is, in fact, in a position to delegate in a discreet way those aspects of his work which would detract from his respectability or his prestige. The elite of those professions or specialties practiced in organizations (social workers, clergy, the academics in law and medicine) are those who are in positions of high rank and influence in outstanding institutions in their fields. In the professional schools, as in other institutions of higher education, the elite are those who have the reputed pick of aspiring students and the best resources for research. Certain government positions and membership on commissions are signs of success in some fields.

Some students—numerous and vocal enough to be heard—reject these canons of success at least insofar as success is achieved by not serving the poor and those least sophisticated about what good professional services are and how to get them. The canons of success put little or no emphasis on equitable distribution of professional services. Some professional students talk of establishing special clinics of lawyers, physicians, and ministers to serve the poor and disadvantaged. Some have actually established such units. It is too early to know whether these are essentially missionary efforts, from which the young professionals will resign under pressure from spouses who want better prospects or from frustration at lack of hoped-for results. The clergy have known the missionary career as a special one with its own rewards and disappointments. It is doubtful whether in the middle run, let alone the long run, there will be many in the other professions who will last out missionary work until middle age. An alternative is changing the whole system of distribution of medical, legal, and social services. Such change has already occurred in Canada, Britain, and a number of European countries, in fact, in all countries that are as urban and industrial—or postindustrial—as we are.

Many students, teachers, and professionals want the poor and the minorities to be better served in this generation. These people—the poor, disadvantaged minorities—are also pressing for a more adequate distribution of services. And middle-class people also feel the pinch as their needs for professional services increase and costs soar.

There are thus two directions that the change could take to meet the stated wishes of the discontented students. They and their whole generation would be converted to a new style of work and career; or the whole system of distributing professional services could change so as to bring about a reorganization of professional institutions, hence also careers. The students and most others who are talking of reform of both professional education and of the distribution of services often propose smaller movements and experiments rather than basic institutional change. They often feel themselves so without power that to work on more revolutionary changes would be fruitless.

The question of the social characteristics of the professional in relation to those of his client is implied in talk of better access of minorities, women, and the poor to the ranks of the professions and to services of all kinds. What things do women do for women, men for men, women for men, men for women? One may ask the same questions concerning rich and poor; people of less or more education; people of the same or different religions, social classes, ethnic groups, or races. Lawyers, physicians, and clergymen are predominantly male. Rank-and-file social workers are women, as a rule. Men rise more quickly to positions as administrators or policy makers.

Women are served by men in the professions of higher rank; men are less often served by women. By and large, the longer the course of training beyond the bachelor's degree, the greater the proportion of men in a professional rank. Class and ethnic category also play a role. Some professional offices have so much charisma that the incumbent may serve laymen of any category. This seems so with the higher ranks of clergy, although it is not often put to the test with respect to race. Black bishops are still rare in churches with white laymen. Indeed, there seems to be a tendency for religion, and even medicine, to be ethnic and racial, for minister and ministered to be of the same ilk. Notable exceptions occur in professions or specialities entered out of proportion to their number by members of some ethnic group.

Many professional students seek change in some of these arrangements as to social characteristics of professional and client. It seems impossible that middle-class people could be served by professionals of lower ranks, since middle-class behavior and acceptance by middle-class teachers are prerequisites to becoming a professional. The people of minority status are themselves carrying on the battle for admission, as are some students. The same people seek to change the distribution and character of professional services—a change of effective mandate. This implies a change of styles of careers. How they are to be changed is open to question. Studies of the relative prestige of occupations in industrial societies show a great similarity of ranking in spite of differences of political and economic philosophy.

There is much discussion of the number of years of study for the professions, and indeed of all young people in our society. Some would reduce the number of years in preparation, especially for medicine and law. This proposed reduction is thought of as one way to get more people into the professions and to make them available to do less specialized work. In most professions there is a myth that any professional may perform any task in the province of the profession, that the man with a license to practice has a very broad latitude. The myth that he can do all things is a protection for the whole profession. The years of common study serve to maintain some feeling of colleagueship even after many have gone into separate specialties requiring special skills and subjecting them to special risks.

Experiments in shorter medical or law courses might weaken this sense of colleagueship, of being in the same boat. The result might be increased stratification in the professional work system—even beyond that which comes from the use of auxiliary occupations. It seems unlikely that those with fewer years training and education will remain equal in prestige and in admission to inner circles to those who study longer. To make "general practice" equal in prestige and income would run counter to the general temper of American education and professional values.

The people who take shorter courses may later find it impossible to resume studies in order to rise to higher levels. They may find themselves as firmly fixed in their rank as are paraprofessionals and treated with a similar approving condescension, which implies, "What could we do without him (her)?" There might also be a question of recruiting people ambitious enough to study for a profession but who will settle for a career with a low ceiling. That might depend a good deal on the development of social economy. Careers with bureaucratically fixed ceilings of middle height may be the salvation of many people in the future. They allow people to have a sense of helping in the delivery of professional services, and even of correcting some of the errors made by the full professionals, without taking full responsibility.

THEORY AND PRACTICE
It seems to be generally assumed that there is need for a much larger number of physicians, lawyers, religious workers, and social workers who will carry on the ordinary, "general" work of these professions, as against the more specialized and often more difficult parts. When a plea is made for a shorter training, it seems generally to mean training for this ordinary, general work. It also seems to imply a change of the balance between theory and practice. The division of time and attention to these two aspects of education has always been an issue. In the sixteenth century, medical education at Oxford and Cambridge consisted of reading "certain approved

authors" and their commentators. A famous physician of the time said that " . . . one had as good send a man to Oxford to learn shoe-making as practising physick . . ." (Charlton, 1965, pp. 166–167). Civil law was also at that time scarcely taught in the English universities, and Roman canon law was forbidden after the Reformation. In the university professional schools of our time, the student moves from theory to practice, and — if he continues into still higher study — back to theory again, although it may be mixed with practical study of some specialized sort.

But theory and practice are very loose terms. Theological theory is elaborated doctrine about the nature of God, man, and the church; each denomination proves to the satisfaction of its adherents that the claims it professes (and that was the original meaning of profession) are true. The three "learned professions of divinity, law and medicine" all once claimed a body of truth upon which their practice was presumably based. But the application of such knowledge was by no means all that was done in their fields. Much of medicine was based on knowledge very like the "science of the concrete" described by Levi-Strauss (1966, Chap. 1) as being so elaborately developed among so-called primitive people. Much of law has always been the settling of small quarrels about property and personal matters. Much of religion had to do with birth, death, illness, visits to shrines, and the committing and purging of smaller sins. Only in more recent times has science of the experimental kind found its way into professional education and practice in a significant degree.

Perhaps the significant thing about contemporary education is the great increase in the amount of theory and practical skill to be taught and learned. With the great development of science and with the great complexity of modern institutions, there is more to be learned about practice in any profession; there is also much more of systematic knowledge to be learned about law, religion, medicine, and social welfare. Each profession teaches its candidates some selection of the immense body of both theory and practice. The distinction between theory and practice is reinforced by separating them into courses which emphasize one or the other. It is reinforced by the setting in which the teaching is done, the classroom, the laboratory, the hospital, the social agency, the law office.

While the student is acquiring his professional knowledge, he is also being inducted into a fraternity. Much that passes for theory, and much that is called practice as well, is the ideology of the profession including its conception of the nature of the phenomena it deals with—the nature of disease as seen by physicians, of law as seen by lawyers, of social problems as seen by social workers. No profession does its teaching without implanting its philosophy concerning the aspects of nature, society, culture, and knowledge involved in its work. Part of that philosophy is a set of convictions about what knowledge and what skills are most important. No one can know more than a small part of the theory and practice of any of these professions. Each specialty has its own notions about which part is essential to its work. The prestigious specialities are thought to require both more theory and more practical skill than does general practice. But as one comes to the lower ranks of the professions themselves and to the occupations called paraprofessions (in medicine, the allied health professions), the emphasis is put on practical skills. The community college is thought especially appropriate for training in the allied professions because it does not hold aloof from teaching practical—the so-called vocational—skills.

The question of theory and practice, then, is not merely one of the length of time spent on each, or of the total length of time of professional education. It is also a matter of selecting certain kinds of practical training to be learned in certain settings upon certain clients and problems, and of selecting certain parts of scientific knowledge, social knowledge, and ethics to be inculcated in the professional students. The students, generally inclined to acquiesce in the views of their teachers, nevertheless develop their own notions of what is most important to learn. They work out an economy of time and effort that is often quite different from that proposed by their teachers; the teachers themselves differ in choices and emphases, according to their specialties, class philosophy, or idiosyncratic tastes. The teachers as a group may differ from their fellows in practice on the selection of things to be taught. In addition there may be, and there appears to be now, a distinct generational mutation in values.

If there is a constant politics of the several parties to professional education by which content and material of the curriculum are determined, it is not peculiar to professional education. We are clearly in a period when the balance between theory and practice and the whole economy of emphasis in higher education are matters of general public concern.

2. Professional Education in Medicine

by Barrie Thorne

Training for the medical profession is longer and probably more demanding, intense, and cloistered than for any other. Since the turn of the century, the period of study and initiation leading to formal entry into the profession has become highly standardized in length, sequence, and content. This standardization—the development of a lengthy training program under the control of physicians themselves—has combined with licensing regulations and the power of professional associations to strengthen the monopoly of physicians over nearly all of the practice of healing. The long-range consolidation and maintenance of power by the medical profession lie behind more specific developments in the training of physicians.

The first theme of this chapter is the history of medical education in the United States. Under the impetus of Flexner's criticisms and proposals in 1910 (Flexner, 1910), medical education moved away from variation in types of preparation and toward a homogeneous program of study. Within this century it has become standard for the training of physicians to take place in relatively isolated educational institutions, linked with both universities and clinical facilities. The period of study has become uniform in length and sequence: from three to four years of general liberal arts education, four years of medical school (divided into basic science and clinical phases), and additional years of internship and residency. The so-called Flexner revolution established a structure and set of priorities which continue to dominate medical education (and which provide a base point for this profile) but which, within the last decade, have been subject to widespread criticism and proposals for change. Recent trends in medical education will be described along several dimensions. The first concerns the scheduling, sequence, and length of medical education; the relation of preclinical to clinical training; and the underlying question of how theory is related to practice.

Discussion will then turn to the professional mandate—the rights and prerogatives which physicians assume; their definition and evaluation of problems, clients, and responsibilities; and their philosophy concerning the distribution of services. The traditional mandate of the medical profession has been widely challenged by critics both inside and outside the profession. In raising questions of priority and organization, this challenge is having an impact on medical education.

Approaching the subject from a more institutional perspective, we come to a third theme—the ecology of medical schools: their relation to the surrounding community, the practicing profession, the medical work system (including paramedical training programs), and the university. The concluding section centers on the medical student and the process of initiation and socialization into the profession, including student cultures, cloistering, changing patterns of recruitment, and student activism.

THE HISTORY AND STANDARDIZATION OF MEDICAL EDUCATION

In the seventeenth and eighteenth centuries, apprenticeship was the prevailing type of medical instruction in the United States, although a few practitioners acquired formal training by attending lectures in English or continental universities. In 1730, of the 3,500 practitioners established in the colonies, only 5 percent held degrees, and no more than 400 had received any formal training (Shryock, 1960).

When practicing physicians set up lecture and demonstration courses for groups of students, more formalized instruction supplemented apprenticeships. The next step, which began in the United States in 1765, was the founding of medical schools; there were four of them in the United States by the end of the eighteenth century. The early medical schools combined academic instruction with several years of apprenticeship. Apprenticeships also continued as the sole means of training for many who entered the practice of medicine. Although graduates of medical schools became practitioners of the highest prestige, they held no monopoly. The work of healing was carried out by a variety of practitioners—physicians of varying degrees and kinds of training, midwives, barbers, clerics, and others who operated independently of the physician.

By the mid-1820s there were 17 medical schools, enrolling 2,000 students a year, a number far short of the demand for physicians. The bulk of physicians continued to enter practice by routes other than formal training. In 1839 there were at least 30 medical schools, and the number expanded to 65 by 1860 (Shryock, 1960; *Journal of the American Medical Association,* 1915, p. 694). The mass of practitioners were still "second-class doctors but—unlike the medical men of that type in 1820—they had at least a bowing acquaintance with formal education" (Shryock, 1960, p. 150). In the latter half of the nineteenth century the number of medical schools rapidly increased, reaching a peak of 160 by 1900. With the founding of more medical schools, alternative forms of training dwindled, sometimes at the expense of practical experience, since some schools had no preceptorship or clinical arrangements. As medical schools began to establish hospital-based clinical programs, the apprenticeship style of learning became a supplement to rather than a substitute for academic training.

Nineteenth-century medical schools varied in institutional and financing arrangements, medical philosophy, and sense of mission. Prior to 1820 most United States medical schools followed the continental-Scottish tradition of affiliation with a university (which, in the United States at that time, meant a liberal arts college). Sometimes medical schools were created as an integral part of a well-established collegiate institution; in other cases the tie was loose and nominal, the result of "grafting" between a self-constituted medical faculty and a college (Norwood, 1941). Other patterns developed which did not involve university affiliation. In the 1840s a few medical schools were established within hospitals. Independent proprietary medical schools flourished in the middle and late nineteenth century; competing for profit and usually seeking large enrollments, they often had poor facilities and low standards. These proprietary institutions, many of them small and short-lived, helped account for the large number of medical schools at the turn of the century.

Schools also differed in medical philosophy. By the 1850s various medical sects had evolved, and some founded their own training institutions whose names often included a sectarian reference (for example, the Homeopathic Medical College of Pennsylvania and the California Eclectic Medical College). Some colleges were designated for groups excluded by the usual requirement that students be white and male; special schools were formed for blacks (there were five of them in 1901) and for women (starting with the Women's Medical College founded in Philadelphia in 1850). A few evening schools catered to part-time students, and several colleges were founded to train medical missionaries.

The length of training varied in different times and places. In New York City in 1792 a law required three years of apprenticeship for those lacking a college education and two years of apprenticeship for those with an arts degree (Shryock, 1960). Three years was the customary length of apprenticeship, although some were longer and many shorter (Norwood, 1941). In the colleges of medicine which were founded in the late eighteenth century, it was common to require three years of apprenticeship (on a private basis under a respectable practitioner), attendance at two terms of lectures, a thesis, examinations, and a minimum age of 21 years before one was granted an M.D. In subsequent years the requirement of three years of apprenticeship was gradually modified and often not enforced. Some individuals set themselves up as physicians with no background of practical experience. In 1873 only one medical school offered longer than a two-year course of academic training, and some proprietary schools offered a degree after only one year of study (*Journal of the American Medical Association.* 1901, p. 778). In the absence of state licensing laws, many entered practice without having completed the formal training period. Norwood (1941) estimates that prior to the Civil War, as many as two-thirds or three-fourths of medical school matriculants did not remain long enough to graduate, although many of them still entered practice.

In the early 1900s the quality of medical education became a focus of public attention. The large number of proprietary schools, often amounting to little more than diploma mills, dramatized a general decline in the quality of United States medical education. At the request of the Council on Medical Education of the American Medical Association and the Carnegie Foundation, Abraham Flexner visited all the existing medical schools and in 1910 published his highly critical findings (Flexner, 1910). Flexner's critique had an immediate overhauling effect on medical education. Many proprietary and second-rate schools folded or merged, and other schools began to upgrade their standards. Between 1900 and 1920 the number of schools declined from 160 to 87 (*Journal of the American Medical Association,* 1950, p. 115).

Flexner's study affected not only the number of medical schools, but also their form of organization and program of study. The diversity which had characterized training for the practice of medicine prior to 1900 consolidated into one standardized and relatively homogeneous pattern of education. Drawing his model from the Johns Hopkins University School of Medicine, which followed the German tradition, Flexner emphasized the importance of a science and research orientation, a university affiliation and a full-time faculty, clinical instruction provided through a teaching hospital, and standardized admissions requirements.

Medical education became, by and large, a form of university education with an academic and research focus. Its isolation from the world of practice was reinforced by the hiring of full-time instructors as well as practitioners who taught part-time. A sequence of two years of basic science instruction followed by two years of clinical experience in a teaching hospital became widespread and reflected an assumption that theoretical studies should precede practice. Upgraded admissions standards and a gradual lengthening of the educational sequence made medical schools more selective in recruitment and made the course of training a greater investment of time and money.

The Flexner report and its recommendations helped the medical profession tighten its control over recruitment, training, and practice. In the twentieth century, medical licensing became widely established for the first time, and state boards began excluding graduates of low-grade schools from licensing examinations. The advancement of research and an accepted scientific basis for medical practice helped buttress the claims of the medical profession to a monopoly over the practice of healing. As the scientific basis of medicine developed, knowledge became more standardized, and one philosophy absorbed and replaced the competing perspectives of the nineteenth century. Recruits to the profession began to share a long and standard period of training, which partly functioned as an initiation rite, separating them from other types of practitioners, establishing a public identity, and strengthening their mutual identification.

With uniform training, every licensed physician could be expected to have a basic technical education more or less equivalent to every other's and distinct from that of any other kind of healer. With a sound technical basis of his training, the physician could win confidence and establish the justice of his claim of privilege. And finally, with mass education the public developed knowledge and belief that became more like that of the physician himself and therefore it became more receptive to his work. The outcome was control over the practice of healing that has never before been enjoyed by medicine (Freidson, 1970a, p. 2).

Since the dramatic results of the Flexner report, the basic framework of medical education has remained relatively unchanged, although there have been alterations in the length, complexity, points of emphasis, and, of course, content of medical knowledge. Medical schools, as Flexner recommended, have assumed multiple responsibilities reflected in the complex institutional arrangement of the university medical center, with university ties, teaching hospitals, clinics, research institutes, programs of graduate study for basic medical sciences, and affiliated schools for training paramedical personnel. The proportion of full-time faculty has increased rapidly, creating career possibilities in teaching, research, and administration in an academic medical setting.

Flexner stressed the importance of scientific research, which, since his time, has developed into a major activity in most medical schools. After World War II, federal financing of biomedical research increased, providing as much as 50 to 60 percent of medical school budgets by the 1960s. Largely due to this outside boost, medical school budgets have expanded into millions of dollars (*Journal of the American Medical Association,* 1970). This trend strengthened the research focus of medical schools and created a pattern of fiscal dependence on the government.

Since Flexner's time, medical knowledge and technology have expanded rapidly, and specialization has become a significant and steady trend, resulting in more complicated patterns of medical practice and training. An extensive division of labor has developed, with a proliferation not only of specialties but also of paramedical occupations, which form an elaborate work system under the control of the physician. As medical practice began to require large amounts of capital equipment and a group of supporting workers, the work of physicians moved into large institutions and organizations such as hospitals, clinics, and group practices.

Strengthened by trends such as the growth of scientific research in medicine, Flexner's model has had consequences which are now a subject of public discussion and criticism. An immediate consequence was a reduction in the number of physicians being trained, a situation which was not significantly reversed in subsequent years.

In 1900 there were 157 physicians per 100,000 population, but by 1929 this ratio had dropped to 125 per 100,000. Thereafter it rose until 1940, when it leveled off. Since then the ratio has hovered around 133 per 100,000 (Lerner & Anderson, 1963, p. 222).

Another consequence of the model Flexner proposed was isolation—medical training takes place in a context set apart from the everyday world of health problems and practice, and even during the clinical phases of training, most students see only the selected types of patients found in teaching hospitals. Academic medical centers became increasingly aloof from their surrounding communities and from the problems of primary medical care. In some medical schools a research emphasis began to take precedence over issues of patient care, and highly specialized careers in academic and research medicine became more valued than the role of practitioner. A new and powerful professional elite based in university medical centers began to assume a central role in the shaping of the medical profession and to challenge the traditional dominance of the AMA and private practitioners.

These consequences have bearing on the role of medical schools in the delivery of services, an issue which has gained significance as attention has shifted from Flexner's focus on quality to a more quantitative and organizational concern with the distribution of medical care. Increasingly described as a failure or at least as being in a state of crisis, the United States medical system provides second-class or no professional services to large segments of the population and has a shortage and maldistribution of manpower, inadequate facilities, and rising costs. In terms of indexes of public health, such as infant mortality rate and life expectancy, the United States ranks relatively low, especially given its level of affluence and advanced medical technology. These facts have been emphasized by consumers (or would-be consumers) of health services, especially members of disadvantaged communities, and by activist segments of the health professions, and have become a familiar theme in the media and in government rhetoric. Many current criticisms of medical education can be traced to this issue.

While medical schools are not in the throes of a dramatic transformation such as occurred early in the century, they are the focus of rising dissatisfaction and criticism, and changes have been proposed and in some cases are being implemented. The Flexner model, which continues to dominate the form, structure, and assumptions of medical education, provides a background for tracing the points of greatest controversy and possible change.

THE SCHEDULING OF MEDICAL EDUCATION With the standardization of medical education, a uniform schedule and timetable of training replaced the variations in length and type of education which were prevalent before this century. The now-accepted belief that the shaping of a competent physician requires a fixed period and sequence of schooling has been reinforced by licensing regulations and degree requirements. Compared with previous centuries, there are more formal hurdles required of those seeking membership in the profession.

Medical education has steadily increased in length. By 1900 most medical schools required, or at least professed to require, four years of attendance for the M.D. degree, and in the aftermath of Flexner's report, this period of schooling, divided into two years of basic science and two years of clinical study, became a stable pattern. More time was added by making academic terms longer and by lengthening the course of study at both ends of the medical school years.

Increase in Length Premedical requirements have increased. In 1900, some medical schools did not even require that entrants be high school graduates, and only five required as many as two years of college. By 1918 state licensing boards had fixed two years of college (including prerequisite science subjects) as necessary for admission to medical school; in 1938 the Council on Medical Education recommended three years of college. Although the bulk of schools do not require a bachelor's degree for entry, by 1950, 72 percent of entering medical students had a B.A. degree, and the figure had risen to 89 percent of those entering in 1969 (*Journal of the American Medical Association,* 1950, p. 116; 1970, p. 1514).

Originally, granting the M.D. degree marked the end of formal training, but it gradually became only a milestone along the way. By the 1930s the internship had become an accepted stage in the education of physicians, and as specialization became more common, from two to four additional years of residency were added (Field, 1970). The dramatic increase in the duration of training is illustrated by the fact that while in 1850 one could become a surgeon after only one year of training at the Harvard Medical School and the Massachusetts General Hospital, by 1940 the period of formal study for a surgeon had reached 14 years beyond high school, and at the point of entering practice, the average surgeon was over 30 years old (Cope, 1965).

Since 1850 medical knowledge has developed extensively, a fact often used to account for the much longer period of training required of today's physicians. But other factors, related to the structure and power of the profession and to the way physicians organize and control their work, have also shaped the trend toward a steady lengthening of medical training. The length and sequence of professional training are historical products; apart from social definitions and convention, there is no "right" time of schooling—that is, a fixed time, necessarily, functionally, and in every case the period required for learning the skills needed for competent practice. A long and uniform period of higher education—four years in a liberal arts college, from three to four years in a professional school, followed, in medicine, by an added stage of clinical training—has, by convention, become the professional timetable, used both as a symbol and a justification for the status and prerogatives of the professions.

Of all the forms of modern professional training, medical education is seen as most grueling and demanding, an image which substantiates the profession's claim to special control over its work. The longer and more esoteric the course of training, the more firmly can an occupation insist that it has best claim to monopolize a given sphere of work, including the right to delegate tasks (the taking of temperatures, for example). With the aid of the state, physicians have established a more thorough monopoly than any other professional group, a position reinforced by the length of medical training.

A prolonged, uniform, and demanding period of training also facilitates the medical profession's control over the recruitment of physicians. By setting exclusive standards of admission (including the selection implicit in the fixing of prerequisites and in the demand that the training phase start relatively early in the life cycle and continue for many years, full-time and uninterrupted), the profession regulates the number and type of people allowed to enter. This system strongly favors recruits who are white males of the higher socioeconomic classes; it has made it difficult for persons who lack any one or more of these qualities to become physicians, and if they do, to enter the mainstream of medical activity. It has also been used to limit the number of recruits to suit the economic advantage of physicians.

Medical training is widely perceived as a significant investment of time and money, an investment likely to lead to a high level of individual commitment to the occupation. Medical students tend to make relatively early gestures of commitment; about three-fourths of the medical students in one study had decided to enter medical school at least two years before they actually did so, compared with one-third of law students who had decided on legal careers by that time (Thielens, 1957). Early decisions are partly required because prerequisites for admission to medical school necessitate taking as long as two years of specified courses as an undergraduate. Among medical students, the age of crucial decision—the point at which recruits make choices and investments which definitely identify them with given careers—is relatively early.

The professional timetable reflects assumptions about the life cycle. Long training programs start at an early age and keep recruits in school until they have reached what is perceived to be the age and level of maturity appropriate to carrying out various professional services. A standard timetable helps guarantee that a person starts at a certain age, learns at the right rate, goes through status grades in the right order, and then arrives at an age ripe enough to enter the full duties and role of his profession, while still humble enough not to get above his station.

Movement toward a Shorter and More Flexible Timetable

The length of time required for medical education has become so great that public opinion, various social interests, and students themselves question both its necessity and its feasibility. The shortage of doctors has become a public issue, and one way to increase quantity is to shorten the period of training. That the military produces medical manpower in a shorter time indicates that the traditional civilian timetable is somewhat arbitrary and could be shortened. With the institutionalization of a post-M.D. phase of training, medical schools no longer have to prepare physicians to enter practice immediately after graduation. Entering students are better prepared than in the past, high school and college science courses have improved, and more students enter college with advanced standing in the sciences, providing reassurance that the traditional medical school program could be shortened without sacrificing quality (Page, 1969).

The post-M.D. stage of training is now being rearranged, and possibly shortened. Since medical schools have increased the length of clinical training prior to the M.D., and since residency training has become widespread, the year of internship has begun to seem redundant. Internships have been eliminated in psychiatry, and the AMA has resolved to phase out the freestanding internship by 1975 (Millis, 1971).

On the other hand, the expansion and complexity of medical knowledge create continual pressure to further extend residencies; specialty boards have lengthened, but in no case have they shortened, required periods of residency. With the elimination of the internship, residency experience—and hence training as a specialist—may become virtually a requirement for practice.

At the premedical and basic science level, a number of medical schools have experimented with ways to decrease the length of medical training. Through early admissions, advanced placement, advanced credit, and summer school, some students have completed baccalaureate degrees in three calendar years. Boston University, Northwestern University, and four other schools have introduced an option which allows students to finish both B.A. and M.D. in six years (*New York Times,* Nov. 14, 1971). At Johns Hopkins University, a specially selected group is admitted to a five-year medical school program after two years of college. These programs both shorten the period of training and have the effect of lowering the age of crucial decision.

A 1969 survey found that one-third of all United States medical schools have either instituted or thought they might introduce three-year programs; 19 schools had started or were planning to start programs which would allow students to graduate in three calendar years; and 14 other medical schools were considering implementing such programs in the foreseeable future. These courses were of three kinds: those based on advanced placement, those which compressed a four-year course into three by eliminating vacations, and programs with many electives so that students could proceed along different timetables (Page, 1970).

The trend seems not so much to be an across-the-board reduction in the number of years of study (as there was a uniform increase to four years after the Flexner report) as a move toward greater flexibility, toward providing students with alternative timetables and programs of study. All the schools with a three-year option continue to offer four- or even five- or six-year sequences leading to the M.D. Less than 20 percent of college students enter with advanced placement, and not all medical students want the relatively early isolation and demanding program involved in the accelerated six-year course. While, in general, admissions requirements have tightened and continue to favor students with strong science backgrounds, in some cases medical schools have loosened admissions requirements to give various minority groups greater access to the medical profession. Some schools have lengthened the years of training available to students lacking the educational background of those admitted by traditional criteria.

Stanford University Medical School was one of the first schools to break the conventional timetable. Seeking to encourage careers in academic, research medicine, it shifted in the late 1950s to a five-year M.D. degree. In 1968, partly, some observers have noted, in response to growing social and political awareness among students and a shift toward concern with community service, Stanford changed to an elective system which offers a three-year option, as well as the possibilities of graduating in four, five, or six years. One of the aims of the program was to "open alternative 'pathways' through medical school to fit graduates for the differing roles played by physicians today" (Walsh, 1971).

Lockstep Education and Its Loosening Length of time is just one aspect of the scheduling of professional training; sequences and courses of study were also standardized in the early 1900s, resulting in what is often called "lockstep education." Nearly all medical schools settled into a uniform and prescribed program of study starting with two years of sciences related to medicine (such as anatomy, biochemistry, physiology, pathology, and pharmacology), studied in a given order with didactic lectures and a cookbook kind of laboratory instruction, and followed by two clinical years, also arranged in a rigid sequence. Writing in a critical vein (since he favored enough variation of program to suit different backgrounds and interests), Flexner (1925, pp. 137–138) described lockstep medical training as it was in 1922:

[Students] were grouped in fixed classes, the personnel of which was practically unchanged, except for outright losses due to failure, from year to year; they followed in fixed order, day by day, the same subjects, for the same length of time, in the same year and at the same hour. From 8:30 to 1, from 2 to 4:30, all students in their respective classes pursued an identical routine. And, at regular intervals, all alike, in the same rigid groups, performed precisely the same practical exercises, attended the same quizzes and submitted to the same monthly, semi-annual, and annual examinations. Anything more alien to the spirit of scientific or modern medicine or to university life could hardly be contrived.

Some of today's medical students would find Flexner's description close to their present experience; lockstep education has by no means disappeared. But there is a trend toward greater diversity in curricula and courses of study. The increase in medical knowledge, specialization, and variation in the background and career plans of students have made it difficult to justify a single prescribed curriculum for all four years of medical school. Medical educators are finding it difficult to define a core curriculum—a basic sequence of study necessary and relevant to all types of medical careers (research scientists, community practitioners, and highly specialized physicians, for example).

In the 1950s a few schools, with Case Western Reserve University as pioneer, tried to reduce the required core of the curriculum and introduce electives and blocks of free time. Out of 42 medical schools sampled in a 1966 study, all but 3 anticipated a move toward more elective time, and 29 described the change as major. At least 3 schools planned to make the equivalent of a full academic year elective (Littlemeyer, 1969; DeMuth & Gronvall, 1970). In 1968 at Duke, Dartmouth, Harvard, Pennsylvania, Stanford, and Yale, from 1½ to 2 or more years of the 4-year medical curriculum were devoted to elective studies (Funkenstein, 1968).

THE CONTENT OF PROFESSIONAL EDUCATION: THEORY AND PRACTICE

Although medical students now have a greater choice of pathways through medical school, with varying timetables and curricula leading to the M.D. degree, the basic sequence of study remains essentially as it has been: three or four years of liberal arts college; one to two years of science training followed by several years of clinical study, both under the aegis of the medical school; and a post-M.D. phase of internship and residency.

This sequence reflects assumptions about the appropriate order for acquiring professional knowledge and skills, assumptions which have shaped the mode of training in law, theology, and other professions, as well as in medicine. It has become the custom for general education to precede later, more specialized and narrow professional learning. Professional recruits share an initial period of liberal education in undergraduate colleges with those who will not be their future colleagues. The sequence of more strictly professional training, involving isolation from other types of students and learners of other professions and occupations, begins with emphasis on theory. This reflects a second assumption: that the learning of theory or induction into the abstract and systematic core of the mysteries held by the profession should come before practical training and experience. Professions tend to keep recruits as long as possible from the actual situation in which work is to be done.

The division between theory and its application is less in occupations which are learned within the actual work setting. In this situation (typical, for example, of training for various skilled manual trades, and more characteristic of medical education when it was organized on an apprenticeship basis), there is more overlap between what is learned and what is needed, in a practical way, when one is at work. Learning and doing tend to coincide (Geer et al., 1968).

With the development of the professions, learning was increasingly separated from the actual doing of work. The learning phase was shifted out of work settings and into special training institutions, isolated from the world of practice. This shift accompanied the development of an abstract and systematic body of theory, sufficiently complex and esoteric to justify the profession's claim to unique competence over its chosen sphere of activity. In contrast with other occupations, preparation for the professions involves considerable preoccupation with systematic theory, a preoccupation tied with formalized, university-based education.

As the medical profession laid claim to greater scientific expertise, medical schools began to impart an abstract body of knowledge not directly related to the doing of specific tasks. Flexner's strong belief in university-affiliated medical schools was related to his emphasis on the scientific roots of medical knowledge. He stressed the advantages of an academic setting in nurturing and promoting a scientific attitude, and he advocated two years of study in the basic sciences (chemistry, physiology, pathology) as the appropriate foundation for later clinical training.

Medicine shares with other professions a tension between the theoretical and the practical, between the scientific and more professional or applied dimensions of work.

[M]edicine has been plagued by this conflict through many years. The marriage between clinic and laboratory is still an uneasy one. The wonder-working surgeon (they do work wonders) is still not quite at ease with the skeptical pathologist down in the laboratory. The practicing physician, meeting as best he can the emergencies of patients who refuse to get made-to-order troubles, feels inferior before his patient and learned brethren of the great research schools and foundations; he also resents their detached, leisurely criticism of his hasty blunders (Hughes, 1971a, pp. 360–363).

The separation of the medical school curriculum into two disjunctive stages, the preclinical and the clinical, reflects the division between theory and practice. The division also appears in the location of training and in medical school faculties. The sciences of biochemistry, physiology, pathology, and pharmacology are learned in classrooms and laboratories, that is, in formal academic settings. More practical training, in clinical arts such as internal medicine, obstetrics, and pediatrics, takes place in hospital clinics, within actual institutions of delivery.

Medical school faculties tend to be divided between the Ph.D.'s and M.D.'s, between teachers of basic science and those in clinical programs. More firmly located in the university, basic science faculties became full-time in an era when many medical schools still relied on medical practitioners to teach clinical subjects on a part-time basis. Even with the growth of full-time clinical faculties, the dimension of practice distinguished them from the teachers of physiology or biochemistry. Medical schools tend to be highly departmentalized. Departments, in turn, cluster into the basic science and clinical divisions, and there is often friction between the two (Bloom, 1971; Bucher, 1970).

The division between basic sciences and clinical study is perhaps the most obvious discontinuity in the sequence of stages involved in medical education. But other parts of the sequence—the move from undergraduate college into medical school and the later transition to internships and residencies—also lack continuity. The report of the Citizens' Commission on Graduate Education in Medicine emphasized the problem of continuity in medical education, noting that the stages of medical school, internship, and residency "are independently planned and separately organized and controlled. Often they overlap in content and sometimes they leave unfortunate gaps" (The Citizens' Commission on Graduate Medical Education, 1966, pp. 9–10).

One type of gap is the experience of "reality shock"—a sharp sense of disjuncture between one's preparation and expectations and what is actually encountered. This sort of shock can happen to a student whose ideas about medical training do not match the situation he or she discovers on entering medical school. A later shock often occurs when the student moves from the isolated, preclinical phase into contact with the realities of practice.

Clinical clerkships, internships, and residencies are designed to teach students the complexities of actual practice, but the practical or "doing" phase of the training sequence only partially resembles what many recruits eventually encounter when they become full-fledged practitioners. Practical instruction takes place in teaching hospitals, which are highly specialized and oriented to acute medical situations. The outpatient departments of teaching hospitals, where learners get some exposure to ambulatory patients, provide a "fragmented, discontinuous, crisis-oriented ambience" (Bosch &

Banta, 1970, p. 2101), and the inner-city poor are the typical clientele. In the world of actual practice, 90 percent of all medical care is delivered in settings other than the hospital, and teaching hospitals provide relatively little medical care (James, 1967). Students learn on the poor (a symbiosis which will be discussed later), but when they enter practice, the vast majority will have patients from higher socioeconomic classes. The practical experience which medical students receive is often only marginally relevant to their future careers; as they move into a position of fuller colleagueship within the profession, new physicians often go through yet another experience of reality shock.

Many of the recent changes in medical school curricula can be described as an attempt to overcome the fragmentation of medical education. Some programs purport to achieve a better integration between the premedical and the medical school stages of training; there are efforts to lessen the division between the basic sciences and clinical instruction; and there are some moves toward broadening the learner's exposure to the realities of medical practice.

Changes in the Relationship of Premedical to Medical Education

There have been some recent attempts to overcome the sharp division between premedical and medical school training. Medical schools in close geographic and institutional proximity with undergraduate schools are in a better position to develop coordinated programs than schools lacking a university affiliation or located at some distance from an undergraduate college.

At the University of Michigan an undergraduate with advanced science standing can take medical school courses while not yet formally enrolled in medical school. This option is a forerunner of a proposed new program which would integrate premedical and medical education and shorten to five years the total time of study required for both a baccalaureate and an M.D. degree. The University of Vermont allows selected students to mix the course work of the final year of college with the first-year medical school curriculum during a transitional two-year period. Six-year curricula leading to the B.A. and M.D. degrees require coordinating undergraduate training with professional stages of training. Such programs, however, are small and experimental. The bulk of medical students still move in a discontinuous way from undergraduate college study into the almost wholly separate world of the medical school.

Basic sciences are taught both in college and in medical school — a fact which provides possibilities for rearranging both the sequence and place of training. Recognizing that college instruction in biology, chemistry, and other basic sciences has improved, some schools, for example, Duke University School of Medicine, have compressed basic sciences requirements into one year. This reduction in the number of required courses is accompanied by an increase in elective time. There have been proposals for shifting the basic science part of the medical curriculum onto the main campus of the parent university (Carnegie Commission on Higher Education, 1970). This type of proposal has bearing on the relation of preclinical or basic science to clinical studies.

The Relationship of Basic Science to Clinical Study

In the period of reform following Flexner's report, medical schools institutionalized a division between the first two years of basic science study and the later two years of clinical instruction. In the last decade there have been varied efforts to change this format — in some cases by even further separating the stages of training, and in others by trying to achieve a closer integration of preclinical and clinical studies.

Because preclinical and clinical phases of instruction take place in different settings, it is feasible to relocate medical training. Some medical schools are shifting away from a unitary location and toward a program which would offer the basic sciences in university locations and use community hospitals to provide separate centers for clinical instruction. This arrangement facilitates expanding the number of medical students by using existing institutions (adding a teaching component to community hospitals). It also disperses medical instruction to a wider territory, which may help redistribute medical services. The University of Illinois, for example, is reorganizing medical education to locate the initial year of basic science study on the university campuses at Champaign-Urbana and Chicago. In the last three years, students have dispersed to clinical training centers located in hospitals throughout the state. A similar arrangement has been proposed for a regional education program in the Pacific Northwest.

In contrast with plans which would locate basic science and clinical studies in different places (with the likely effect of reinforcing their separation), another, more widespread trend is toward greater integration of the entire medical school curriculum, crossing departmental barriers and introducing students to both basic sciences and clinical subjects in what is hoped to be a more coordinated and concurrent way.

Case Western Reserve Medical School was the pioneer of this sort of curricular revision. In the early 1950s it implemented a program of instruction organized not on a departmental basis but according to functional units.

The heart was no longer described structurally in anatomy, functionally in physiology, with structural and functional alterations covered in pathology, and the drugs which modified such alteration considered in pharmacology. Instead, a single-subject committee provided a period of joint instruction on the cardiovascular system using lecture, conference, and laboratory methods. The committee members were, themselves, still members of a department, still carried out their own research within disciplinary boundaries, but did not cling to this categorical pattern in their teaching. It was the first profound and fundamental departure in 50 years from an increasingly rigid departmental program of instruction (Miller, 1962, p. 108).

Other schools, especially in the last few years, have followed this lead. The University of Michigan Medical School, for example, has introduced a course entitled Neural and Behavioral Sciences which draws on several disciplines (anatomy, neurology, psychiatry) to teach the basic structure and functions of the nervous system. Another integrated course, which is also given in the first and second years, deals with the relationship of basic sciences to the practice of medicine, in a specific attempt to correlate preclinical and clinical study.

The traditional division between preclinical and clinical study means that student contact with patients is postponed until at least the third year of training. As a result, basic science courses often appear irrelevant to the realities of medical practice, a hurdle to be passed before the student can get down to the "real" and highly valued business of actually dealing with patients and disease (Becker et al., 1961; Bloom, 1971). In an effort to sustain student interest and to encourage careers as practitioners (under the theory that isolation from the world of practice reinforces academic research careers), some medical schools have started to bring students into contact with patients earlier in the course of study.

The early innovations at Case Western included a program which assigned each entering student to a family, usually with a pregnant mother, to follow the evolution of medical needs through the duration of the student's training. Other schools have set up "correlation clinics" which introduce patients almost as audiovisual aids, for example, bringing children to be observed in courses in growth and development. This attenuated form of contact with real patients —that is, not in the capacity of practitioner or even full-fledged apprentice, but more as an observer—characterizes many programs of early clinical study.

With the shortening and condensation of basic science training into 1 or 1½ years, clinical clerkships can begin earlier, even where some version of the customary sequence is followed. At the Downstate Medical Center of the State University of New York, required clinical clerkships start in the second half of the second year and can be completed within one year, leaving a final period of electives.

Yale Medical School has introduced a six-week required clinical experience, under a preceptor in a community hospital or in group practice, at the end of the first year. The stated objective is to demonstrate to students "in a very forceful way that a knowledge of basic science is, indeed, a necessary prerequisite to clinical competence," but, according to report, some students return to the second year of basic study with great reluctance:

For a few of the students, the excitement, the challenge, and the stimulation of early clinical experience has whetted their appetites for increased clinical work and has, perhaps in a naive way, diminished their enthusiasm for the study of basic science. Their requests for increasing numbers of clinical correlations, clinical rounds, and other experiences that bring them in contact with patients, reflect their impatience with the return to basic science and the consequent delay before they go on to their clinical clerkships ("The Case for First Year . . . ," 1970, p. 9).

Some schools are trying to extend the elective philosophy into sequencing. In an experiment at the University of Pennsylvania, entering students can choose the order in which they take the first two years of required preclinical and clinical courses. The last two years of study are completely elective.

These experiments raise questions about what have customarily been defined as prerequisites—for example, the assumption that basic science study must precede satisfactory clinical learning. But changes which have been made in length and in sequence constitute more of a reshuffling than a basic reorganization of the form and assumptions of medical training. Questioning of the medical profession, especially of the organization and distribution of services, is taking place at a far deeper level, with significant implications for educational institutions. The next section explores current challenges of the structure and prerogatives of the medical profession.

THE CHANGING PROFESSIONAL MANDATE Professionals hold an extraordinary power of definition; the most successful (physicians are a prime example) have established the right to set the very terms of the problems and services involved in their sphere of work. These matters of definition are central to the professional mandate—the right which physicians claim to define the nature and treatment of disease, to control admission to their ranks, to fix the limits of their responsibility, to define more or less legitimate and desirable problems and clients, and to determine the way in which medical services ought to be distributed and paid for.

Professional mandates change. As physicians consolidated their monopoly over the practice of medicine in the nineteenth and especially the twentieth centuries, their mandate expanded, encompassing more problems, clients, resources, and other occupational groups. Gradually one basic philosophy, rooted in the tenets of scientific medicine, came to dominate professional thinking about matters of health and disease, and one large but relatively homogeneous and organized colleague group assumed the prerogative of defining, providing, delegating, and distributing medical care. As Eliot Freidson (1970a) documents in some detail, of all occupational groups, physicians have established the greatest monopoly and the most extensive mandate over their domain of work.

As the general mandate of the medical profession expanded, specialties developed within, which, like orders within the Catholic church, represent distinctive subdivisions and philosophies, a narrowing of technique, identity, and definition within an encompassing context. Some specialties grew out of movements of reform; for example, pediatrics developed when some physicians turned their attention to the special problems of infants' and children's disease and health. It was part of the child-welfare movement. Other specialties, like anesthesiology and radiology, developed with changes in medical technology. Although rooted in the medical profession, specialties have their own philosophies, networks of colleagueship, procedures for certifying new recruits, and preferences with regard to clients.

Bucher and Strauss (1961) describe specialties as one kind of professional "segment"; other segments may be less formally instituted and recognized. Embodying distinctive identities, ideologies, problems, and social organizations, segments constitute the basic unit of social change within professions. From this perspective, professions may be seen in process "as loose amalgamations of segments pursuing different objectives in different manners, and more or less delicately held together under a common name, at a particular period in history" (ibid., p. 326). The notion of segments draws attention to the changing nature of professions, to the fact that their mandates are not fixed, but constantly shift, with inner variations, subdivisions, and conflicts.

In recent years professional mandates have been widely and basically questioned by powerful outside groups (such as state and federal governments), by clients (who have begun to organize into protest and reform movements), and by a small but vocal group of activists within professional, and especially student, ranks (a group that can be described as an emerging professional segment). Criticism has shifted from the issue of standards to problems of social organization and the distribution of services. This includes questioning of some of the most basic professional assumptions about what services should be provided, who should receive them, what the basis of payment should be, and what the scope and limits of professional responsibility are.

Professional Individualism At issue is a deeply ingrained individualism, endemic to the professions since their origins. Professionals have traditionally regarded the individual client as the unit of service, and in carrying out their work, they have insisted on a high degree of autonomy and individual judgment. Although affirming a service obligation, professionals have tended to define responsibilities in terms of the individual client rather than society or the public as a whole. The balance between duty to the client and duty to the community has been weighted toward the client.

It is precisely such an emphasis on individual judgment and independence, founded on a conception of the character of the work, which allows the self-regulatory process of professions to shift from the ideal of responsibility for the actions of one's colleagues to concrete responsibility for one-self, to shift from belief in the ideal of responsibility for the public good to the practice of responsibility for the good of one's personal clientele (Freidson, 1970*b*, p. 154).

Doctors and lawyers have traditionally regarded solo practice as an ideal, in which services are delivered on a one-to-one basis, in a private transaction between professional and client, with the client paying a fee for the services received. This ideal reflects not only the values of individualism and autonomy but also the entrepreneurial side of the professional's role. Under a fee-for-service arrangement, professionals provide services primarily to those who can pay, and the success of one's practice is measured in terms of the class of people whom one serves. Care of the poor is either ignored or handled through various forms of charity.

One result of professional individualism has been a stratification of the services delivered.

The professional man cannot spread his services, he cannot, except within narrow limits, distribute his skill through subordinates. He is unable to go in for mass production and is forbidden to offer cheap lines for slender purses. Since he works for a limited market it is not surprising that he should choose one which is solvent and concentrate on the wealthy individual client. In other words, he must find an employer, and the general public was not organized for his employment. The doctors, whose sense of public duty has always been strong, got round this difficulty to a large extent by giving free service to the poor while living on fees taken from the rich, and by organizing unofficial insurance schemes in country districts under which the villager paid his penny a week while he was well and received the attendance he needed when he was ill. But speaking generally this state of affairs led to a maldistribution of professional services in terms of social need, a maldistribution due to economic motives among professional men but not necessarily implying any disloyalty to the principle that service must not be sacrificed to profit. . . . Big-scale social activities only became possible when the initiative was taken by the State and the local authorities, by public corporations and rich charities. And by that time the professions had built up their tradition of individualism, which meant not so much the pursuit of individual self-interest as the service of individual clients in a relationship of individual trust. They were therefore disinclined to press for the establishment of corporation agencies for the distribution of professional services and reluctant to work for them when they appeared (Marshall, 1939, p. 332–333).

Individualism remains a deep-seated value in the professions, even though there have been extensive changes in the context of medical practice since the nineteenth century, a result of changes in technology, processes of institutionalization, and shifts in financing. There has been a steady decline in the number of physicians both in solo and in general practice, and more physicians work in organized settings. The medical division of labor has become increasingly complex; rather than an individual practitioner, there is frequently now a team of workers (or, more accurately, a hierarchy of health workers under the control of the doctor). The private office is giving way to clinics and hospitals, and medical centers and teaching complexes have assumed strong institutional power, especially in urban areas.

Outside agencies have become more involved in the distribution of professional services. After World War II, various forms of third-party payment—Blue Cross, commercial health insurance, schemes run by unions and companies, and, in the 1960s, Medicare and Medicaid—emerged, attempting to spread the risk and cost of medical care and adding an outside, fee-paying party to transactions between physicians and patients. The result has been a double system, with some patients still paying on a fee-for-service basis and others through third-party arrangements (which apply primarily to hospital-based care).

In spite of greater institutionalization, centralization, and some outside intervention in financing, medicine has not become a public business or responsibility; it remains a private but highly subsidized enterprise. The traditional mandate—giving professionals the right to select their clients and the client the responsibility of paying for the care he seeks—still underlies most of medical practice. Medical care is still dispensed in accordance with people's ability to pay. The quality of services varies along class lines, with the poor cared for within the framework of charity, welfare, and teaching hospitals (in a form of symbiosis—receiving care in return for being learned upon).

The poor receive inferior care not only because of an inability to pay, but also because professional services are geared to the lifestyles of the relatively affluent. From the beginning, recruits to medicine have come from the middle and upper-middle class, and these origins have shaped the mandate and mores of the occupational subculture, putting clients from other classes at a basic disadvantage. For example, according to the occupational code, professionals are prohibited from advertising and are supposed to wait for referrals or for the client to take initiative and seek out services. Since *knowledge* of the need for services and how to procure them, as well as the ability to pay, is differentially distributed along class lines, the poor have an added difficulty in gaining access to medical care.

The rule against advertising favors clients and professionals with good middle-class connections, who are in the circle of knowledge and referral; it excludes the poor and minority groups and their needs.

The reason the medical systems have not reached the poor is because they were never designed to do so. The way the poor think and respond, the way they live and operate, has hardly ever (if ever) been considered in the scheduling, paperwork, organization, and mores of clinics, hospitals, and doctors' offices. The life styles of the poor are different; they must be specifically taken into account. Professionals have not been trained and are not now being trained in the special skills and procedures necessary to do this (Strauss, 1967, p. 8).

This situation is reflected in medical education, recruitment policies, curricula, and the careers to which training is geared. The goal of medical school has been to create successful doctors, which has come to mean doctors who are serving profitable clientele. In traditional career lines care of the poor has been relegated either to a stage of learning (the internship and residency, where young physicians often learn disdain for patients from lower socioeconomic backgrounds) or to failed, little-valued, or ethnically specialized careers.

Distribution as a Public Issue

Within the last decade, the traditional, individualistic professional mandate has been under strong attack. Health care issues have not remained the private, esoteric domain of physicians; the structure of the medical profession, especially as it concerns the delivery of services, has become a public, and a very political, issue.

Facts and statistics about the failure of the current health care system are widely publicized and discussed—the fact, for example, that although the United States ranks first in the world in the percentage of its gross national product spent on health care, it ranks fifteenth in terms of infant mortality and eighteenth in male and eleventh in female life expectancy (Cray, 1971). Much has been written about the shortage and maldistribution of health personnel; 5,000 American communities have no doctor at all (Michaelson, 1971). Hospital outpatient clinics have become the primary care facilities for the urban poor, who cannot gain access to less crisis-oriented types of care. Rising costs and basic shortcomings in current forms of third-party payment are an added dimension of what has become generally known as the health care crisis.

Organized consumer groups, outside critics, some policy makers, and activist medical students, practitioners, and health care workers have launched various lines of attack which can be described as a multistranded movement of protest against the organization and traditional mandate of the medical profession. These groups have begun to insist that health care is a right rather than a privilege, and they have begun to demand that the medical profession be held publicly accountable for an equitable distribution of services. This would entail shifting from an individual and toward a more collective definition of responsibility, in some sense coming to regard the community rather than the individual as the patient. Such a shift would involve reevaluating the structure of practice, the philosophy and organization of distribution, and, hence, redefining favored and legitimate clients and problems.

The medical profession itself is divided on the issues of structure and responsibility. One writer has described the situation as a "medical war," with three main factions:

. . . the politically conservative American Medical Association, representing generally the interests of the traditional, fee-for-service entrepreneur; the academic, generally "liberal" hospital-and-medical-school-based practitioners, with their complicated affiliations and sources of power; and a third faction loosely defined as a "health movement" of radical professionals, consumer, community, worker, and student groups, which is beginning to emerge (Michaelson, 1971, p. 33).

In addition to factions within the profession, controversy over the the basic structure and assumptions of medical practice has come to involve groups of health consumers, state and federal governments, large insurance companies, manufacturers of drugs and hospital equipment, and labor unions.

As both socializing and delivery institutions, medical schools figure prominently in current assessments of the health care system. Medical schools have a direct hand in shaping the composition and orientation of the profession and in transmitting the assumptions of the professional mandate. They also play a direct role in the delivery of health services, a role which has expanded with the growth of large university medical centers and networks of affiliated teaching hospitals. Some look to the medical schools as agents of social reform, to help solve the health care crisis. Others regard medical schools as very much a part of the problem.

The government, community and consumer groups, and activist students are pressing medical schools to respond to the crisis of health care delivery. The dispute over professional mandates has shaped some of the most recent and dramatic trends in medical education: programs to increase enrollments, to recruit more minority students, and to bring medical schools into closer relationship with their communities; changes in curricula (for example, the addition of new, experimental programs in social, preventative, and family medicine); and the emergence of protest and activism among medical students.

Government Pressures   Federal and state governments are no casual bystanders with regard to medical institutions, Federal activity has rapidly expanded in the areas of health and medicine. Since 1963 Congress has enacted more than 32 major laws involving health programs, with an increase in federal health expenditures from $3 billion in 1960 to an estimated $13.9 billion in 1968 (Lee, 1968). The Medicare and Medicaid programs accounted for a significant part of this increase, drawing the government into direct financing of patient care.

The government has given funds for special projects, construction, and student loans and scholarships, but the bulk of federal aid to medical schools has been indirect, in the form of research grants and the subsidy of service functions. In the 1950s and 1960s the rapid expansion of government spending on biomedical research had the effect of making medical school budgets dependent on federal money. By 1967, federal research grants constituted 42 percent of total medical school income.

Sponsored research funds (including overhead) accounted for more than one-half of the total increase in medical school receipts between 1947 and 1967. Federally sponsored research accounted for almost 90 percent of that growth (Fein & Weber, 1971, p. 215).

This pattern of federal financing encouraged medical schools to emphasize research; thus it had an impact on their educational climates, sense of purpose, and curricula. Admissions committees favored students with strong science backgrounds, and highly specialized research-oriented careers were rewarded. Medical schools became increasingly aloof from their surrounding communities and from the goals of direct patient care and training for practice. Funkenstein (1969*b*) calls this period, which he dates from 1959 to 1969, the "scientific era" of medicine.

As the distribution of health care became a national priority, with widespread concern about the crisis in the delivery of services, medical schools began to change their orientation, moving into what Funkenstein has labeled the "community era." In the last few years the federal government has cut back its funding of biomedical research, and service and delivery activities have assumed higher priority (a shift which still means that the educational mission is supported by other activities). The purchase of patient care in teaching hospitals has provided a growing means of support for education, a trend encouraged by the introduction of Medicare and Medicaid. Between 1967–68 and 1968–69, the medical school income derived from services to patients increased by 36 percent, becoming the third largest source of support for regular operating programs (in 1958–59 this income source was in eighth place) (*Journal of the American Medical Association,* 1970, p. 1523).

There has, however, been no simple shift from research to service. The decrease in government research grants, combined with inflationary trends and recent cutbacks in Medicaid, has thrust many medical school budgets into a state of near collapse. The financial crisis has forced some schools (for example, the University of Buffalo, California College of Medicine, Seton Hall, and Marquette University) to shift from private to public or semipublic status. Legislatures in at least six states have begun giving financial aid to private medical schools to help them avoid continuing deficits. More than half of the nation's medical schools have received special projects grants from the National Institutes of Health "on the basis of conditions of financial stress." Some medical schools have warned that they may soon be forced to close ("Financial Cutbacks . . . ," 1970).

Recent legislation promising any kind of aid to medical schools tends to be directed not toward research, but rather toward issues of manpower and delivery. Both state and federal governments have offered financial incentives for medical schools to increase enrollments, a push which reflects widespread concern with the shortage of health personnel. For example, in Illinois, both private and public medical schools can qualify for special subsidies from the state on the condition that they expand enrollments. In 1971 Congress passed new amendments to the Health Professions Educational Assistance Act, which will provide $3.5 billion for medical education over three years. The main objective of the legislation is to increase the number of practicing physicians. To be eligible for these grants, medical schools must increase their student enrollments (*New York Times,* Nov. 4, 1971).

Medical schools are being rewarded not only for producing more physicians, but for producing physicians of a certain kind. The same bill offers medical schools incentives to train family physicians. Programs for recruiting students from minority groups and low-income families have received a degree of financial support from foundations and the government. Office of Economic Opportunity community health centers, which often have ties with medical schools, offer another example of the way in which government programs are drawing medical schools toward concern with the organization and delivery services.

Although academic research medicine remains a strong segment within the profession and a continuing force within medical schools, the rhetoric of government officials and some medical educators has begun to shift toward concern with problems of service and distribution. Medical schools are under pressure to increase enrollments, especially of members of indigent minorities (who are in greatest need of financial support), to help expand the numbers of allied health personnel, and to provide new forms of training and community service, perhaps even taking a leading role in restructuring the delivery of medical care. But funds have been drastically curtailed just at a time when medical schools are being pressed to follow new directions. This is one of the most basic problems which today's medical schools confront.

Community Demands

Consumer and community groups are another force pressing medical schools toward greater concern with issues of delivery. Medical schools have traditionally remained somewhat aloof from their surrounding communities, apart from drawing on them (especially the poorer segments) for "clinical material" to use for teaching and research purposes. The research focus of the 1950s and 1960s reinforced this detachment from community- and service-oriented concerns.

In recent years, however, medical schools have been forced to reexamine their relationship to surrounding communities. Community groups, especially those drawn from the lower socioeconomic classes and from black, Puerto Rican, and Mexican-American populations, are better organized than in the past. Health care has become a highly politicized issue and a focus of protests and demands.

Some of the government health programs of the sixties, for example OEO neighborhood health centers and community mental health centers, call for formal community participation. Although these provisions have often been implemented in a superficial way, becoming a source of frequent conflict, they have had the effect of drawing communities together around health issues.

As of 1970, New York had more than a dozen black and Puerto Rican neighborhood organizations concerned solely with health. Even in smaller cities, like Fresno and El Paso, and in Southern rural areas, there are beginnings of black and brown movements for community control of health institutions (Ehrenreich & Ehrenreich, 1971, p. 238).

Protest movements among indigent health consumers have special relevance to medical schools and their affiliated hospitals, which are often the only source of medical care in urban ghetto areas. This is in part the result of a historical trade-off. Unwilling to give up paying clientele, the practicing profession let medical schools, who needed patients for teaching and research purposes, have access to charity cases. Many medical schools are located near large ghetto populations or at least have teaching affiliations with hospitals in those areas.

The result has often been a double standard of care. Patients who can pay receive the respect and privileges of private care; poor patients admitted to the same hospital receive services in return for being used for research and teaching purposes, which often means impersonal and denigrating treatment (Duff & Hollingshead, 1968). Medical centers have placed other priorities above service to the community—an orientation which consumers have begun to protest.

Patients from disadvantaged communities are increasingly resistant to being used as clinical material, and with the growth of third-party payment, especially Medicaid and Medicare, many of them became paying, rather than charity, patients. Although these programs are now being cut back, they have had the effect of raising health expectations among segments of the population traditionally denied access to medical care.

Community protests have been directed specifically at medical schools and teaching hospitals. In 1969, a coalition of Columbia medical and nursing students and people from the surrounding community launched a protest against the dual standards of care at the medical-school–affiliated Presbyterian Hospital. They demanded that the hospital be run by a community board and that the hospital decentralize into more accessible neighborhood settings. There have also been protests against the physical expansion of medical school complexes into surrounding neighborhoods. In 1969, the community surrounding the Harvard Medical School organized opposition to a long-range construction program; this protest halted plans for immediate expansion.

The Student Challenge to the Professional Mandate

Mandates are being questioned not only by government policy makers and by clients but also by recruits to the professions. Student unrest and protest first took hold in undergraduate colleges, but soon began to appear in professional schools. Compared with their predecessors, the most recent generation of medical students are more socially conscious and politically aware, less willing to follow traditional roles and careers and to take the existing system (including the practices of medical schools) for granted. This change will be discussed more fully in a later section on student cultures, but it is important to note that professional mandates—the basic assumptions, structure, and priorities of the medical system—are a central target of protest.

Student complaints often center on the "irrelevance" of their training, on its narrow research focus and its separation from primary patient care and the needs of disadvantaged communities. The content and direction of student demands vary from place to place, but the general thrust is to insist on basic changes in the traditional mandate of the medical profession. Activists have called for an elimination of fee-for-service and the assumption that health care is a commodity rather than a right. They have demanded an equal distribution of health services without regard to ability to pay and increased minority enrollments in medical schools. Critical of medical centers for being oriented to research and for neglecting the needs of surrounding communities, activists have urged a shift in emphasis toward patient care, including programs in preventative, social, and community medicine. In some cases, medical students have joined community groups in calling for consumer participation and even community control of health institutions.

Activist students have pressed their concerns with leaflets, picket lines, and demonstrations. Disruptions have become an almost predictable part of professional meetings; for example, in 1969, 150 medical students disrupted a national meeting of medical school deans and accused them of being "unresponsive and unaccountable to the consumers and victims of health care in America." Students have organized service projects in disadvantaged communities, many, until 1969, under the aegis of the Student Health Organization, a nationwide activist organization of health care students, which was founded in 1965.

Episodes of protest erupt and die down. In 1970, observers on a number of campuses noted a lessening of student activism compared with the previous two years. Active protest seems to be more common among first- and second-year medical students slackening as they disperse to separate clerkships and to the demands of clinical training, and as they become more absorbed into the profession. Nevertheless, in the last few years, students have emerged as a vocal and persistent voice for change both in medical schools and in the health care system of which they are a part.

The Mandate Issue in Relation to Medical Education

A number of recent trends in medical education reflect efforts to cope with problems of distribution and to redefine professional mandates in terms of the needs of the community rather than the individual patient. These trends include changes in admissions policy, with emphasis on increasing the number of students and broadening the base of recruitment to include more members of minority groups; a shift toward earlier and more diversified clinical programs; and the addition of courses in fields like community and social medicine.

Increase in Enrollments

The doctor shortage, and the need to increase the number of physicians, has become both a shorthand phrase and a suggested palliative for the current crisis in the health care system. Federal and state funding of medical schools is increasingly contingent upon expanded enrollments. The American Medical Association, which traditionally sought to limit the number of recruits into the profession, has, in the last few years, begun to change its tune, joining a chorus of voices calling for more doctors. In 1968 the AMA and the American Association of Medical Colleges issued a joint statement which urged that:

Increased emphasis be given to support of the educational component of academic medical center activities with the intent that the production of physicians and other health personnel by such centers be assigned the highest possible priority (*Journal of Medical Education,* 1968, p. 1009).

Partly as a result of these pressures, in the late 1960s medical school enrollments began to climb. For about 36 years prior to 1960 the total enrollment went up an average of 325 students a year. From 1960 to 1968, the average annual increase rose to about 506. In 1968, all but eight of the medical schools in operation increased enrollments (*Journal of the American Medical Association,* 1968). The following table summarizes the acceleration of medical students enrollments from 1968 to 1971:

Enrollment in United States medical schools, 1968–69 through 1970–71	*1968–69*	*1969–70*	*1970–71*
Number of schools	99	101	103
Total students	35,833	37,690	40,238
Increase over previous year	3.7%	5.2%	6.8%
Total first-year entrants	9,863	10,422	11,360
Increase over previous year	4.6%	5.4%	9.0%

SOURCE: *Journal of Medical Education,* January 1971, p. 96.

Related to this increase in enrollments is an expansion in the number of new and developing medical schools. Between 1910 and 1915, in the aftermath of the Flexner report, there was a rapid drop in the number of schools. From 1929 to 1953, the number of schools stayed between 76 and 80 and slowly increased to 86 by 1960. Between 1960 and 1970, 17 new medical schools were developed, bringing the total to 103 (including 6 schools of basic medical science) (*Journal of the American Medical Association,* 1950, p. 115; 1970, pp. 1484, 1516).

Producing more doctors has clearly become a priority among medical planners and educators, a priority reflected in larger class sizes and promises for even more increases in the future. But even if the number of medical graduates sharply increased, it is doubtful whether the current crisis would be solved, because it is not simply a problem of manpower but one of distribution and structure, involving fundamental questions of mandate.

Simply increasing numbers does not entail a basic restructuring of the health care system. This may be one of the reasons why even the most established segments of the medical profession have been so ready to translate the health care crisis into a problem of a shortage of physicians. If the main remedy is only to increase the number of doctors, traditional individualism, medical care as a private enterprise, and the mystique of a doctor and his patient as a sacred dyad can be retained—as values if not realities—in an era of hospitals, third-party payment, and large work systems.

Those who have taken a closer and more critical look at the health care crisis have come up with a more complicated picture. From the consumer's point of view, there is a shortage of available medical services. Availability is a more acute problem for consumers in geographical areas (such as ghettos and rural communities) and for some types of practice (such as primary care) than for others. In some areas and specialties there may even be an oversupply of practitioners. The problem is one of distribution, exacerbated by rising costs and inadequate financing. Not only physicians, but also allied health personnel and facilities, are in short supply. The crisis reaches into the heart of the health care system, and its solution will require more than enlarging the number of physicians-in-training.

Minority Recruitment People from poor, black, Mexican-American, Puerto Rican, and American Indian communities have limited access not only to medical services but also to the medical profession. From its beginnings, the guild of physicians has drawn from elites; in Europe and later in America its recruits have overwhelmingly been white, male, and middle- or upper-middle-class. In 1967 almost two-thirds of all medical students came from families with incomes over $10,000, and only 9 percent came from families earning less than $5,000, although 25 percent of all American families fell into that category (Crocker & Smith, 1970). In 1969 only 2.8 percent of all medical students were from nonwhite minorities, compared with 11 to 12 percent in the United States population (*Report of the Association*

. . . , 1970). Although women constitute over half of the population, in 1968 only 9 percent of all medical students were female (*Journal of the American Medical Association,* 1970, p. 1512).

Until recently, the exclusive composition of the medical profession has gone relatively unchallenged. But the growth of political movements among blacks, Puerto Ricans, Mexican-Americans, and women has brought demands for equal access to the professions. Activist medical students have also taken up the recruitment issue. In Philadelphia in the fall of 1969, a Health Professions Minority Admissions Campaign was organized, led by white and black medical students and by some junior faculty members. This group demanded that blacks constitute at least one-third of the entering freshman class in each of the five Philadelphia area medical schools. The same year in Boston, a coalition of black community groups and the Student Health Organization proposed that all black and Spanish-speaking residents of Massachusetts who had completed the prerequisites be offered admission to medical and nursing schools. Their open admissions proposal noted that "for health care, black and Puerto Rican people remain dependent on a system that refuses to educate their children but demands retention of the power to plan which services will trickle into their communities."

In the late sixties, the American Medical Association and the American Association of Medical Clinics (AAMC) appointed various task forces to study the issue of minority recruitment; these professional bodies began to voice the goal of expanding the number of black, Mexican-American, and Puerto Rican physicians. (Women were not included, and are often mentioned tangentially, if at all, in discussions of minorities within the professions.) Foundations and the government, through the Office of Economic Opportunity, provided funds to support some of the initial studies and programs (Dove, 1970).

By the 1968–69 school year, 54 medical schools had initiated special minority recruitment programs (Crowley & Nicholson, 1969). A variety of enterprises emerged to form what some call "the minority recruitment industry": special recruitment trips and publicity efforts, often with minority medical students participating, designed to make opportunities more visible among populations where access to the medical profession seems inconceivable; summer programs to introduce high school and college students to careers in health care; special admissions committees for minority applicants, with the authority to waive traditional criteria such as minimum Medical College Admission Test scores and college grades; provisions for tutorial and remedial academic help; and financial aid (essential for recruits with limited personal resources and having non-middle-class perspectives on loans and long-range career investments).

Minority recruitment efforts vary from school to school. The University of California San Francisco Medical Center has perhaps the most far-reaching official objective: to reach at least 25 percent minority students in the entering class of its medical, dental, pharmacy, and nursing schools. Out of 136 students in its 1969 entering medical school class, there were 22 blacks, 8 Mexican-Americans, and 1 American Indian (*Chronicle of Higher Education,* Apr. 20, 1970). Some schools have increased class sizes specifically to allow places for minority students admitted under special criteria; in 1969, Stanford Medical School added 10 extra places with this in mind.

Rather than cooperating, medical schools have often been in competition for minority students. Some schools have no special recruitment programs. More elite and well-financed medical schools have had an edge in attracting minority students, and Howard and Meharry, which have traditionally trained the bulk of black physicians, have begun to lose students. In 1968 these two schools accounted for almost two-thirds and in 1969 for a little less than half of the nation's black medical students (Curtis, 1971, p. 33).

Recent cutbacks in funds from the federal government and other sources leave the future of these recruitment drives in some doubt, but in the last few years there has been a steady increase in the number of medical students from nonwhite and poor communities. In 1968 there were a total of 226 (or 2.7 percent) blacks in the entering classes of medical students; in 1969 the number had risen to 440 (or 4.2 percent) and in 1970 to 697 (or 6.1 percent). Between 1969 and 1970, the number of entering American Indians increased from 7 to 11, Mexican-Americans from 44 to 73, Puerto Ricans from 96 to 113 (including the University of Puerto Rico Medical School), and Asian-Americans from 140 to 190 (*Journal of Medical Education,* 1971, pp. 96–97). Of the 12,263 students who entered medical school in the fall of 1971, 11 percent, or 1,376, were nonwhite (blacks, Mexican-Americans, American Indians, Puerto Ricans, and Asian-Americans) ("A Record Number . . . ," 1971).

During the last few years the number of women medical students has also increased, going from 9 percent of students entering in

1968 to 11 percent of students admitted in 1970 (*Journal of Medical Education,* 1971, pp. 96–97).

This movement toward broadening the base of recruitment may help change the mandate of the medical profession. Control over entrance to their ranks (a basic prerogative of the professions) has been one source of the power of physicians to define what services are distributed and to whom. The profession is composed of people from the community it tends to serve best—those who are white and affluent—and success in the professions has generally meant having a middle-class, paying clientele. A narrow base of recruitment is tied to an inequitable distribution of professional services.

An increase in minority enrollments, some have argued, will help effect more equality in the delivery of health care. The gap of social class and culture between the mass of physicians and their more disadvantaged clients contributes to the maldistribution of medical care. Medical students and house staff are often shocked by the realities of poverty and are unaware of the details of daily life of patients from nonwhite and poor communities. According to the traditional pattern, medical students learn on the poor, picking up the disdain embodied in the phrase "clinical material," and when training is completed, they move on to paying, usually white, clientele.

Physicians recruited from disadvantaged communities are likely to bring to their training a different set of values and assumptions, having more sympathy, knowledge, and ability to communicate with patients from minority subcultures. Some argue that recruits from these communities may be more willing to follow careers among the urban poor, rather than seeking clients of high status and income.

At least one minority recruitment program is specifically designed to direct students from black and other disadvantaged communities into careers among the inner-city poor. Through a pilot project called the Urban Doctors Program, which began in 1972, Northwestern University has committed itself to annually admitting 25 inner-city high school graduates to a six-year program leading to the M.D., starting with two years of intensive premedical study in a community college. In an effort to keep the students in emotional and social contact with their communities of origin, students will be encouraged to commute from home to medical school. Curricula will emphasize urban health needs and will involve the students with health services in their home areas.

Some have cautioned that it is both unrealistic and discriminatory to expect minority recruits to forgo the careers most valued by the medical profession and to practice among the urban poor. The expectation that blacks will (and should) become primary practitioners in the inner cities is continuous with a historical fact: rather than following the distribution patterns of the profession as a whole in terms of choice of career and type of practice, minorities have traditionally clustered in certain kinds of careers, largely because there are significant barriers to other kinds of work. For example, a 1942 study found that black physicians were less likely than other physicians to be found in specialties or in group practice (Cornely, 1944).

If the number of minority recruits and practitioners in the medical profession is significantly increased, there may be important, long-range changes in the structure, values, and career lines of physicians — a possibility discussed in the section on student cultures. But it is obvious that it will take more than doubling class sizes and introducing minority recruitment programs to effect an immediate change in the distribution of services. The effort to move from a conception of medicine as an individual, private business toward a more collective sense of professional responsibility involves basic definitions of work and rewards. New kinds of careers will emerge only if they are made financially attractive and are held in fair esteem. The next section reports on efforts to create new types of practice, more oriented to the community and toward basic problems of distribution.

An Emerging Professional Segment

Critics have pointed to the ways in which the structure and content of medical education contribute to the maldistribution of professional services. As medical schools became more isolated from their surrounding communities, with highly specialized and research-oriented faculties, students were exposed to few models of community-based practice. With clinical training postponed until the last two years of training and often limited to teaching hospitals (which are far from representative of community practice), students were encouraged to enter academic or highly specialized medical careers. Students remained in the isolation of the hospital, seeing patients referred and preselected for their "clinically interesting" (or unusual) problems. Primary and preventative medical care implicitly became dirty work, "clinically uninteresting," the domain of less valued careers.

A new direction of effort is promised in a variety of programs developed by medical schools in recent years. The issue of delivery, the goal of providing good medical care to the entire population, has become an organizing point and stated mission for new departments, curricula, special electives and programs of study, new kinds of internships and residencies, and even entire medical schools. The delivery issue has emerged as an enterprising nucleus within the medical profession.

Concern with the delivery of health care is behind changes in the sequence and timing of medical education. By integrating preclinical and clinical study and by bringing students into earlier contact with patients, some educators hope to encourage students to choose careers as community-based practitioners. There are also efforts to expand clinical programs beyond the restricted setting of the teaching hospital, to draw students into experiences more typical of the work of the practicing profession.

The curriculum of the University of Massachusetts Medical School, which opened in 1970, includes a three-week clerkship in the first year, during which students are placed in a variety of practical situations — solo urban and solo rural practices, health departments, nursing homes, neighborhood clinics, general and group practices — to observe consumers and providers of health care. The goal is to sensitize students to community problems and to expand career horizons early in medical school careers. At a professional meeting, one of the planners of this program asserted that "every medical student today needs to study the health problems of communities as intensely as they study patients." This statement indicates a shift from the traditional individualistic professional mandate.

In 1971 the University of Missouri–Kansas City Medical School began a program which assigns students to docent units, or learning teams, under the guidance of teacher-practitioners. Under this arrangement, from 30 to 50 percent of the student's experience will be gained directly in the health care system, in community hospitals and neighborhood health centers, as well as within the setting of the medical school.

Drawing medical education into the community often means familiarizing students with the problems of the disadvantaged — a client group which figures centrally in the delivery issue. Some medical school programs promise exposure of this type. Other programs have been initiated by activist students, who want their training to have both more "relevance" (which often translates into more practical experience) and a closer tie to groups traditionally denied access to medical services.

Students have initiated a variety of service projects among the poor. Although not institutionalized in medical school curricula, participation in these projects is becoming an almost standard learning experience for many students. In its February 1971 newsletter the Student American Medical Association estimated that as many as 80 percent of medical students will participate in extracurricular health service delivery programs before graduation.

From 1965 to 1968 the Student Health Organization ran summer service programs for medical, nursing, dental, and social work students. During the first summer, students conducted an audiovisual screening program for children in Watts, California, acted as patient advocates for migrant workers in the San Joaquin Valley, and did surveys of the health of ghetto residents. Supported by federal grants, the summer projects expanded over the next three years, giving participants "a first-hand exposure to the health problems of the poor and a glimpse of what the health system looks like from the bottom up" (Ehrenreich & Ehrenreich, 1971, p. 244).

The Student American Medical Association developed a more activist cast in the late 1960s and began to organize student service projects in poor communities. In 1969, 94 medical and 20 nursing students were placed for the summer with private physicians in the Appalachian region. The goal was to expose students to the problems of the rural poor and to encourage them to return to Appalachia to practice medicine. Other projects have been run by groups of medical students; for example, Stanford students set up a free clinic for migrant farmers in the San Joaquin Valley, and Howard medical students established a health care project in Mississippi.

These service projects have shared a similar set of goals: to provide health services where they are most needed, to expose middle-class medical students to disadvantaged communities, and, as a result, to encourage careers among the rural and urban poor. The results have not always been encouraging. In some communities, students found that they were not welcome as practitioners. Paradoxically (since the programs were designed to improve on an inequitable delivery system) student service projects are in line with the traditional pattern of learners distributing services to the poor. Some communities made it clear that they preferred experienced doctors and regular, institutionalized health care services over temporary patchwork programs run by novices who are present for only a few months.

As for the theory that these programs would encourage careers among the poor: at the end of the summer program in Appalachia, a survey of the 114 participating students found that only 20 might be willing to return as practitioners. Apparently it takes more than exposure to encourage a shift in career choices.

New Programs, Departments, Careers

Within the last decade a spectrum of new names—*community medicine, social medicine, preventative medicine, family medicine* —has been added to the roster of medical school departments. It is difficult to differentiate these fields, and their content is less clearly specified than that of more institutionalized specialties. One professor of public health (a field related to these new programs) remarked in a meeting devoted to the subject of training in community medicine:

There are wide varieties of things around the country which are taught under the heading of community medicine and preventive medicine. These fields are now into public favor. Everyone wants them, but no one is sure what they are. These might be called the specialty of question-mark. More and more students are showing an interest in them, and faculty are hard pressed to know what to do with this interest. It is not clear what the graduates of community medicine will be doing. One can't start with a job description and work backwards.

These fields have developed in response to the crisis in health care delivery. They share an orientation to larger groups such as society, the community, and the family rather than a narrow focus on the individual patient; and they emphasize primary, community-based medical practice. One can document the rise of these fields— in the names assigned to new academic departments and training programs and as designations accepted by some, especially younger, physicians. Taken together, and grouped with various attempts to create new kinds of careers oriented to the issue of health care delivery, they can be described as an emerging, but still inchoate, professional segment. Their greatest strength seems to be within medical schools; they have yet to gain a firm institutional and economic foothold within the medical profession.

Training in these fields is a hodgepodge of medical school courses, special elective programs, and internships and residencies.

There is no general agreement about the stage and sequence of learning appropriate for becoming a "community" or "social" physician. Some doubt whether these fields should constitute full-fledged specialties, believing that it is more appropriate to regard them as background for other kinds of practice. One questionnaire which asked 62 medical school deans if their schools offered "an instructional program for medical students in Community Medicine" got a confused pattern of response. The question was intended to refer to discrete instructional programs, but some of the 42 deans who responded "yes" were referring to the fact that in their schools something like community medicine was covered in courses or clerkships primarily devoted to other subjects (Littlemeyer, 1969).

A number of schools, especially newer ones, have begun to use the notion of community medicine as a specific organizing theme in their educational programs. One of the first of these programs was initiated by the University of Kentucky Medical School, which established a Department of Community Medicine nearly 10 years ago and began to send fourth-year students into clerkships in the surrounding community. Meharry Medical College, which has long had ties with the poor black community of Nashville, recently attracted government funds for expansion under the new federal emphasis on community medicine. Referring to the grant, the president of Meharry noted, "We are an idea that has come of age" (*New York Times,* Nov. 29, 1970). At least two relatively new medical schools—the University of Massachusetts and Pennsylvania State University—claim a special delivery orientation by supporting undergraduate programs in community medicine which give students practical experience in the surrounding community.

New internships and residencies are also appearing in these delivery-oriented fields. Albert Einstein College of Medicine and the Montefiore Hospital and Medical Center in New York have begun internships and residencies which combine social medicine with internal medicine or pediatrics. After training, a physician receives a diploma in social medicine and is eligible for "boards" in one of the other two fields. Those who direct the program claim that the addition of social medicine makes the residency experience

. . . general rather than specialized, with the emphasis on developing competence in managing common diseases and the focus on psychosocial preventive, health maintenance and rehabilitative aspects of medical care (Wise, 1970).

Family medicine is the only field in this new spectrum to be formally designated as a specialty. In 1969 the Council on Medical Education of the AMA approved residencies in family practice— the first new specialty to be added in 21 years. In 1970 the American Board of Family Practice gave its first examination to 2,000 physicians seeking certification in the specialty. Hospitals around the country, many of them without teaching affiliations, have developed residencies in family medicine. In 1970 it was estimated that less than 15 percent of medical school graduates were entering the field (*New York Times,* Mar. 1, 1970).

A New Breed of Doctor? Training programs in community, family, preventative, and social medicine are part of a trend which some claim will result in a "new breed of doctor." Medical schools and hospitals have found that establishing programs which focus on delivery issues can bring direct institutional gains: government grants (for example, a special federal subsidy for programs in family medicine and Office of Economic Opportunity assistance with projects in community and preventative medicine); and manpower (some hospitals, especially those lacking a close tie with a medical school and therefore facing acute shortages of house staff, have added internships and residencies in family or social medicine, partly hoping to attract more personnel).

In taking a long look ahead, however, one must ask to what extent medical schools, even with government help, can open up new kinds of professional careers. Not every new mission and movement within the history of medical education has been successful. In the 1950s, for example, several medical schools developed programs in "comprehensive medicine," a conception with some resemblance to the more recent notion of "family medicine." Although they began with optimistic claims, hoping to be a prototype of a new kind of medical practice, training programs in comprehensive medicine gradually faded out. The orientation did not take hold within the practicing profession or result in lasting careers.

Although within the last decade official rhetoric has turned to the issue of medical care distribution, there is no guarantee that even a part of the profession will firmly reorient itself in the direction called for by community, social, and family medicine. Establishing a new professional segment requires more than a few training programs and an initial corps of enthusiasts; it takes supporting institutions: financial and social rewards; legitimation within the profession and access to its resources of capital, referral, and skill; and the cooperation of clients.

Training programs in the new delivery-oriented fields have just gotten underway; it is too early to predict their long-range outcome. But several patterns can be traced in terms of supporting institutions for these new kinds of careers.

First, the financial support for work in community and social medicine is not likely to come from fees paid by individual clients; some type of third-party payment will be necessary. Fee-for-service as a form of payment runs against an orientation to a more comprehensive and communitywide distribution of services. The new fields tend to focus on the problems of disadvantaged communities — on clients whose health needs have been ignored in the past precisely because they were unable to pay for medical care. Government programs seem the most likely source of funding, and some community-oriented careers have emerged within OEO neighborhood clinics and in the Public Health Service (a new law enables health professionals to enlist in the Public Health Service to provide medical care to slum and rural areas). But the OEO is in financial difficulty, and federal support of health care has been generally cut back. It is becoming clear that careers which depend on federal support of medical care for civilians are precarious.

In additon to financing, the establishment of new career lines required both formal and informal legitimation within the profession and in the eyes of clients. Of the newly named community-oriented fields, only family medicine has received formal certification as a specialty; the leaders of the field regard this achievement as an important step toward making family medicine a stable and attractive career. Those wanting careers in community or social medicine can get specialty certification only in other fields (for example, pediatrics or internal medicine, as in the Einstein Medical School residency program at Montefiore Hospital). The result tends to be a hybrid rather than a coherently defined type of practice.

In seeking respect and a degree of prestige, family, community, and social medicine run against a deep strain in the recent history of medicine: the trend toward specialization and away from more general kinds of practice. In 1958, 38 percent of medical students intended to go into general practice; in 1966, the figure was 13 percent (Bartlett, 1969). Within the medical profession, the various specialties are strongly ranked in prestige, and general practice and public health (traditional fields most akin to the new types of practice) have low positions on the scale. To many physicians, and clients as well, fields like family and community medicine connote general practice, and thus low status and an image of being relatively untrained and unskilled. To become fully established with sufficient prestige to attract both recruits and clients, these new fields will have to overcome widespread bias in favor of physicians who practice the more traditional specialties based on organ systems and diseases.

There are signs that the systems of rewards and the definition of favored work are beginning to change, especially among the younger generation of physicians and medical students. Problems of delivery and the health needs of communities are more widely acknowledged, and medical students have a concern with social and political action which distinguishes them from their predecessors. According to some observers, the changed character of medical students is likely to support career choices in the direction of community, social, and family medicine. Daniel Funkenstein, who for two decades gathered detailed information about Harvard medical students, claims that, starting with the class entering in 1968, students have had distinctly different values and expectations:

This new breed of students first became the majority of an entering class in the Harvard Medical School in 1968. Their personal characteristics and career plans can best be described as appropriate to the Community Era of medicine in which health care would be delivered to all segments of our society without regard to financial means, in which action would be taken on social factors that impede health and breed disease, leading to a true preventive medicine, and larger numbers of students from minority groups would be provided with the opportunity of becoming physicians (Funkenstein, 1969*b*, p. 15).

The orientation of the more socially aware students, Funkenstein claims, differs from that of the medical school faculty and the bulk of practitioners:

Faculty members see their social responsibility to be scientists and to do research; students see theirs to deliver medical care to all segments of the population, largely primary care, to take action on social problems related to health, and to see that more minority group students are admitted to medical schools. . . . Today's students reject the faculty and the physician in private practice as role models (Funkenstein, 1969*b*, p. 21).

It is unclear whether the "new type of student" is a lasting trend (in 1970 and 1971 some medical school observers noted a resurgence of the old-style, science-oriented student), or whether socially oriented values will be retained through the long process of induction into the medical profession. One possibility in both medicine and law is that service to the community will be a youthful career stage rather than a long-range focus. An increasing number of graduating M.D.'s may serve for a period in OEO clinics or in the Public Health Service, but, especially as they assume more family responsibilities and look to more secure futures, they may eventually drift toward middle-class clientele and more traditional forms of practice. Thus far in OEO neighborhood health centers there has been a large turnover of doctors — a trend that suggests that service to the poor has a long way to go in becoming a lifelong, fully established career in medicine.

Experiments in the Social Organization of Practice

The movement toward community and social medicine involves basic changes in the social organization of practice. These are more than new specialties, which may be built around a technological advance or greater knowledge of an organ system. With the goal of providing more equitable delivery of health care, advocates of community and social medicine propose fundamental shifts in the social and economic arrangements of professional practice. There have been a variety of experiments with more comprehensive and community-oriented ways of delivery medical care — some in OEO neighborhood clinics, and others, like a clinic opened by the North East Neighborhood Association in New York City, the result of independent initiative.

These new types of practice are a far cry from the solo, fee-for-service model. They uniformly depend on some form of third-party payment, and physicians are usually salaried. Doctors in these kinds of practice do not pick and choose their clientele; they are responsible to a given community, and responsibility tends to be defined in collective rather than individual terms. Physicians and other health workers often become advocates for those they serve, defining them as constituents as well as clients. In these experimental settings, doctors have less autonomy than in traditional forms of practice. Clients often have a voice in clinic policy (although not in questions such as diagnosis), and in some of the new experiments (for example, that run by the North East Neighborhood Association in New York City), work is governed by the principle of community (or lay) control.

In these experiments with new forms of delivery, traditional definitions of favored and legitimate clients are turned around, and specific preference and attention are given to the disadvantaged, to the urban and rural poor, and to racial and ethnic minorities. This also means a redefinition of dirty work — screening for lead poisoning and innoculation campaigns become important tasks, in contrast with the work most valued in highly specialized types of practice.

There are other departures from the preferences and code traditionally governing the doctor-patient relationship. Rather than waiting for clients to take the initiative, physicians often go into the community, trying to persuade people to seek medical care.

In contrast to perpetuating an air of mystery, the physicians in community medicine may strive to reduce the mystery of disease and to encourage and "educate" a population toward more rational patterns around health. Then too, while the patient comes to the doctor in private practice, the health team goes to the community in preventive efforts and moves to bring patients into clinics. The physicians in private practice may be repelled at the suggestion of "advertising for patients," but the community medicine program may advertise to bring people to a mobile chest X-ray unit and to come in for Pap tests. Persuasion in the form of calls and reminders and posters and handbills to draw the attention of "target groups" fit in with the goals and commitments of community medicine. But these same actions do violence to the ethos held with near reverence by many private practitioners (Mumford, 1970, p. 226).

The concept of community or social medicine includes emphasis on the work team, and training programs in these fields often try to combine the education of physicians with that of nurses and allied health personnel. This is true, for example, of the University of Kentucky program in community medicine (Eichenberger & Gloor, 1969). Experimental programs in community medicine carry out the idea of rearranging the medical work system, trying out different combinations of tasks and new roles. The role of the pediatric nurse-practitioner, who is delegated some of the doctor's functions of diagnosis and management, has developed in neighborhood clinics; another new role combines elements of the public health nurse, the social worker, and the doctor's assistant (Rosen, 1971). There have also been experiments with trying to break down the traditional medical hierarchy, making the jobs less stratified in terms of salary and prestige. Frequently these clinics draw paramedical workers from the surrounding community, thus providing another link between the delivery institution and its clients.

Conflict over Questions of Mandate

These developments in community and social medicine remain at a tentative and experimental stage. They lack strong institutional supports and are regarded with skepticism and even disapproval by many physicians who hold the traditional mandate of the profession as an almost sacred premise. Like other segments which have emerged in the history of the profession, an orientation to community medicine will become firmly established only if it can command financial and institutional resources, and the process is likely to involve strong conflicts. This is especially true in the case of these new delivery-oriented fields because they tinker with long-standing assumptions about delivery of and payments for services, about favored and legitimate problems and clients, and about the doctor's role with regard both to patients and to his fellow health workers. Emily Mumford (1970, p. 226) notes some of the reasons why the medical profession resists this new orientation:

Presently, the ethos of community medicine is closely related to medical schools and the behavioral sciences — in some places more closely than it is related to the community of local practitioners. At first, it seems paradoxical that the local physicians, whose primary work and experience and skill relate directly to the lay community, are probably among the physicians farthest away from both planning and effecting community health efforts for the future. . . .

But the paradox is less marked when we see that the paths of community medicine and solo practice are divergent. The relationship between patient and *the* doctor is the lodestar of private practice; but in community medicine the team and the hospital become involved in cooperative efforts on behalf of the patients. There may be many "third parties" as the team works in the large organization to pull together the work of many specialists and sometimes many agencies on behalf of all people who need it in a community. The patient sometimes in turn tends to become loyal to the hospital, the doctors, the clinic. . . .

The acts that the educator in community medicine sees as progress toward large health goals, the man in solo practice may see as subversive of the very essentials of the system to which he is committed. The final incendiary social fact in the antipathy of local doctors to a program in community medicine may be that they sometimes direct their efforts toward some of the same patients.

On closer examination, many of the changes in medical education which are advertised as efforts to reorient the profession to problems of distribution seem to be more rhetoric than reality. The accepted mode of discourse now includes talking in terms of community needs and expressing concern with the delivery of patient care. Proposals and programs in medical education as well as other health institutions are packaged in new ways. Professional individualism may no longer be taken for granted, but powerful vested interests continue to uphold traditional institutions and assumptions. There is great room for skepticism in assessing the actual changes of recent years.

THE INSTITUTIONAL ECOLOGY OF THE MEDICAL SCHOOL

The modern medical school is part of a complicated network of institutions which span the worlds of practice and of higher education. Medical schools have ties with universities and colleges, research facilities, the practicing profession and professional associations, delivery institutions (hospitals, group practices, neighborhood clinics), and powerful third parties (federal and state governments, health insurance programs, drug and hospital equipment companies). The medical school is a large, multipurpose institution; recurring debate over the priorities of teaching, research, and patient care indicates that the purposes often conflict. Taking an institutional perspective, this section will trace the ecology of professional training in medicine.

Delivery Institutions, the Practicing Profession, and the Community

Formal training in medicine has traditionally involved a practical element, in which students devote some of their time to learning on actual patients. According to a long-standing practice, these patients have predominantly come from among the poor, receiving professional services in return for being learned upon. This symbiosis was partly the result of the reluctance of the practicing profession to give up any paying patients, which left medical schools with charity cases, whose care, incidentally, was defined as involving lower stakes than that of middle-class clients. In choosing a location, many medical schools established facilities in or near large indigent populations in order to ensure an adequate supply of "clinical material."

Through these patients, medical schools have always had ties with their surrounding communities, but only in recent years have medical schools begun to claim special responsibility for the delivery of health care to a given geographic area or population. Medical schools have become more directly and fully involved in the delivery of health care, adding large networks of hospital affiliations and initiating new enterprises such as prepaid group plans and neighborhood clinics.

In cities like New York, Boston, and Chicago, virtually every municipal and veterans' hospital is affiliated with a medical school, creating large institutional complexes with medical schools drawn into the center of the health care delivery system (Ehrenreich & Ehrenreich, 1971). Institutional arrangements vary, from loose affiliations with some hospitals to a situation in which a hospital is entirely owned and operated by a medical school or university.

Within the last two years at least seven schools of medicine have set up prepaid group practices as "models" of medical care delivery. Harvard Medical School established the first, the Harvard Community Health Plan, which is underwritten by commercial insurance companies and which operates a health center backed up by four Harvard-affiliated hospitals. According to the plan, 20 percent of the membership is to be drawn from the medically indigent, whose fees will be paid by the federal and state governments.

Medical schools have also helped found and operate neighborhood health centers, many under the auspices of the Office of Economic Opportunity community health program. In the late 1960s, for example, Stanford Medical School developed links with three OEO-sponsored health centers: one in Palo Alto in an area populated by low-income blacks, a second serving a largely Mexican-American community in Alviso, and a third clinic located in a rural area. As a result of student initiative, Stanford also developed a health care facility in the San Joaquin Valley.

The expansion of medical schools into the delivery of health care is partly the result of a traditional motive: to gain more patients for teaching and research purposes. There have also been financial incentives—third-party payment (which has made hospitals more financially independent and has altered traditional charity arrangements) and special funds, such as those from OEO, earmarked for delivery purposes. Philanthropic, federal, county, and municipal government agencies have begun to invite medical schools into the management of community and veterans' hospitals, since medical school affiliations bring hospitals prestige and help them obtain a better supply of interns and residents.

Medical schools have moved more squarely into the realm of health care delivery, but there is debate over the wisdom of this trend. Some have urged medical schools to assume an even larger role in the distribution of services, becoming institutions of reform in the health care system. Federal health reorganizational programs such as Regional Medical Programs and Comprehensive Health Planning look to large medical centers to help restructure and rationalize the delivery system. The Carnegie Commission on Higher Education (1970) has proposed a distribution of health science centers according to population, so that each school can be integrated with the medical delivery system of a given geographic area.

Opposition to this trend has come from within medical schools, from some parts of the practicing profession, and from some client groups. Some medical educators believe that the functions of teaching and research suffer when medical schools become centrally responsible for community medical services. They dispute the new community focus which has taken hold within medical schools. Donald W. Seldin (1966, p. 979) takes this line of argument:

We are now confronted from all quarters with the demand to undertake clinical services responsibilities far beyond what is required for academic purposes. The University is regarded, not as an institution of learning, but as the agency to solve the medical service needs of the community. These needs, to be sure, are pressing, and no responsible citizen can question the social value of legislation designed to bring the fruits of medical science to all people. However, for the University to become the prime agency for the solution of community service problems is a very grave step. The University is not a community service institution. Its prime function is the cultivation of learning. Once responsibility for broad patient care is assumed, this must, for moral reasons, take priority over every other activity. It is difficult to see how, under such circumstances, the qualities of academic life can be preserved. We hear much, in these days of regional medical centers and similar programs for broad medical care, of the need to "dismantle the barriers." But the University barriers are designed to preserve those functions unique to the University. The price for the solution of community service requirements may be the inexorable erosion of academic activity.

The practicing profession has had a history of resisting the expansion of medical schools into the delivery of services. In some places, acute problems in delivery institutions have reduced these objections; in New York City, for example, the hospital system reached such a point of crisis that the organized profession was willing to give medical schools a larger hand in delivery. But there have traditionally been strong conflicts of interest between local practitioners and physicians attached to medical schools.

In 1965 Patricia Kendall published a study of the relationship between local practitioners and medical educators in a number of communities. She found that conflict between town and gown had several dimensions. Medical school faculty generally came from outside the community and, partly because of large research grants, remained cosmopolitan, oriented to a national circle of colleagues, often in other university medical centers. Local physicians found medical educators aloof, condescending, and lacking in respect for community institutions; they also disagreed with the medical school emphasis on research and specialization, which, they claimed, neglected practice. Local practitioners were not always able to gain access to hospitals affiliated with medical schools, which often restricted use of the facilities to those with board certification. Finally, in the cases where medical educators also had private practices, they were in direct economic competition with local practitioners, who felt at a disadvantage because of their lower status.

Conflict between the medical school and the practicing profession is likely to accompany greater medical school involvement in the delivery of services. For example, there are plans to establish a large academic medical center in Milwaukee, consolidating teaching, research, and clinical facilities on one site, and treating private patients as well as those financed by Medicare and Medicaid.

The rise of a comprehensive medical center to replace the hospital for the indigent poor will mean a change in town-and-gown relations in the medical community. Until now there has been no real conflict of interest between local medical men and the medical faculty. As a medical center began to attract larger numbers of private patients, local physicians and private hospitals might begin to feel frozen out. It is not impossible that opposition to the medical center idea in its present form could develop ("Marquette School . . . ," 1969, p. 20).

On a broad scale, the conflict between local, private practitioners and the academic, institution-based medical establishment is reflected in a division between the American Medical Association and the American Association of Medical Colleges. The AMA represents the sentiments of small-town and rural practitioners and upholds the traditional individualistic, fee-for-services, entrepreneurial model. The AAMC is based in large, urban institutional complexes controlled by university-based medical centers. In recent years these two medical establishments have come into increasing conflict:

Criticism of the expanded role of medical schools in the delivery of services has come from community and consumer groups as well as members of the practicing profession and some educators. In this case, the issue of public accountability is primary; those concerned with patient care fear that the goals of teaching and research will divert attention away from community needs. In line with this criticism, some medical schools have professed to be reexamining their priorities, to be adopting a new mission: responsibility for the health care of entire communities.

New enterprises in social and community medicine forge stronger ties between medical schools and their surrounding communities. Minority admissions programs also focus attention on the medical schools' relationship to the community and bring into the profession representatives of the groups who have been most deprived by the current system of care. Partly due to community pressure, many medical schools have begun special programs to train people from adjacent communities to assume paramedical roles. This type of health worker will always be under pressure to work as an advocate for the patient and the community.

This is part of his role and his *raison d'être.* This makes him less fully committed to the institution that employs him than are the professionals with whom he works, and subjects their relationship to inevitable strain. To the degree that these institutions fail to meet the demands made on them, the new careerist will be prone to see the failure as a reflection of professional shortcomings (Rosen, 1971, p. 20).

As more links have been forged between the medical school and the community, there has been increased debate over the goals, priorities, and responsibilities of the medical center. This debate is part of a general questioning of the traditional isolation of institutions of higher education. Universities as a whole are more community-oriented than in the past, and the shifting ecology of the medical school is only one part of this trend.

Universities Although they have assumed more responsibility for the delivery of services, medical schools have not left the world of higher education. On the contrary, Flexner's proposal that medical education should be brought within the university system has become an established fact. Of the 83 four-year United States medical schools in full operation in 1966, all but 11 had university affiliations (Blumberg & Clark, 1967).

This institutional arrangement has been reached from a number of directions. In some cases, an existing college and an existing medical school joined; for example, Emory University School of Medicine came into being in 1917 when the Atlanta Medical College, an independent professional school, affiliated with Emory University (Weiskotten et al., 1940). Some medical schools and universities were founded at the same time; a medical faculty was part of the original plan for the University of Virginia when it was established in 1825 (Norwood, 1970). In other cases, existing universities created new medical schools; this is true of all but 2 of the 21 medical schools currently in development *(Journal of the American Medical Association,* 1970, p. 1493). In no cases have medical schools themselves created universities, but the University of Alabama Medical School, which is located in a city remote from the main campus, has plans to expand into an entire university at its site in Birmingham (Souter, 1967).

The phrase "university affiliation" covers a variety of geographic, administrative, and academic arrangements. Of the 72 four-year medical schools with university affiliations in 1966, 20 were located in metropolitan areas different from their affiliated universities, in sites often determined by hospital facilities and patient populations. Eighteen of the twenty were public institutions, many affiliated with a land-grant institution in a rural area; for example, the university of Maryland School of Medicine is in Baltimore, while the main university campus is in College Park. Twenty-four of the medical schools were in the same metropolitan area but on a campus separate from the main university; for example, Tufts Medical School is located in downtown Boston, and Tufts University is in a more suburban location several miles away. Twenty-eight of the schools in operation in 1966 were located on the general campus of the affiliated university; Duke, Minnesota, the University of Chicago, and Case Western Reserve are examples (Blumberg & Clark, 1967).

In financing, organization, and administration, medical schools tend to have more autonomy than other divisions of the university. Medical schools have become financial operations of considerable magnitude; in the 1968–69 academic year they spent an average of $15,700,000 *(Journal of the American Medical Association,* 1970, p. 1485). The money came from a variety of sources: state, local, and federal governments; gifts and grants; endowments; tuition and fees; university income and reserves; and payment for service in teaching hospitals and clinics. Direct federal grants have become the backbone of operating budgets; in 1969–70, 48 percent of all full-time medical school faculty had part or all of their salaries paid from federal research and training grants (ibid., p. 1511). This has given medical schools a relatively high degree of fiscal independence from their affiliated universities.

The current crisis in the funding of medical education has led some schools to shift affiliations. In 1967 Marquette School of Medicine severed its ties with Marquette University in order to receive state appropriations, which were legally prohibited when the school had church connections. The relative ease with which this shift was made illustrates the loose ties which link many medical schools and universities.

The separation from the university actually required no major surgery. Since 1918 the medical school has had its own board of directors, and the school has always been self financing. The medical school was operated as a department of the university but in practice had wide latitude to conduct its own affairs ("Marquette Schools . . . ," 1969, p. 20).

In some cases, especially where medical schools and their affiliated universities are located at a distance, ties are largely nominal. Tufts Medical School relates to Tufts University primarily through accounting facilities; there is little sharing of faculty or resources. Both the University of Illinois and Harvard University have some joint faculty appointments that link their medical schools with university departments, but the medical schools have their own separate departments of anatomy, biochemistry, and other basic sciences. The University of Chicago School of Medicine has a relatively high degree of integration with its parent university; organizationally the medical school is part of the university division of biological sciences, and medical students and graduate students share some classes. When it opened in the fall of 1965, the College of Human Medicine of Michigan State University followed a similar arrangement; it established few new university departments, drawing instead on the resources of the existing departments of physiology, biochemistry, sociology, etc.

One observer, referring to the "common-law marriage of medical schools and their universities," has concluded that isolation rather than integration is the general rule:

Although it is fashionable to speak of "the university medical center," there are literally fewer than a dozen instances in the United States where a medical school and a university are geographically, administratively, and academically integrated. Therefore, it is largely in theory that the intellectual resources of the university stand available to medical centers as they analyze their new responsibilities and attempt to launch bold new programs (Sanzaro, 1969, p. 147).

Training in all professions tends to be isolated and self-contained. The professional claim to monopoly over an esoteric and unique body of knowledge leads to exclusiveness and to separation from other disciplines and pursuits. On the other hand, professions also claim that their work rests on some branch of universal knowledge or science, a claim which leads to integration with the world of higher learning. The result is a chronic strain between the exclusive and the general, between intellectual isolation and ties with other disciplines.

When the medical profession began to develop and emphasize its roots in biological science, it sought a university base for training and research. But the thrust toward exclusiveness and isolation continued. By establishing their own faculties of physiology, anatomy, and biochemistry, medical schools have been able to draw on other fields, to affirm a relation with general science, while remaining relatively self-contained.

Medical students study anatomy and biochemistry, but usually a version more or less adapted to the paradigm and outlook of the medical profession and learned apart from students specializing in the basic sciences. In contrast with clinical teachers, Ph.D.'s who instruct medical students in the basic sciences are not training future colleagues. These instructors are marginal both to the medical brotherhood and to their own academic professions. Within medical faculties there is often friction between physicians and nonphysicians, a strain which is related to the traditional division between basic science and clinical departments and curricula.

Medical school faculties

Until well into this century most medical school teachers were also private practitioners. The trend to full-time medical school faculty began with the growth of basic science departments, many of them staffed by Ph.D.'s. There has also been a steady movement toward establishing full-time members in United States medical schools. In 1960–61 the number had climbed to 11,111, and by 1969–70 it had more than doubled, to 24,706 (Fein & Weber, 1971; *Journal of the American Medical Association,* 1967, p. 747; 1970, p. 1509).

Physicians who teach clinical subjects combine the roles of academician and practitioner in a variety of ways which are usually categorized by the form of compensation. A "strictly full-time" faculty member derives his income entirely from salary, with any fees from private patients reverting to the medical school or teaching hospital. A "geographic full-time" faculty member has his only office at the medical school or teaching hospital and is allowed to supplement his medical school salary with fees from private practice. "Part-time" and "volunteer" faculty members maintain their own practices while teaching; the former receive some payment for teaching, while those in the volunteer category do not.

Although the trend is to employ more faculty on a strict or geographic full-time basis, part-time teachers still constitute a majority of clinical faculties. In the academic year 1966–67 clinical departments had 35,853 part-time faculty members. Some schools, like Chicago, Case Western Reserve, and Yale, had nearly all full-time faculties. At the other extreme, there were schools with more than five times as many part-time as full-time faculty members (Fein & Weber, 1971).

Government spending on biomedical research and the growth of full-time, research-oriented faculties have helped consolidate and strengthen the segment of the medical profession located within medical schools and teaching hospitals. This segment has developed into an itinerant national network of colleagues, often isolated from, and in conflict with, local practicing physicians. On the other hand, with their involvement in patient care and with ties to hospitals and the practicing profession, medical educators have also remained marginal to the mainstream of the academic world. Those who teach in medical schools are rarely active in general university faculty affairs; rather than using the faculty club, they tend to eat in white coats in a special section of the teaching hospital cafeteria, a detail which illustrates their isolation.

There have been divisions within medical school faculties. One which has already been mentioned is the conflict between clinicians and Ph.D.'s teaching the basic sciences. Another is between research-oriented faculty members and those more oriented to practice. The growth of biomedical research was accompanied by a decline in the prestige and importance of clinicians. In part, this was a struggle between generations; research scientists tended to be younger, while clinicians had traditionally derived prestige from years of practical experience. Rapid technological change and scientific advance give an advantage to younger members of the profession, who tend to be more in touch with recent innovations. In many medical schools clinicians began to assume a second-class status.

According to some observers, the recent emphasis on problems of health care delivery has created a new source of conflict within medical schools. The greatest friction is between students, who are increasingly oriented to community service, and faculty, who retain the values of the era of biomedical research (Funkenstein, 1969b). But some faculty members, many of them young and sharing the activist spirit of the current generation of students, are pushing for a shift away from research and toward problems of delivery. These faculty members differ from the old-style clinicians in their concern with changing the mandate and social organization of practice. The recent shift of government priorities and the cut in federal grants for biomedical research have helped strengthen the position of this segment of medical educators, although they remain a minority.

Noting the gradual displacement of part-time teachers by full-time faculties, the way specialists replace general practitioners, and the shift of prestige from clinicians to those engaged in research, Patricia Kendall (1965, p. 142) has concluded that "the history of medical education in this country, at least over the last decade, might be written in terms of the successive displacement of one group by another." The latest chapter in the history of shifting orientations and faculty conflicts may revolve around issues of health care delivery and the mandate of the medical profession.

Medical students and the university
Like their teachers, medical students tend to be isolated from the rest of the university. This is especially true if the campuses are separated, but even where the medical school and the university are in close proximity, medical students spend at least half of their four years in clinical settings, removed from university institutions and activities. Schedules as well as places set medical students apart from the university; at the University of Michigan, for example, medical students find it difficult to take courses in other divisions of the university because the schedules rarely coincide. As medical students begin clerkships and long, even night-time, schedules, their sense of separation from other students increases further.

It is rare for medical students to register for classes in university departments or divisions outside of the medical school, although a few schools have begun to experiment with interdisciplinary arrangements and joint degrees. Stanford Medical School, for example, has developed curricular ties with the psychology department, business school, and engineering school. But these programs are likely to attract only the relatively few students who want a form of hybrid training or unusual specialization. The bulk of students are likely to continue to find that their main business lies inside the medical school and away from the rest of the university.

The isolation of medical students does not mean, however, that the undergraduate segment of higher education is unaffected by post-B.A. professional training programs. Through prerequisites and highly competitive admissions procedures, medical schools heavily influence the experience of undergraduates who intend to seek careers as physicians. Writing about the general impact of the professions on the undergraduate college, Robert P. Wolff (1969, p. 14) has described the functions which professions rely on a college to perform:

First, [a college] must sort the undergraduate out into two groups—those who are acceptable as candidates for admission to professional programs and those who are unacceptable. Second, it must rank the acceptable candidates along a scale of excellence in aptitude and achievement in order to facilitate a fair and efficient distribution of scarce places in the more desirable professional programs (the crunch to get into Harvard Medical School is probably the most familiar example). And third, it must prepare undergraduates for professional training through inclusion in its curriculum of material which the professional schools wish to require as prerequisite to admission. The first two of these functions are inseparably bound up with process of grading. . . . The third touches upon the large question of the proper conduct and style of undergraduate education.

In many colleges those who declare themselves "pre-med" (which in some places is a designated major) constitute a relatively isolated subculture, welded together through shared curricula and concern with passing the hurdle of medical school admission. In effect, this experience is the opening stage of professional training.

The uncertainty, the doubt, the restrictiveness concerning the admission to medical school have led students interested in medicine to prepare themselves for the gauntlet of acceptance many years before their actual application to medical school. Thus, there has been a clearer awareness of the specific requirements for medical school. . . . For better and for worse, the college students arrive in medical school with much of their education already significantly influenced by the need to gain acceptance to medical school. This need has been an inspiration and an incentive, as well as a chronic source of anxiety and intellectual inhibition (Bartlett, 1969, p. 131).

The new six-year combined B.A. and M.D. programs initiated by Boston University and Northwestern are designed to smooth the transition between college and medical school, to lessen repetition, and to shorten the length of training. The result has often been relative isolation of the participants both from other undergraduate students (since those in the six-year program have a close timetable to follow and have already assumed a kind of preprofessional identity) and from medical students following the standard four plus four sequence, which involves different scheduling. Liberal arts or general education and professional training tend to lead to different directions; as students orient themselves to a given profession, they begin to be isolated and set apart.

Although medical students have not been significantly drawn into the activities and programs of other parts of the university, medical schools have expanded their own training programs, drawing in other categories of students. Many medical schools have established Ph.D. programs in the basic sciences; they have also assumed responsibility for more interns and residents.

While the number of M.D. candidates grew from 26,191 in 1950 to 34,304 in 1967 (a growth of 31 percent), the number of interns grew from 1,786 to 4,309 (141 percent), the number of residents grew from 4,259 to 17,501 (311 percent), and the number of graduate students in the basic sciences grew from 2,720 to 8,785 (223 percent). As the total number of full-time students (including clinical postdoctoral fellows) representing the teaching responsibilities of the faculty increased by 101 percent (about 4.2 percent per annum), the percentage that M.D. candidates were of the total declined from 75 to 49 percent. The responsibilities of the medical school had shifted and had grown (Fein & Weber, 1971, p. 54).

The training of the medical hierarchy
Within the last few decades there has been a significant growth and rearrangement of the medical work force. The number of workers in the health occupations has increased at a greater rate than in all service occupations taken together. In 1975, at the current rate of growth, over 4 percent of the civilian labor force will be employed in

health occupations (Allied Health Professions . . . , 1967). The greatest area of expansion has been in the paramedical occupations. In 1900 each physician had an average of one helper; by the 1960s, there were 10 paramedical workers to each physician, and some estimate that by 1975 the ratio will be at least 20 to 1 (Schreckenberger, 1970).

The medical division of labor constantly shifts. New occupations emerge as technology changes, specialties are developed, and some groups move up in the hierarchy, while casting off tasks to new categories of subordinate personnel. There are over 100 separately designated occupations in the health field, with over 200 further subdivisions. New categories continually appear; for example, the physician's assistant, the physician's associate, and the pediatric nurse-practitioner are occupations recently created to work at a level close, but still subordinate, to the physician.

Paramedical fields are distributed according to medical specialties: surgeons have an array of assisting occupations beneath them; pathologists have a different array (including, for example, laboratory technicians); dentists have developed their own group of assistants (such as the dental hygienist). But each specific work group remains under the dominance and control of the physician or dentist. Although the word *team* is in vogue, the situation is more accurately described as a rigid hierarchy organized under one key profession which delegates and supervises work and retains control over subordinate occupations (Freidson, 1968).

The medical hierarchy is in many ways a caste system. Its varied strata and substrata (referring to the various categories of nurses, for example) remain intact, and their members have little vertical or horizontal mobility. If an individual enters the system at one level — for example, as a licensed practical nurse or as a physical therapist — that is where he or she will remain. Formal training requirements and "credentialism" reinforce this stratification; diplomas, certificates, and licenses seal off one stratum from the next.

Recruitment patterns also reinforce the occupational caste system. The majority of doctors are white males, and are from relatively affluent backgrounds. The percentage of women, of racial and ethnic minorities, and of people from lower socioeconomic classes increases as one moves down the ranking system. The lower the status, the less rigid the occupational entry requirements. While medical students are relatively homogeneous in age, class, and education, as are students in four-year nursing programs, those training to be licensed practical nurses or laboratory technicians range more widely in background.

Secondary characteristics reinforce the formal differentiation of training, uniforms, titles, and income and prestige, with a vast gap separating doctors from the middle and lower orders. In 1967 self-employed physicians had median net earnings of $34,730; the median income of staff nurses in public health services ranged between $4,669 and $8,449; practical nurses received a median annual salary of $4,695; and, at the bottom of the hierarchy, aides and attendants typically earned less than $3,000 a year (U.S. Bureau of the Census, 1970; "Salaries Paid . . . ," 1967; Langer, 1971).

The fact that doctors control their own training—and that of the other health occupations as well—is basic to their position of dominance. The medical profession develops much of the technical knowledge learned by paramedical workers and in many cases directly controls their training and certification. The AMA, for example, formally accredits educational programs for medical technology, occupational therapy, radiologic technology, and 12 other paramedical fields (*Journal of the American Medical Association,* 1970, pp. 1529–1533). While nurses have more formal independence in shaping their training programs, they remain subordinate to the medical profession's body of knowledge and delegating powers.

The proliferation of new categories of workers and the gathering of a variety of occupations around a central one have important implications for professional training and for the educational system. Allied health workers are trained in a variety of institutions: hospitals, laboratories, vocational high schools, independent and proprietary schools, junior colleges, universities, medical schools. The situation has a strong element of the haphazard and unsystematic, but more and more programs are being drawn out of the hospital and into formal educational institutions.

Training programs for registered nurses illustrate trends typical of many allied health fields. Nurses are schooled in three kinds of educational institutions: junior colleges, with two-year associate degree programs; hospitals, which offer three-year diploma courses; and universities, which give B.A., M.A., and Ph.D. degrees in nursing. The various categories of nurses are arranged in a hierarchy, depending on length of training. With the exception of the B.A. program, which may precede study for an M.A. or Ph.D., each level is supposed to be complete in itself rather than a step in an educational sequence. The American Nurses Association favors an eventual two-level system: "technical nurses," trained in junior colleges, and, at a higher rank, "professional nurses" with at least a B.A. degree. Although hospital-trained nurses still predominate and are resisting the trend, there has been a significant shift toward these two types of university-based training. In 1968–69, 60 new junior and community college programs and 19 new B.A. nursing programs were instituted, while there were 33 fewer hospital-based programs in existence ("National League for Nursing," 1970).

The rapid growth in the number of paramedical workers and the general movement of training programs out of the hospital and into colleges and universities have led to a re-sorting of the functions of various schools. Junior and community colleges are assuming an expanded role in paramedical training, universities have added more baccalaureate-level programs to train the middle ranks, and medical schools and their affiliated hospitals have begun to educate allied health workers as well as physicians.

The hierarchy of educational institutions, ranked by level and length of training, as well as by prestige, parallels the medical hierarchy; "the longer, the more formal, and the closer to the university, the higher the position in the division of labor" (Freidson, 1968). Postbaccalaureate and baccalaureate degree programs, whose graduates work at or near the top of the hierarchy, are concentrated in university settings. The lower-ranked occupations, such as radiologic technology, inhalation therapy, and associate degree nursing, which require from one to two years of formal training, are shifting from hospitals to junior colleges. Practical nurses and various types of aides are trained either on the job or in vocational high schools.

Among paramedical training programs that have been drawn into colleges and universities, there are wide variations in administration and organization. At Michigan State University, for example, the departments of nursing, nutrition, social work, and veterinary science are relatively independent and are separate from the medical school. At the University of Pennsylvania, the School of Allied Medical Professions offers degrees in medical technology, occupational therapy, and physical therapy. In addition, health curricula are offered in five other units of the university: the Dental School (a dental hygiene program), the School of Social Work (a program in medical social work), the Graduate School of Arts and Sciences (biomedical electronic engineering and clinical psychology), the University Hospital (inhalation therapy, radiologic technology, medical technology), and the Graduate Hospital (histologic technology, medical records science, and radiologic technology).

Paramedical courses have increasingly been drawn into a single division of the university, in many cases administered by the medical school. In 1967 at least 16 medical centers had developed schools of allied health professions, and an additional 50 universities with medical and dental schools offered three or more programs of education for paramedical fields (Allied Health Professions . . . , 1967). The paramedical boom has entailed new functions and responsibilities for the medical school.

The education and increased use of paramedical workers have created new lines of contact between medical schools and their surrounding communities. While student physicians are recruited from a wide, even national, area, paramedical training programs draw students from a more local population. In some cases, local communities have demanded that area residents be trained and employed in medical centers.

The creation of schools of allied health professions has also linked medical schools with local educational networks. Developing its ideas from the notion of a "university of health sciences," the Chicago Medical School has begun to look to various community colleges to form combined programs. Since the school is not affiliated with any university, it plans to rely on neighboring community colleges to provide the general and liberal arts component of degree programs in physical therapy, nursing, and radiologic technology.

Although their future jobs are, by the "team" description, interrelated, the various categories of medical and paramedical students are usually isolated from one another during training. Those at any particular level of the medical hierarchy resist being taught in the same room as any lower category, and separate uniforms, curricula, and schedules mark off the various strata of students. This is the cloistering phenomenon, discussed more fully in a later section. Medical students rarely, if ever, have academic contact with nursing, inhalation therapy, or social work students; their classes, faculty, and routines are separate, even where the programs are administered within the same medical center or university. The only noticeable movement toward integrated training programs has been within some schools of allied health professions, where those in similarly ranked occupations occasionally share courses. For example, in some schools, students of physical therapy, occupational therapy, medical records administration, dental hygiene, and nursing take the same pathology and microbiology courses.

Even at the clinical level, the experience of each student group tends to be walled-off and isolated; medical students follow one set of rounds and rotations, and students of nursing, nutrition, and physical therapy have their own separately structured experiences. Contact between the categories tends to be a chance occurrence. Members of various health occupations apparently learn how to relate to one another—including how to delegate and receive instructions and how to supervise work—not through formal education programs, but through later on-the-job experiences. Isolation during the period of training implicitly teaches some of the behavior that goes with the hierarchical, castelike structure of the medical work system.

Student isolation and the rigid medical hierarchy may be drawbacks to efficient teamwork, communication, and coordination of patient care. In some recent experiments in health education, different categories of students are trained together. In the University of Kentucky community health course, students of physical therapy, dental hygiene, clinical nutrition, social work, and medicine share a field experience in Appalachia; the medical students serve as "team captains" (Eichenberger & Gloor, 1969). Case Western Reserve has tried sending interdisciplinary groups of medical, nursing, dental, social work, and law students to investigate the various health needs of Cleveland in order to assist the city in establishing new medical centers. According to one teacher, the students found that discovering how to relate to each other sometimes took up more time and energy than the specific work tasks: "medical students, in particular, are very problem-oriented; they got impatient with all the talk that they had to go through to get team decisions."

Student Health Organization and Student American Medical Association summer work projects have involved students in a range of health fields and have included emphasis on greater equality among prospective members of the "health team." Medical students, however, have tended to dominate even those interdisciplinary projects which have an egalitarian ideology. A degree of isolation and condescension toward occupations lower in the hierarchy seems to be a basic part of the professional attitude.

Various protest movements have tried to swim against the dominant tide of rigid credentialism, formal academic training, and blocked mobility in the health occupations. The "new careers" movement, for example, seeks to create more chances for advancement in the medical hierarchy and to make promotion less dependent on formal academic training. Proposals have been made to upgrade workers on the basis of job experience and in-service training rather than relying solely on academic credentials. It has been suggested that admission to training programs be more flexible; that programs be created that mix work and study, thereby allowing continuity of employment; that individuals be allowed to transfer to related programs without loss of credit; and that work experience be regarded as a basis for advancement.

An example is the new careers focus of the Training Center for Community Programs at the University of Minnesota. Candidates for the two-year A.A. degree are admitted on the signature of the dean, whether or not they have a high school diploma; 45 percent of those enrolled in the new careers program in 1968 had not graduated from high school. Students are granted two units per quarter for supervised work experience, and have a choice of courses in the regular liberal arts division of the university, in special sections of the two-year general college, or in the more vocational division specifically geared for those in the new careers program (*"Flexible New Careers . . . ,"* 1968).

The new careers idea is an effort to loosen access, to provide second chances and alternative routes to the paraprofessions. In the dialectic between learning on the job and learning in a formal, isolated school, the movement would weight the balance back toward the world of work. But the trend predominantly moves the other way. Employers and the gatekeepers of the professions and paraprofessions continue to insist on educational credentials. A study by the National Committee on the Employment of Youth found that experiments with new careers had not made much headway in cracking the credentials barrier. Without a college degree, "opportunities for genuine career advancement for paraprofessionals are either severely limited or completely nonexistent" (*"Dead End . . . ,"* 1971).

Relationships among Medical Schools

What patterns of communication, competition, and coordination exist among the nation's medical schools? This dimension—as well as the relation of medical schools to delivery institutions and to universities—can be considered part of the institutional nexus or ecology of medical education.

The training of physicians is more standardized and centrally controlled than that of any other profession. There are night or part-time schools of law, but not of medicine. Unlike theological seminaries, medical schools are not separated by dogma or belief. The medical paradigm or body of knowledge is relatively universal; within bounds of specialty, those holding the M.D. are considered to be formally, if not always in fact, interchangeable. This standardization is in part due to the control exerted by the medical profession. The American Association of Medical Colleges and the Council on Medical Education of the AMA accredit schools, help license graduates, coordinate resources, compile statistics, and in other ways provide formal ties among medical schools.

But the picture of homogeneity can be overdrawn. Medical schools vary in ownership, mission, constituency, student and staff origins, typical careers of graduates, prestige, and value climates. On the basis of these variations, medical schools cluster in a series of orbits or networks of relationships.

In a study of career choices in medicine, Lyden, Geiger, and Peterson (1968) classified a sample of 12 medical schools according to ownership (public or private), size (large or small), geographic location (a variable they found had little effect per se), and variations in traditional output (whether the school tended to produce chiefly specialists, general practitioners, or teachers and research workers). They found that the distinction between state-supported and private schools had a strong relation to choice of internship and specialty. In their sample, public schools produced a much greater proportion of general practitioners (in 1954, 33 percent of the public school graduates and 8 percent of the graduates of the private school were general practitioners). A higher proportion of the public school graduates terminated their training with an internship rather than a residency. Graduates of the private schools were more likely to obtain internships in major teaching hospitals, to have at least two years of residency training, and to obtain specialty certification (ibid.).

As the study indicates, the sorting of individual physicians into different types of careers and circles of colleagueship begins during the years of training. This sorting—the career lines typical of graduates of various schools—is one way in which medical schools tend to divide into "national," "state," and "local" orbits.

The more national or elite medical schools (for example, the University of Chicago, Stanford, Harvard, and Johns Hopkins) graduate a relatively high proportion of physicians headed first for prestigious internships and residencies (in teaching rather than community hospitals), and then for careers in teaching and research or in highly specialized types of practice (Miller, 1969; Mumford, 1970). These are the kinds of careers most valued within the medical profession. The national schools draw students and staff from around the country; their faculty members are "cosmopolitans" rather than "locals," and tend to look for colleagueship, not within the local profession, but in other prestigious medical centers. The Lyden, Geiger, and Peterson study indicates a connection between private ownership of a medical school and presence in the elite orbit, but the relationship is far from exact. The national orbit includes some public schools, for example, the University of Michigan and the University of California San Francisco Medical Center, and many private medical schools have a state or local orientation, for example, Emory, Jefferson, and schools with religious origins or connections, such as Loma Linda (Seventh-Day Adventist) and Loyola (Catholic). As medical school budgets have come to reflect a greater mixture of government and private sources, the distinction between private and public schools has become more fuzzy.

Schools which fall within state or local orbits draw their students from relatively circumscribed populations and head them toward careers in practice (often of the less specialized kind) rather than toward teaching and research. These schools tend to be oriented to the local profession rather than to a national circle of colleagues. Constituencies, missions, and functions vary widely. For example, Meharry Medical College has traditionally trained physicians, many of them general practitioners, for black communities; 80 percent of the graduates of Meharry practice in ghetto and rural areas (Elam, 1969). Founded by the Jesuits, Saint Louis University School of Medicine draws a high proportion of its students from Catholic universities and colleges in the Midwest, schools which reflect its basic constituency. Loma Linda School of Medicine was originally founded to train medical missionaries, but it has expanded its training to include those not seeking careers with a religious overtone. Like colleges and universities, medical schools seek formulas for survival; to remain going concerns, to retain students and resources, they shift missions and add new functions, while usually trying to keep their original monopolies (Hughes, 1971*a*, Chap. 6).

Variations among medical schools may reflect an implicit division of labor. Harvard Medical School operates in a national, even an international, orbit; it draws students from throughout the country and from abroad. It trains them to become part of the elite of teachers, researchers, and practicing specialists at home and abroad. In contrast, the new University of Massachusetts Medical School specifies that its students must come from the state, draws a significant portion of its funds from the state government, and has adopted the explicit mission of training community practitioners, presumably encouraged to work in Massachusetts. Tufts University School of Medicine and Boston University School of Medicine also tend to draw students from the surrounding region, or at least from the East Coast, and to train more for practice than for academic careers.

Many of the differences between medical schools remain implicit rather than explicit. Although schools vary in the kinds of careers their graduates choose, every school is presumably equipped to prepare its students for the range of available careers. There have been proposals for an explicit division of labor among medical schools. Daniel Funkenstein (1969a) suggests that there should be a "bioscientific tract," training researchers and specialists (as schools like Harvard now do); a "biosocial track," emphasizing fields like family medicine, public health, and psychiatry; and a "biomedical engineering track" (an orientation embodied in a new school now being jointly planned by Harvard and MIT). According to Funkenstein's plan, some schools, such as Harvard, would have all three tracks available; other schools with fewer resources would focus on one or the other of the tracks—as some are in fact now doing.

The fact that schools like Meharry, Michigan State, and the University of Massachusetts have explicitly declared a "biosocial" mission indicates movement toward a more formal and specific differentiation of function among medical schools. Like other aspects of professional organization, medical orbits change over time. There have been shifts in the ranking and evaluation of different kinds of careers. While some physicians had careers in biomedical research and teaching before World War II, it was only after the war that large amounts of money made possible the organization of institutions and laboratories in all medical schools. As suggested in the section on mandates, career lines in community medicine have begun to receive more resources and attention, and provide a focus for a new sense of mission, for individual schools as well as for medical students and physicians. The emergence of minority recruitment programs has drawn medical schools into new patterns of relations; for example, in Washington, D.C., an arrangement was worked out between Howard, Georgetown, and George Washington Medical Schools to develop jointly an M.D. and Ph.D. program for black students (Harden, 1969).

Both individuals and schools may seek to change orbits. A school can specialize or create a new sense of mission, advertise itself as unique in some way, seek applicants from a wider area, and raise admissions standards. Internships and residencies provide a means for the top graduates of state and local schools to shift to elite career networks (Miller, 1969).

There is little available information about the actual structure of medical school orbits. How much contact and communication are there among schools within a given orbit? National schools seem to be in closer contact than local schools. How much contact, communication, and mutual influence are there across orbits, that is, among national, state, and local schools? People in the lower leagues are often more aware of those in the upper leagues than vice versa. But it is unclear whether there is a diffusion of standards and procedures from the elite schools downwards, or if the various segments of medical education are shut up in themselves, without much mutual influence.

MEDICAL STUDENTS: INITIATION AND SOCIAL- IZATION

The process of becoming a doctor is one not only of socialization, of learning the skills, knowledge, values, mores, life-style, and world view of the medical profession, but also of initiation into a club and brotherhood. This final section explores the socialization and initiation of medical students in terms of cloistering, recruitment, and student cultures.

Cloistering

During the period of formal training, medical students are relatively isolated—physically, socially, intellectually, and psychologically. They are cut off from equal and close fellowship with those outside the world of medicine and, more narrowly, the medical school. This isolation or cloistering begins relatively early, often during undergraduate years, when premed students focus almost single-mindedly on gaining admission to medical school. Upon entering medical school, recruits to the profession are cut off from daily contact with those preparing for other occupations, even those related to medicine. As described earlier, even when medical schools are tied to universities, they tend to be geographically, administratively, and academically set apart.

Unlike Catholic seminaries, medical schools do not formally regulate all aspects of the student's life. But the heavy workload, the demanding routine, and the isolation of the medical school have a cloistering effect. Entering medical students find that every hour is scheduled and that they have little time, interest, or opportunity for contact with anyone except future professional colleagues.

The homogeneity of students contributes to the secluded quality of medical training. Medicine, law, and theology had their origins as vocations for gentlemen; historically the ideal professional student (who learned Greek and Latin as a symbol of high social standing) was a male, unmarried, of a young age, and from the upper class (Reader, 1966). This status limited claims on the individual who might compete with the demands of training. Without family or economic obligations, the student was more available for thorough socialization, for full absorption into the business of becoming a physician, a lawyer, or a clergyman.

Medical students are still predominantly young, male, and white, and from relatively affluent backgrounds (a fact documented in the earlier discussion of minority recruitment). The "latent culture" (Becker & Geer, 1960)—the values, etiquette, code, and outlook— of physicians is rooted in the white, male, middle and upper-middle class, just as the occupational subculture of licensed practical nurses assumes that recruits will be female, from lower socioeconomic classes, and from a variety of racial and ethnic backgrounds. As Freidson (1970b, p. 16) suggests, the shared social background of physicians and the fact that they tend to come from the most powerful segment of society reinforce their position of dominance and high visibility and contribute to a "homogeneity of outlook among doctors which significantly distinguishes them from people in such occupations as nursing and social work, who have typically more humble backgrounds."

The homogeneity and isolation of medical students help set them apart not only from the lower strata of the medical hierarchy, but also from ordinary laymen. This separation, this sense of being exclusive, is basic to professions. Given special license, for example to violate bodies and to obtain guilty knowledge, and granted considerable autonomy from outside judgment and control, professionals identify strongly with their colleagues. This feeling of brotherhood is in some measure a product of isolation and close association during the period of training. One can neither enter nor leave the medical profession on a casual basis; the investment of time, ego, and money and the cloistering of medical students strengthen commitment and loyalty to the guild.

The Experience of Minorities Physicians, paramedical workers, and patients expect medical students and doctors to be white and male; females, blacks, and Mexican-Americans who attempt to enter the exclusive community of doctors violate these expectations and are continually reminded of their anomalous position or contradiction of status (Hughes, 1945). Female doctors, for example, often find that both colleagues and clients focus on their sex status rather than their occupational status. Compared with men, the family and sex status of a professional woman is more often used in evaluating her work; the greater the occupational achievement of a woman doctor, the more likely she is to be accused of neglecting her family or being "unfeminine" (Epstein, 1970a, 1970b). Responding to a questionnaire distributed by Dr. Helen Glaser, women medical students revealed

"an ambivalence about being thought of as one of the boys. . . . and consequently, as a result of that identification, being thought of as less of a woman. They expressed vague anxiety about being a member of the third sex." Some of this confusion may come from their minority position: medical school lecturers automatically address their audiences as "gentlemen" or "you guys," a phenomenon which is universally noted by women students (Lopate, 1968, p. 81).

Women in male-dominated professions and professional schools have reported that their colleagues and teachers seem to expect less of them than of men and that every failure is ascribed to their sex (Epstein, 1970b; Lopate, 1968). Similarly, a black medical student felt that his instructors used two standards for judging performance; if his examination score reached the average, it was considered phenomenal ("Impact of Cultural and Economic Background . . . ," 1969). As they move into the "higher" professions, minorities often find themselves being treated as "special cases," a situation which may be double-edged.

Provisions especially designed for members of minority groups may help them elevate their position as a group, but it may also be used to maintain them in the very inequality that they hope to escape (Lopate, 1968, p. 20).

Since student subcultures, traditions, and networks of association often follow along lines which exclude those who are not white and male, minorities report an experience of isolation. Describing the experience of blacks attending a predominantly white medical school, a student noted:

As far as interaction with classmates is concerned, Earl seems to feel he had an almost non-existent social life. He and his classmates had very little to talk about outside of the academic sphere. This situation seemed to have improved over the last couple of years, but there is still a lack of complete social interaction among classmates. John, a first year student, typifies this by saying that all the relationships among students eventually have one dimension, racial. Seemingly, no matter what the topic or under what conditions one meets a fellow student or begins to engage in conversations or outward activities, the dynamics of the relationship will inevitably become racial ("The Impact of Cultural and Economic Background . . . ," 1969, p. 67).

Analogously, Lopate (1968) describes the isolation experienced by female interns and medical students, who feel themselves excluded from an all-male "buddy-buddy system."

Isolation is one sign that an individual has not been accepted into full and easy colleagueship. Related to this is the fact that minorities often end up in types of practice which separate them from the dominant circles of the profession (Hughes, 1945). Female physicians tend to enter pediatrics, psychiatry, and public health, which are specialties of low prestige (Lopate, 1968; Epstein 1970*b*). Women more often than men can be found in salaried rather than private practice and in relatively low paying jobs such as in community health centers. Blacks are less likely than whites to be found in group practice or specialties, and have traditionally found their clients among blacks. Although they may hold the formal credentials of the medical profession, minorities are often relegated to types of work and clients less valued by white male professionals.

The difficulties experienced by those who enter medical school and are not male, white, or middle-class reveal the ways in which these secondary characteristics infuse the structure of the medical profession. It is assumed, for example, that physicians will follow full-time, uninterrupted careers of study and then work. If a doctor has a family, it is assumed that these obligations will not significantly interrupt or cut into his full-time professional performance (i.e., it is assumed that a wife will handle the bulk of child care).

However, female physicians with children often experience conflicts between work and family demands, and may have interrupted career lines, which are taken by the profession to indicate less than full commitment.

The financial arrangements behind medical training assume that students will be middle- or upper-middle-class. In this country medical students receive little if any financial aid; they typically rely on family support and long-range loans, looking ahead to lucrative practices which will compensate for the years of low income and debt. Students from low-income families lack financial backing and are usually less willing to undertake a large debt on the basis of projected future earnings. The inadequacy of financial aid poses a major barrier to individuals from low-income, often nonwhite, backgrounds, who might otherwise qualify for medical school (*Report of the Association,* 1970).

Changes in Recruitment

Since the nineteenth century medical schools have loosened some of their criteria of admission. Married medical students were rare before World War II, but by 1967–68, 23 percent of all first-year and 61 percent of all fourth-year medical students were married, with about 50 percent of the income of married medical students coming from the earnings of their spouses (AAMC figures cited in *Report of the Association,* 1970).

Medical schools still discriminate according to age, giving preference to students just out of college (and for accelerated, six-year programs, drawing students into medical training even earlier). But some have made exceptions and admitted at least a few students in their late twenties and early thirties. The University of Miami, for example, has instituted an accelerated M.D. program for those already holding Ph.D's in the sciences (Harrington et al., 1971).

The traditional preference of medical schools for students who are white, upper class, and Protestant has gradually expanded to include other ethnic and religious groups. Quotas for Jews have been eliminated, and various immigrant groups, such as Italians, have gradually advanced into the medical profession. As discussed in the section on minority recruitment, in the last few years blacks, Puerto Ricans, Mexican-Americans, Indians, and women have demanded better access to medical training. This focus on minority recruitment has raised the number of nonwhites and females in medical schools. In 1970–71 about 6 percent of all medical students were nonwhite and 9 percent were women (*Journal of the American Medical Association,* 1971, pp. 1217, 1221), but these groups still remain vastly underrepresented in medical schools and in the profession.

If the composition of the medical profession broadened to include a significant number of women, blacks, Mexican-Americans, Puerto Ricans, and others who do not share the auxiliary characteristics now expected of physicians, what would be the consequences?

Under these circumstances (which are not likely in the foreseeable future) the occupational subculture and code of physicians would probably undergo basic changes. The clublike aura of the medical profession is partly based on the homogeneity of doctors; if the composition of the profession were more varied, definitions of colleague loyalty, common interests, demeanor, and career lines could no longer be based on a white, male, middle-class ethos.

For example, as more women enter medical school, there are pressures to change assumptions about career lines—to provide more flexible types of internships and residencies, practices which allow for interruptions and family obligations, and institutional provisions for child care (Kaplan, 1970; Lopate, 1968). If physicians received relatively better compensation during medical school and the early phases of their careers (a policy essential if the profession is to recruit more minorities), doctors might be less concerned with being highly remunerated to make up for a long period of indebtedness. They might then be more ready to follow less high-paying careers—for example, in community medicine.

The segregation of minorities into specified professional roles, types of practice, and clientele has not significantly altered, and may well continue (witness current assumptions that blacks will go into ghetto medicine). However, if the composition of the profession were to shift radically, different groups of clients and types of practice might become valued. Nonwhite medical students and physicians may be more oriented to their communities of origin than to their colleagues, which challenges the tenet of primary loyalty to the professional club.

These speculations suggest the basic way in which the medical profession assumes that its members will be of a certain sex, race, and class. There are powerful vested interests behind the current structure and ethos of the medical profession. To change its basic composition, which might entail altering the way it is organized and oriented, would require tremendous pressure.

Student Culture

The term *socialization* can be misleading, implying that students are passive receptacles whom the socializers mold, train, and condition according to a preset model. But students are neither *tabulae rasae* nor essentially passive. They take an active part in their own education; they may resist or evade aspects of the formal training; evolve their own goals and directions of effort; and learn attitudes, values, and behavior from unofficial sources, such as peers, nurses, and patients. There are important informal sides to the training of physicians.

Studies of medical schools have pointed to the existence of student cultures, of a rich underlife of interaction and shared understanding which develops among cohorts of students. This theme is central in *Boys in White* (Becker et al., 1961), a study of the Kansas University Medical School. The authors found that in confronting shared problems (for example, the tremendous amount of material they were expected to learn), the students evolved their own set of goals, working agreements, and solutions, which sometimes conflicted with official definitions of the student role. The isolation of medical students as a group and the interaction fostered by shared classes, labs, and work teams encouraged the development of understandings, for example about ways to cooperate to meet examinations and other crises and to share a heavy load of work in the clinics. Medical students constitute a community of fate and of suffering. They face similar adversities which help bind them together, and by joining hands (at least in the Kansas situation) they found a way to cope with shared and chronic problems.

Descriptions of other medical schools indicate that the Kansas situation is only one possibility. At Cornell, as described by another team of sociologists (Merton et al., 1957), students had a subculture which, compared with the Kansas case, was more integrated with the formal educational system, functioning to "maintain the communications network of the school, clarifying standards and controlling behavior based on norms that are mutually held by students and faculty" (Bloom, 1965, p. 155). The Cornell students are portrayed as physicians-in-training; the Kansas students, as "boys in white," which reflects the difference between a context in which students are already accepted as colleagues, proceeding more or less smoothly to full membership in the profession, and one in which students and faculty are set apart, with distinctive and even conflicting interests and with students in an isolated and subordinate position which makes it clear that they are not yet professionals.

As Bloom (1965) suggests, the two studies began with different conceptions of the medical school and its relation to the profession, but they also were conducted in different kinds of schools: Kansas is traditional, state-supported, and Midwestern, and Cornell is more experimental in curriculum and philosophy, private, and Ivy League.

Other studies suggest that a variety of educational climates, types of student, and student-faculty relations may be present in the nation's medical schools. Bloom (1965) cites an unpublished study by Louise Johnson which indicates differences in value climates among 14 medical schools, and Christie and Merton (1958) describe differences among three schools. A recent monograph on the State University of New York Downstate Medical Center (Bloom, 1971, p. 5) describes a student culture which is "notable more by its absence than by its clear and definable character."

No secret society exists; nor does a "little society" of doctors-in-training. One might say that this medical school is a way-station, a place to come to study and to leave. This is as true, apparently, on a day-to-day basis as it appears to be in the total career pattern of its students. A school of utilitarian value, a place mainly in which to be trained, but not where strong loyalties and identifications are made: these appear to be the outstanding characteristics of this institution from the point of view of students.

After surveying the literature on student cultures in medical schools, Bloom (1971, pp. 3–4) extracts two polar types which approximate the Kansas and Cornell situations: in one "the student is treated with relatively little respect and is 'on probation' until he receives his degree;" in the other "the student is thought of as a member of the profession—a junior member—but a full fledged member of the team." The difference is partly one of initiation. In one case students have to prove themselves through a trial by ordeal until they are finally accepted into the professional club. In the other, students are granted a degree of acceptance by virtue of having been admitted to medical school, and their dealings with the faculty have a collegial tone.

Behind these differences, and a crucial factor in determining medical school cultures, is the type of relation between faculty and students. The trial-by-ordeal model emerges where faculty and students are separated and have a sense of conflicting interests. In the Downstate Medical Center, as Bloom describes it, faculty and students rarely interact on a close and accepting basis. The faculty perceive students as practically rather than academically motivated, and therefore as holding values opposed to those of a good professional. On the other hand, the students regard the faculty as remote and impersonal, more oriented to research than to teaching, and failing to provide the advanced educational experience which they had hoped for. The response of both sides is to withdraw; the students experience great anxiety and discontent but have not created their own subculture.

The Kansas study also describes a high social barrier between students and faculty. The student culture is both within and apart from the school. In dealing with faculty members, students present a face of cooperation and acquiescence, but when interacting with their peers, students are more autonomous and critical, regarding the faculty as a group opposed to their own. The student culture sometimes works to evade and subvert faculty demands and to direct efforts away from official educational goals.

The Medical Student Experience

When asked about their experiences in medical school, students usually refer to competition and anxiety. A sharply competitive atmosphere often emerges among groups of premedical students who, in many undergraduate colleges, come into contact through a shared preparatory curriculum. In recent years there has been an upsurge in the number of applicants to medical schools; in 1961–62 there were 14,381 applicants and 8,682 were accepted; in 1970-71 the number rose to 24,987 applicants with 11,500 accepted (*Journal of the American Medical Association*, 1971, p. 1217). This increase makes the process of gaining admission to medical school even more competitive than in the past. Being an applicant to medical school is a role in itself, requiring preparation, energy, and investment; Bojar (1961) maintains that many entering medical students are prepared for being medical school applicants but not for being medical students or physicians.

For those who are successful applicants, being admitted to medical school does not end the anxiety. According to Bloom, students in the Downstate Medical Center were in a continual state of tension. Even though the attrition rate was not exceptional, students conceived of the school as a "flunk-factory"; they were uncertain about what was expected of them in the student role and were "unclear about the continuities between the values of the school and those of the future profession" (Bloom, 1971, p. 20).

Referring to medical students in general, Funkenstein (1970, p 741) makes a similar comment:

Across the nation medical students are restless, unhappy, and markedly dissatisfied with the education they are receiving. They feel that medical school is a poor learning experience and that their personal development is being impeded. These future physicians are disenchanted with medical school policies, which they blame for the inadequacy of the health care delivery system. The majority of students complain that they experience constant anxiety and stress. A "dehumanizing experience" is their most frequent characterization of medical school. Other typical remarks—from a sophomore: "I was not sure the day after I entered whether I was in a prison or a kindergarten, and I still haven't made up my mind." From a junior: "Every day I like being a medical student less and a doctor more."

The student who suspected he had returned to kindergarten echoed a theme voiced by others who have found medical school a regressive educational experience, involving rote learning, a highly structured curriculum and classroom routine, and authoritarian, paternalistic instruction. Much of what students are asked to learn, especially during the preclinical years, may seem of little practical relevance to their future work as physicians. Medical students often adopt an attitude of postponement, putting up with a difficult present, and waiting for the clinical years and even more for after graduation to get gratification and expected rewards.

The suffering and sacrifice which medical school entails may be related to building commitment to the profession; recruits stake something of value, investing time, ego, and money, in training to be physicians (Becker, 1960). Writing along these lines, Wilbert Moore (1970, pp. 77-78) sketches a "punishment-centered theory of socialization." Training for the professions, he notes, involves putting initiates through a difficult and unpleasant set of tasks and duties.

Some of the difficult tasks are commonly ritualized and in that sense arbitrary. The medical student bound for a career in psychiatry must memorize the bones of the human body; the law student looking forward to a practice in establishing trusts for wealthy clients must learn endless cases in torts. . . . Marks of success, too, are commonly ritualized: awards, election to honorary fraternities, certificates, and diplomas. Yet the punishment does not stop so quickly, at least for occupations high on the scale of professionalism. The medical intern does the medical dirty work around a hospital; the young lawyer does the dirty work around a law firm. . . .

Like the hazing of newcomers to a fraternity, medical school is a symbolically loaded induction into an exclusive group. The initiates share a challenging and painful experience and develop a sort of fellowship of suffering which is an important ingredient of growing commitment to colleagues and to the profession.

Student Activism

This is not to say that students quietly accept the structure and content of medical training. Complaints and even organized protests have been plentiful, especially in the last few years. Many recent observers have noted a basic change in the outlook, values, expectations, and behavior of medical students. Some speak of a "new breed" of student, more oriented to social issues and community medicine, and critical of the organization both of medical education and of the practicing profession. The recent generation of medical students has been variously described as idealistic, humanistic, and critical, and as having "a lot better social conscience than 10 years ago." One Stanford medical student categorized his classmates into three types: the "new breed"; the "competitive" types, who aim for traditional types of practice and specialties; and "individualistic" students, oriented to academic and research medicine (Walsh, 1971).

Drawing on extensive data about the background of Harvard medical students, Funkenstein (1969b) documents a marked increase in social science majors and a decrease in humanities majors among students entering in recent years (although biology majors still remain the largest group). Funkenstein relates this interest in social sciences to an increased concern with community action.

The change in medical students is obviously connected with the general wave of social and political activism which swept through colleges and universities in the sixties. The civil rights and antiwar movements helped orient students to issues beyond the university; the Berkeley Free Speech Movement launched a series of challenges to the structure and authority of institutions of higher education. As one might expect from their relatively isolated and exclusive position, professional schools were among the last to experience these movements. But student discontent—including organized confrontations, sit-ins, and demands—eventually appeared in medical, law, and theology schools. Furthermore, during their years as college undergraduates, entering classes of professional students were likely to have been affected by the activist trend.

It is difficult to estimate the size or the long-range significance of activism among medical students. As each class enters and moves through a given medical school, one can hear judgments and evaluations of the activist pulse. At some places the classes which entered in 1968 and 1969 were seen as radically different from preceding classes. They formed Student Health Organization chapters, organized projects in poor communities, pressed for more admission of minorities, and challenged curricula and grading policies. Some observers claim that the 1970 class signaled a return to the past—more acquiescent, less willing to agitate, less socially conscious. Others have noted a decrease in activity as a class moves through medical school, especially when students start working in the clinics, an experience which isolates them from each other and draws them into immediate responsibilities for patient care. However, there is little concrete information about these trends.

The appearance of medical students has dramatically changed. In an interview, one medical student referred to what he said was becoming a standard pattern: when students came for admission interviews, they wore their hair short-cropped and were clean-shaven. From the time of interviews to the beginning of school, they let their hair grow, and they arrived in September with long hair, beads, and blue jeans (the requirement that students wear coats and ties has disappeared in most medical schools). For preclinical courses, such as anatomy, which is a "greasy subject," the casual style of dress is quite appropriate. But when students get into the clinics, they tend to cut their hair. At a different medical school the dean referred to a similar sequence, remarking that "the patient is the great equalizer." In the clinics, he said, students end up cutting off long hair and adopting a more conservative style of dress in order to avoid alienating patients. But one still hears of conflict over the issue of dress, with students defying rules of demeanor implicit in the traditional professional code.

The subject of dress is only one source of conflict between the medical students and the faculty and administrators. Students have challenged the structure, content, and quality of their education, arguing that the curriculum is repetitive, rigid, and excessively long and that much of it is of dubious relevance to the realities of medical practice. Student complaints and pressure are related to some of the changes in medical education referred to earlier in this chapter: the opening of more elective time and options of length and sequence, the addition of programs in family and community medicine, the earlier introduction of clinical work, the reconsideration of the balance of theory and practice, and the emphasis on admitting more minorities to medical school.

In many medical schools, grading policies have been a subject of great debate, linked with basic conflicts over authority, student-faculty relations, the problem of competition, and the role of schools in sorting students into future, stratified careers. Since the mid-sixties a majority of medical schools have shifted to a pass-fail grading system; of 90 medical schools surveyed in 1971, 41 had a straight pass-fail system, and 16 had a grading system which involved some pass-fail option (Abrams & Byrd, 1971). Some schools reported satisfaction with the change. Others cited problems such as loss of student motivation, possible difficulty in postgraduate placement, and emotional problems related to lack of a clear definition of the grading system. One respondent to the survey noted "an apparent oscillation from pass-fail to numeral grading and return, at about a five to ten year frequency" (ibid, p. 317).

Like students elsewhere in higher education, medical students have demanded a larger, more formal voice in institutional decisions. In many medical schools student representatives have been added to faculty committees, although some find that their role is limited. Medical students at Stanford, for example, have complained that although they serve on many committees, they have relatively little impact on basic issues such as budget and admissions (Walsh, 1971).

Perhaps the most significant shift in student interest has been toward issues which reach beyond the medical school: concern with restructuring the delivery of health care, providing services for disadvantaged communities, creating new kinds of practices, and broadening the recruitment base of the profession. These movements have been described earlier as part of the challenge to the traditional mandate of the profession. Several student organizations have focused and coordinated activist energy: the Student Health Organization set up summer projects in poor and nonwhite communities, and the Student American Medical Association, originally a close junior companion of the American Medical Association, also established service projects, a shift which is "a significant indication of the new and dramatic shift in the climate of medical education" (Michaelson, 1969, p. 53).

The Student Health Organization was active from 1965 to about 1969, when many of its chapters began to reconsider "band-aid" projects which at best patched up but did not cure a faulty health care delivery system. Activity began to trail off. Some students lost interest or got reabsorbed in the immediate demands of medical school; others turned to political activity within the profession.

Activism has come into conflict with many of the practices, values, and codes of the profession—for example, the sense that strikes, sit-ins, confrontations, and other demonstrations of openly partisan political activity are unbefitting a professional or a learner of a professional role. The exclusivity, social distance, and elite position of physicians conflict with the activists' ideology, which emphasizes egalitarianism, elimination of special privilege, and primary orientation to clients and community (especially those who are disadvantaged) rather than to the professional club. In their concern with the needs of communities and with political and social issues, the activists, some of their professional critics claim, tend to neglect "the individual patient" and fail to learn technical competence. This criticism may in some respects be a retreat to technique, to pleading scientific expertise in the face of a political and social challenge. In any case, it reflects the kinds of issues and ideologies which now divide the medical profession.

The conflict is in part one between generations. The segment of the profession pushing for reorganization and for a radically different philosophy of distribution tends to be youthful. This may be partly because younger physicians and medical students are less invested in traditional forms of practice. The fact of technological advance may enhance the position of the young, since older professionals become technically obsolete faster and thus have less rational authority than in a pretechnological era.

Medical Education and the Behavior of Physicians
With a focus on the institutions of medical education and the period which is formally set aside for learning the role of physician, this chapter has bypassed an important general issue: How much of the skills, knowledge, attitudes, and behavior of the practicing physician is learned in medical school and how much from other sources and in other settings?

It is commonly believed that the long and arduous process of formal medical education shapes recruits to fit the doctor's role, that the socialization process is direct and linear and explains why doctors become the way they are. But there is evidence that the process is more discontinuous than linear. Being a successful medical student involves its own set of problems, obligations, and behavior, which may bear little relation to the eventual role of physician. The reality shock which students experience when they finally graduate to practice, their sense of being unprepared for many facets of the doctor's role, and reports that they pick up skills, techniques, and attitudes while on the job indicate that professional socialization is a complex and lengthy process not limited to the years of formal training (Olmsted & Paget, 1969). Eliot Freidson (1970*a*; 1970*b*) suggests that a preoccupation with the process of formal medical education, at the expense of examining the daily environment and social organization of professional practice, has skewed our understanding. He argues that "education is a less important variable than work environment. There is some very persuasive evidence that 'socialization' does not explain some important elements of professional performance half so well as does the organization of the immediate work environment" (Freidson, 1970*a*, p. 89).

If medical education molds the medical man, the exigencies of practice are likely to be the proof of the mold. It is for performing his role in the circumstances of practice that medical education prepares the physician. And it is in the realities of practice rather than in the class-room that we find the empirical materials for clarifying and articulating the actual rather than the imputed or hoped-for nature of the professional role (Freidson, 1970*b*, pp. 17–18).

3. Professional Education in Law

by Barrie Thorne

Legal education, which for decades has remained substantially unchanged, is now being critically reevaluated. The American Association of Law Schools curriculum committee recently made a lengthy report proposing changes in the organization, length, and content of legal education. The chairman of the committee concluded:

> . . . legal education is in a crisis and . . . fundamental changes must be made soon. It is not only that law students over the country are reaching the point of open revolt but also that law faculties themselves, particularly the younger members, share with the students the view that legal education is too rigid, too uniform, too repetitious and too long (Meyers, 1968, pp. 7–8).

Critics of United States legal education point out that its structure has changed little since the 1920s, when the current model became firmly established. The first section of this chapter traces the historical development of legal education: the substitution of isolated schooling for apprenticeships, the spread of the case method of teaching, and the pattern of three years of law school preceded by three or four years of college. This pattern involves assumptions about the sequence and length of training, which in law schools revolves around a more general issue: the illusion that law is a unified profession with all members sharing a common educational background. The gap between the reality of law practice (which involves specialization) and the uniformity of law school study has led to proposals to make legal education more heterogeneous: to establish training programs of varying lengths and types of specialty and to create a formal work system which will bring paralegal occupations and their training under the control of lawyers.

Another theme is the mandate of the legal profession, the question of which clients it feels called to serve and which problems it should try to settle. Critics from within and without the profession (including many law students) are challenging the legal profession for its orientation to the affluent and their property and its neglect of the poor. This challenge is affecting curricula of law schools and the careers chosen by their graduates.

A related topic is the movement toward clinical legal education, an effort to break down the isolation of the law school and to draw legal training closer to the world of practice. This involves issues familiar in the history of professional education: the conflict between theory and practice, between advocates of isolated, university-based training and those favoring education which is rooted in practical experience. The institutional context of the law schools reflects this tension; the relationship of law schools to the practicing profession and to the university, and the division of labor among law schools themselves, is another general theme.

The final section explores the experience of students in law schools: student culture, unrest, activism, and recruitment policies.

THE HISTORY OF LEGAL EDUCATION IN THE UNITED STATES

In law, as in medicine, it has traditionally been assumed that the training of its members is the business of the profession itself. Apprenticeships with practitioners historically preceded the opening of formal schools. In colonial America some lawyers went abroad to study in the English Inns of Court, but most entered the profession by training in a lawyer's office, often serving as clerk-copyists. In the 1780s a practicing lawyer in Litchfield, Connecticut, established a course of lectures (largely based on Blackstone) which were attended by small groups of students. Proprietary schools of this type were intended as a supplement rather than a replacement for law office experience, and they began to disappear when published editions of Blackstone and other law texts became available at the time of the Civil War (Reed, 1921; Stolz, 1970).

In addition to independent, proprietary ventures, a few early universities included courses in law. In 1779 Thomas Jefferson initiated a professorship in law at the College of William and Mary; he also helped plan the University of Virginia, which opened in 1825 with several chairs in law. In both cases law was taught at the undergraduate level as a relatively self-contained program of study. In 1816 Harvard appointed its first law professor, Chief Justice Isaac Parker. Parker set out to cover only part of the professional training of the lawyer, arguing that "the practical knowledge of business may always be better learnt in the office of a distinguished counsellor" (Reed, 1921, p. 138). At Harvard, from the beginning, law courses were isolated from the undergraduate curriculum; "the precedent of theology rather than of medicine was to be followed; the college was not to build up a law school competing with itself, but to superimpose one upon a college basis" (Reed, 1921, p. 138). However, the connection between the law school and the university was largely nominal, and the law school did not require that its students have prior liberal arts training, nor even enough education to be admitted to college (Reed, 1921).

At the time of the Civil War only a handful of law schools had university connections. The Columbia Law School, which opened under Theodore W. Dwight in 1858, involved "a two-year program of lectures and drill in legal principles, supplemented with moot courts for students, many of whom were already clerking in New York Law Offices" (Stolz, 1970, p. 56). Dwight insisted that his graduates be admitted to practice on the basis of their diplomas; he believed that training in a law school was not just a substitute, but was fully preferable to apprenticing in a law office.

Christopher Langdell, a dean of the Harvard Law School, was another persuasive advocate of law school–based training. In 1870, a year often cited as a turning point, Langdell instituted the structure which eventually came to dominate American legal education: the case method of instruction (geared toward the principles of law rather than the details of practice), the requirement that entering students have at least three years of college and three years as a uniform term of law study.

In the beginning the bar resisted the arguments of the schoolmen such as Dwight and Langdell, who insisted that law schools should replace the law office method of teaching. Training by apprenticeship continued, although with the expansion of law schools after the Civil War, more would-be lawyers had access to some kind of formal schooling. The schools ranged from the more elite, lengthy, university-connected programs to independent and proprietary schools. Part-time law schools catered to students who earned a living during the day, and became a means of social and occupational mobility for immigrant groups. There was a rising demand for law training, and these varied enterprises emerged to fill it, unfettered, until the 1920s, by accrediting procedures or legal controls.

Some who opposed giving law schools monopoly over legal education were concerned that this would limit access to the profession. Law is closely connected with government and public functions, and in the United States there is a strong tradition favoring open access to the bar, and hence to public roles. In colonial times, when the professions were closely shaped by the British experience, the bar had a "shadowy elite status" (Stolz, 1971, p. 145). With the Jacksonian period came strong populist pressures, celebration of the common man, and criticism of formal education as elitist. In this period many law schools were in danger of collapse.

The spirit of professionalism which picked up strength in the late nineteenth century ran counter to this democratizing spirit. Members of the profession justified bar examinations and educational requirements as efforts to raise standards of performance and to protect the public from unqualified practitioners. However, "these standards could easily be converted into monopolistic restriction for the economic benefit of the bar, and they were, accordingly, viewed with suspicion if not hostility by the public" (Stolz, 1971, p. 145).

In time the schoolmen and the professionals won out. The corporate law firm emerged along with industrialism, and Langdell's model of university-based legal training accompanied these changes. The law became increasingly complex, which made the role of the practitioner-teacher more difficult and helped justify the schoolmen's claim that it was more efficient to learn theory and principles of law rather than a mass of details. The invention of the typewriter and the telephone diminished the law office roles of clerk-copyist and messenger, and practicing lawyers had less need of apprentice labor. By the late nineteenth century attendance at law schools had greatly risen, and apprenticeship had declined.

In 1869 there were about 1200 law students in 22 law schools; in 1890 there were 4,500 students in 61 law schools; in 1921 there were 27,000 students in 150 law schools. In terms of the population that was four law school students per 100,000 in 1860, seven per 100,000 in 1890, 23 per 100,000 in 1920 (Stolz, 1970, p. 59).

The movement toward academic legal education accompanied the organization and strengthening of the profession itself. The American Bar Association was formed in 1878, but by 1900 its membership included only 1.3 percent of the nation's lawyers (Stolz, 1971). Admission to law practice became legally restricted only at the turn of the century through the establishment of bar examinations. Langdell, Dwight, and other legal educators at first resisted bar examinations, fearing they would constrain curricula and curtail innovations in law teaching. Their resistance was part of a debate, which still continues, over how much autonomy law schools should have from the organized bar.

Since the bar examination, and not attendance at a law school, was specified for entrance into the profession, the schools continued without legal recognition. Writing in 1921, Reed (p. 219) noted that medical schools were more formally legitimate than schools of law:

Although . . . law school education, as a preparation for practice, has become usual, it still is far from possessing the sanction that the medical school enjoys, in the way of either popular, or legal, or professional recognition. The public regards the LL.B. as only an empty academic distinction. No state requires law school training for admission to its legally privileged bar. . . . The legal profession, as organized in bar associations, has not yet come to the point of insisting that training in any sort of law school must be secured.

Although standards may have been low and public recognition wanting, law schools were clearly here to stay. From 1890 to 1910 the number of schools more than doubled, and the number of students increased almost fivefold. Much of this growth was not in the university-connected programs, but in proprietary, commercial, correspondence, and part-time schools. From 1890 to 1930 the number of part-time schools increased from 20 to 98, while the number of exclusively full-time schools went from 41 to 82 (*Annual Review of Legal Education*, 1930). Some of these enterprises didn't even meet the low standards set by the American Association of Law Schools in 1900: a high school diploma as a prerequisite to admission, access to a library, and a course of study lasting at least two academic years (Stoltz, 1971).

In the 1920s the ABA began classifying schools for the first time, publishing an annual list of those approved and unapproved. This procedure had no legal force, since admission to the bar was based on an examination and not on proof of having graduated from an approved school. Eventually many states began to require law school attendance as a prerequisite for taking the bar examination, but some states (such as California and Georgia) have never specified that the school be approved by the American Bar Association, and in a number of states (such as California, Pennsylvania, and Rhode Island) there is still a legal option, which is rarely followed, of preparing for the bar examination with four years of experience in a law office. These alternatives are partly rooted in the "poor boy philosophy," the belief that access to the profession should be relatively open. In the states where they are still allowed as formal preparation for the bar, unaccredited schools, correspondence courses, and proprietary enterprises have continued to the present, meeting a continuing demand.

There has been no rapid elimination of proprietary and marginal law schools equivalent to that of medical schools following Flexner's report. The Carnegie Foundation, which had commissioned Flexner's report, appointed Alfred Z. Reed to complete a study of law schools, but his results (Reed, 1921), although critical of the existing situation, did not have a comparable impact. The number of medical schools declined from 131 in 1910 (the year Flexner's report was published) to 85 in 1920. During the same period the number of law schools, approved and unapproved, increased from 124 to 146. By 1930 there were 180 law schools; however, the number was reduced to 159 (109 of them approved) by 1944. In 1950 there were 167 law schools (120 approved); in 1960, 159 (132 approved). In 1971 there were 147 approved schools and at least 13 unapproved. Statistics on unapproved schools are not readily available; with professional legitimation comes central records keeping (*Annual Review of Legal Education*, 1926; 1930; 1944; 1960; 1971).

Consolidation of One Model of Legal Training

Although law schools are not as centrally and closely controlled as medical schools and vary more widely in standards of admission, they have concentrated around one pattern of training. In the years between 1870 and 1920 the Harvard model became the standard form of legal education. Professional training was isolated from practice. Law schools developed nothing analogous to the clinical phase of medical education; there is no equivalent of a teaching hospital or clinical faculty. Prior to their first jobs, law school graduates often have no exposure to actual clients.

The more prestigious law schools in this country have always been tied to universities, a pattern which spread. In the early cases (the University of Virginia, Columbia, Harvard) universities founded their own division of law. Alternatively, a previously independent college and law school have merged (as in Alabama, when Samford joined with the almost-defunct Cumberland School of Law in 1949). In a third, more rare situation (exemplified by Suffolk University and School of Law in Boston), a law school developed other organs to expand into a university. Law schools with no university affiliations still exist, although by now they are a small minority among the accredited schools.

While Langdell insisted that law schools belong in universities, he also conceived of law as a self-contained discipline, assuming that "unless law was a package capable of rational analysis within its own confines it has no business being in the university" (Stolz, 1970, p. 63). The familiar professional claim to a unique body of knowledge has inhibited the full integration of law schools into universities. Like medical schools, law schools tend to be autonomous, with little sharing of faculty, curricula, or resources with other branches of learning.

Perhaps the most famous of Langdell's contributions were methods of law school teaching: the case method (which involves studying appellate decisions in an effort to extract broad principles of the law) and the Socratic approach (involving rigorous cross-examination in the classroom). Although law schools vary widely in admissions standards and the careers their graduates follow, nearly all use some form of casebook teaching.

Throughout the hierarchy of law schools, from the most famous national ones to the most locally-oriented, it is the analysis of the appellate decisions through case classes which takes pride of place. The skills developed in today's students tend to be substantially the same as those inculcated in the students of the 1870s largely because the structure of legal education has remained unchanged. Law teaching, no matter how differently the case method is used, is still predominantly a matter of a single professor dissecting innumerable cases before a class consisting of large numbers of students. To be sure, "cases" have given way to "cases and materials," problems have been added to appellate cases, and policy vies with law. But the structure built by Langdell is still visible. Indeed, the concepts of hours and credits and the organization of semesters and years give the impression that form has truly triumphed over content (Stevens, 1970, p. 34).

The curricula as well as the teaching methods of law schools are uniform. The basic first-year course (torts, contracts, procedure, criminal law, property, and constitutional law) reflect the Harvard curriculum at the turn of the century. In the late twenties and in the thirties the "legal realism" movement questioned the case method, charging that there was little relationship between appellate opinions and what was happening in the real world. At Columbia Law School there were systematic efforts to revise the curriculum by shifting from doctrinal classifications to concern with the social and economic problems behind the law. The goals of the legal realists were more ambitious than their eventual achievements, which took the form not of a reorganization of the total curriculum, but of second-year courses in corporations, antitrust law, labor law, taxes, and administrative law (Stolz, 1970).

The length and sequence of legal education became fairly homogeneous after the turn of the century. Although there was an early, largely Southern tradition of including legal topics in the undergraduate curriculum, the study of law gradually became professionalized. Law was not included in liberal arts programs but regarded as more narrow, technical, and specialized—a sequel to general education. In Europe general education takes place in the *gymnasia* or *lycées,* secondary schools which carry the students a year or two longer than high schools in the English-speaking countries. They then matriculate directly into specialized or professional faculties of the universities for training, usually of about four years.

In the early nineteenth century a college background was not a prerequisite for entering law school.

Harvard, . . . and following its lead, all other colleges, let everybody into its law school indiscriminately, and put them all through the same course of study, whether college graduates or not. The two types of prospective practitioners [the one motivated by professional, the other more by commercial ideals] were completely merged, in other words, in the technical portion of their training. The distinction became merely that after leaving the lower schools some students continued to go to college before beginning specialized professional work, while other students short-circuited the college. . . . The four-year college course came to be regarded as something that might or might not be interpolated between [law school] and the lower schools, and that was more closely allied with lower schools than with the law school work (Reed, 1921, p. 313).

A college education gradually became the preferred means of preparation for law study. In another of Landgell's reforms, Harvard in 1866 began to demand that entering law students have at least three years of college. This led to a temporary drop in enrollments. By 1900 Harvard in effect required a college degree. At the time this was unusual; the bulk of law schools either had no academic prerequisites or specified only one or two years of college. Even by 1921, at the time of Reed's report, only three law schools required entering students to have a college degree. That year the American Bar Association endorsed "at least two years of study in a college" as an appropriate law school admissions practice, but the endorsement had no legal sanction until state bars adopted a similar standard.

Six years after the A.B.A. [resolution] only six states required any college education. It took about 15 years, and a good depression, to get the ball moving. In 1935, 30 states required two years of college, 19 required no college at all. By the outbreak of the Second World War, all but a few states required two years. It is clear that in general the legal requirement followed rather than led the growth of college education (Stolz, 1971, p. 143).

Law school and state bar requirements still vary, from a minimum of two years of college (allowed by about one-fifth of the states and by a few unaccredited schools) to a bachelor's degree (required by seven state bars and by over three-fourths of all accredited schools). Most state bars require at least three years of college prior to legal training. Since 1950 this has also been the ABA minimum (*Annual Review of Legal Education,* 1970). The practice exceeds the requirements; 70 percent of those admitted to the bar between 1955 and 1960 had four years of college (Carlin, 1966).

Training for the law, as for medicine, takes longer now than in the nineteenth century. Before the Civil War, law schools offered, at the most, a 2-year course, and many limited training to 1 year (Reed, 1921). Harvard was the first to move to a 3-year law degree, which it instituted in 1878. By 1890, 7 schools had adopted 3-year courses, 45 offered degrees after 2 years of study, and 9 after 1 or 1½ years (Stolz, 1971). The 3-year pattern caught on by the turn of the century partly because the profession was trying to raise standards (which became synonymous with lengthening training) and to reduce the supply of lawyers (many thought the bar was overcrowded, but the move to 3 years did not, as it turned out, result in a smaller bar). By 1921 all but a few schools required

3 years of study (the period was longer in part-time schools which sought to offer an equivalent time of instruction).

In the twenties and again after World War II some schools considered offering a four-year curriculum, but the possibility was never realized. Three years has been a standard period of law training for so long that some call it a fetish. The three-year pattern has no clear justification; Stolz (1971, pp. 159–160) suggests that "perhaps the most persuasive reason is that English custom requires a prospective barrister to dine at an Inn of Court for three years before he can be called to the bar."

THE MYTH OF A HOMO-GENEOUS PROFESSION Since the 1920s legal education has settled into a uniform pattern: the sequence of college plus a homogeneous three years of law school and a set of courses, texts, and a style of teaching which vary little from school to school (although local, less prestigious schools focus more on the specific content of bar examinations, and national schools are more theoretical). Charles J. Meyers (1968, p. 9) criticizes United States law schools for being rigid and uniform:

Rigidity refers to the fact that in any given law school most of the students are doing the same thing: exactly the same thing in the first year, much the same in the second, and only marginally different things in the third year. The defect of uniformity refers to the fact that not only do law students within any given law school do much the same thing, law students in every school are doing much the same thing. For a country as large and diverse as the United States, it is remarkable that law schools are as alike as they are. American legal education is characterized by the same courses, taught from the same books, by the same methods.

Why has legal education remained so monolithic? The answer in part lies in a myth long cherished by the legal profession: the myth that law is a homogeneous profession, that all lawyers are generalists and are equally competent to handle any given case. The ideal of lawyer as generalist harks back to the tradition of the professional as a cultivated gentleman, a man of universal learning. It also has roots in what Reed (1921) calls "the democratic impulse"—efforts to keep the bar accessible and prevent the entrenchment of special privilege.

Unlike medicine, law has resisted overt specialization; specialties are not formally recognized or licensed. Once admitted to the bar by a unitary licensing procedure which varies by state but not by specialty, all lawyers are formally (legally) equal, "presumptively equally trained for their professional role and equally competent to perform any legal task" (Stolz, 1971, p. 146). All law students go through a uniform three years of training; there is nothing equivalent to medicine's internship and residency, when those headed for different types of careers separate for specialized preparation.

The Fact of Specialization   The facts of legal practice have long belied the myth of the omnicompetent lawyer. All lawyers are not, and probably never were, equal colleagues. In a study of the New York City bar, Jerome Carlin (1966) found that lawyers differed in social standing, income, types of clientele, and work settings. The differences clustered into a stable system of social stratification. The elite (21 percent of the bar) were lawyers in large firms, with business clients (largely corporations in heavy industry and major finance) and individual clients who were typically affluent Protestants; their contacts with courts and agencies centered on the federal level. Over three-fourths of them had incomes of $35,000 or more. The middle stratum of lawyers (15 percent) practiced in medium-sized firms, while the lowest stratum (64 percent of all lawyers) were in small firms or individual practice, represented the least affluent and lowest-status clients (including blacks and Puerto Ricans), dealt with the lower courts and government agencies, and had lower incomes (only 13 percent of the individual practitioners earned $35,000 or more). Lawyers entered these different types of practice through a complex process of recruitment and self-selection. The elite lawyers tended to be Protestant, were from higher social-class backgrounds, and were more likely to have a college degree and to have attended a prestigious full-time university law school. Those in the lower strata were ethnically varied, were from lower social-class origins, and were more likely to have something less than a college degree and to have attended a low-status or even a part-time law school. Carlin found that lawyers of different strata had little professional or social contact with each other. They were not, in fact, full and equal colleagues.

As legal problems have become more complex and firms have increased in number and size, specialization has continued to develop; in law, as in medicine, the era of the general practitioner has passed. A recent survey of the California State Bar found that two-thirds of the lawyers regarded themselves as specialists, and nearly three-quarters would prefer to specialize in the future. Most of the specialists concentrated in one or more of six fields of law: negligence, business and corporate law, estate planning, probate and trusts, family law, and criminal law. Specialization increased with the size of the firm and correlated with income (79 percent of those earning more than $50,000 specialized, while only 44.1 percent of the lawyers making under $10,000 were specialists) (*"A Preliminary Report . . . ,"* 1969, pp. 140–187).

The issue, therefore, is not whether the bar should specialize, but whether (and how) specialties, which are now informal and unregulated, should be formally designated, certified, and trained for. The division of labor in the legal profession does not formally begin during the law school years (although the type of law school a student attends and how well he or she performs does lead toward one set of career choices rather than another). Specialization may occur through choice of work setting (a firm of a particular size and orientation, government practice, or individual practice), through division of labor within a firm or law suite, or in an ad hoc fashion (a lawyer takes cases one by one and eventually discovers he is doing primarily divorce or probate work). In any case, the skills and body of knowledge particular to a given specialty are learned not during the law school years, but after admission to practice.

The process is both fortuitous and clumsy. Large law firms will support men while they are learning and provide some guidance some of the time, but the process is apt to be unduly prolonged because the availability of training turns on the needs of clients. A young lawyer's interest in tax may be postponed or totally frustrated if there is no need for an addition to the tax department of his firm (Stolz, 1971, p. 163).

As far back as Reed's 1921 report, critics of legal education have urged the profession to surrender the myth of homogeneity, to recognize specialties, and to gear law school training toward a differentiated bar. For example, Abraham Goldstein (1968, p. 164) argues:

It seems to me that the present structure of the law schools is unsound and that the unsoundness contributes to the delusion that the lawyer-generalist is competent to deal with the increasingly complex areas drawn within legal regulation and control. It is time for us to give up the generalist myth and to develop instead patterns of lawyer specialization adequate to the need.

Goldstein urges law schools to include specialized as well as general courses in their curricula and suggests that elite schools should offer advanced research degrees in areas of specialization.

The nation's law schools are making scattered experiments along these lines. Some schools have developed a specialized focus: the University of Pennsylvania offers a program in securities regulation; Southern Methodist, a specialty in oil and gas law; New York University, a graduate federal taxation course. Some of these programs are organized as institutes for practicing lawyers; others are post-J.D. work, leading to an M.A. or other advanced degree in law. But the three-year J.D. (formerly the LL.B.) remains the basic, multipurpose law degree, sufficient not only for general practice but also (at least for those graduating at the top of elite schools) for careers in law teaching and various specialties. Thus far, the chief function of advanced degree programs has been to permit graduates of less prestigious schools to gain access to elite careers.

Under current proposals to break the uniform three-year program into a variety of sequences, tracks, and specialties, advanced law degrees would assume new importance. The AALS curriculum study committee recently proposed that the three-year course should be replaced by six different course patterns: a two-year standard curriculum for professional generalists (which would replace the three-year degree as the basic professional degree in law), specialized curricula for advanced third-year study, research curricula leading to doctorates in law (for those seeking careers in research and teaching), collegiate curricula for undergraduates (not as a vocational degree but for general education in the law), and limited curricula for paraprofessionals.

The model of the medical profession is clearly behind this proposal. Beyond the degree shared by all members of the profession (M.D. in medicine, J.D. in law), specialty training, involving more years of study, would be oriented to certain kinds of careers. The division of labor would include paraprofessional ranks with their own educational programs. The result would be a work system with formally differentiated levels, reflected in a hierarchy of separate degrees and training programs.

A Two-Year Law Degree? Proposals to shorten the standard law school curriculum from three years to two have become almost commonplace, although Stanford is the only school to make an actual move in that direction by offering a two-year J.M. (master of jurisprudence) degree. For the time being, the J.M. is billed as "nonprofessional" because the state requires three years of law school for admission to the bar, but the degree has symbolic value and suggests that two years is sufficient training for some kinds of legal work. The Stanford J.M. has also been described as a flag in the wind, to test currents which might favor a shorter period of professional training in law. In addition to the J.M. degree (and paralleling the diversification of the AALS plan), Stanford continues to offer a three-year law degree (J.D.), a master's degree (J.S.M.) for students in special programs, an advanced dissertation degree (the J.S.D., or doctor of the science of law), and combined degrees in law and business administration and law and economics. Under this format, the shorter period of basic legal education is counterbalanced by advanced degrees, which might eventually become required training for specialized careers.

Those advocating a two-year curriculum argue that three years is not necessary to turn out a competent lawyer generalist. Entering law students are better prepared than in the past (more of them have college degrees). Students often find law school overstructured and patronizing, and after mastering the case method and the style of "thinking like a lawyer," they find the curriculum irrelevant and dull. The term "third-year malaise" is widely used to refer to the apathy and unrest typical of third-year students. At Yale a recent study showed that second-year students performed much better than third-year students in the same course (Stevens, 1970).

Many law schools have added electives, including clinical programs, as a cure for third-year malaise. In connection with clinical legal education, an increasing number of states now allow third-year law students to appear in court, which suggests a readiness for practice before the degree has been formally acquired. Even in full-time law schools, it has become relatively common for third- and even second-year law students to work part time. These developments all suggest that the third year of law school may be justified more by tradition than by necessity, an argument which has become widespread in law school circles.

Those pushing for a two-year basic curriculum do not want a simple move from a uniform three years to an equally uniform two; they are urging variation and specialization. In both the AALS and the Stanford plans the two-year degree is combined with specialized training which would require an additional one or two years of study.

Since the legal profession does not have formally designated specialties or certification procedures, advanced degrees and training are now optional. Movement toward a formal division of labor would require the cooperation of the bar, which is still attached to the ideal of a homogeneous profession. State bar approval would also be necessary to shift to a two-year degree; resistance is already apparent, in part because a longer period of training is a mark of status and a traditional way of screening and limiting entry into the profession.

Furthermore, law students may resist proposals for early specialization. If law schools became more specialized, students would have to make earlier career choices; the point of crucial decision would be forced down. Law has traditionally been a multipurpose career choice, a way to keep alternatives open, to acquire a useful degree without the narrowing of options and forcing of commitment entailed in medical schools or seminaries. While the ideal of a unitary profession is not, in fact, true, generally training does put off the point of commitment. Student pressure to do away with required courses and to institute electives also runs contrary to the trend toward specialization.

If the bar eventually did accept formal specialization, in education as well as in practice, would the end result be a rigidly stratified profession? Would those holding only the two-year degree be equal with those colleagues who have had additional years of formal schooling? Or if the profession begins to certify specialists, would those who stop with two years eventually be sealed off as a sort of caste, midway between the obviously paraprofessional levels and the elite stratum of specialists? The two-year law degree might end up not as a terminal degree, but as a prelude to further years of specialization (some kind of analog to the internship and residency phase of medical education). The issues being thrashed about in legal circles relate to trends visible in other professions: pressure toward lengthening the total time of training, specialization, and creation of a work hierarchy reflected in different lengths and types of training.

Changing the Division of Labor

Like other professionals, lawyers claim universal jurisdiction over a given body of work, but in law the claim to monopoly has been far from successful. The work of lawyers overlaps with that of accountants, realtors, process servers, bail bondsmen, probation officers, welfare workers, private detectives, and insurance adjusters. These occupations have found a steady demand for their work, which is often cheaper and more specialized than that of lawyers.

Historically the legal profession has fought outside competition by seeking rules which limit the practice of law to licensed attorneys. However, state governments have not always supported the monopoly of lawyers, and even when they exist, unauthorized practice rules have proved complicated and difficult to enforce.

Lawyers have sometimes negotiated with their competitors, establishing interoccupational treaties which recognize the legitimacy of ancillary occupations. Through the years, the American Bar Association has negotiated with nine different groups (including, for example, claims adjusters in 1939, banks with trust functions in 1941, realtors in 1943, accountants in 1951, and social workers in 1965). Joint committees have been established to settle jurisdictional disputes, but these committees lack sanctions, especially over the sizable number of practitioners who are not members of professional or occupational associations (Yegge et al., 1971).

The legal profession is now moving toward another approach to the problem of lay competition. Acknowledging the growing use of lay assistants by lawyers and law firms, the ABA resolved in 1968 that "the profession encourage the training and employment of such assistants" (Yegge et al., 1971). This trend, especially if it leads to formal training and certification of paralegal occupations, would take law along the path medicine followed in the nineteenth century, when physicians absorbed and gained control of other occupations such as bonesetting, midwifery, and nursing. If the experience of medicine is an indication, by drawing other occupations into a work complex with a systematic division of labor and training, lawyers would strengthen their monopoly more effectively than through open competition.

Hospitals became a setting for the integration of healing activity into a central institutional complex. In law, several institutions—the courts, law firms, and legal aid offices—may serve as organizing institutions, though no legal institution has a position as central as the hospital (and hence the legal work system may never be as tightly controlled as that in medicine). Those in occupations whose legal business lies outside the courts or law firms (for example, social workers and insurance adjusters) may retain relative autonomy from the legal profession, just as pharmacists, dentists, and optometrists who practice outside of hospitals have been less controlled by physicians than have nurses or laboratory technicians. If the legal work system develops along the lines of the medical work system, there will be new boundaries and margins of legitimacy and control.

The creation of paraprofessional ranks is part of the trend toward specialization and a more complicated division of labor. Specialization (in fact, if not in professional ideology) has broken down the monolithic structure of law practice, has re-sorted tasks, has led to new patterns of referral, and has created more intricate patterns of cooperation. As specialization advances, some tasks are delegated downward, creating demand for more workers at the bottom of the system. New subprofessional occupations are created—a trend long established in medicine and already visible in law. For example, in many firms legal secretaries and law office managers handle tasks previously done by attorneys; the lawyer appointed to chair the ABA Special Committee on Lay Assistants works in a 3-attorney office employing over 20 subprofessionals (Yegge et al., 1971), and in the late sixties a Wall Street firm with over 100 lawyers had a non-legal staff of 240 (Smigel, 1969). As in medicine, legal specialties may generate their own occupational groups:

In the same way in which radiology generated the X-ray technician, law might generate a non-lawyer tax technician who would be willing to remain on salary rather than becoming a partner, thus avoiding the A.B.A. Canons' prohibition of fee-sharing (Yegge et al., 1971, p. 182).

Some argue that lawyers are overtrained for many of the tasks they perform, and that if these tasks were taken over by workers with less training, legal services would be made more widely and cheaply available, especially to the poor. Since the problems of the poor are relatively routine (involving divorce, bankruptcy, small claims, welfare law) and since these problems are the dirty work, the less desired tasks of the profession, they are seen as especially ripe for delegating to nonlawyers.

The legal system, however defined, faces a critical manpower shortage—a lack of justice-producing persons, 'men of law.' The present crisis of the legal system requires far more than merely educating more lawyers, although in many areas of the country—and in many areas of the law—more lawyers are needed. . . . There is a real need to expand the supply of manpower which can be effectively absorbed into existing legal institutions. An experienced legal secretary can handle a very large number of routine matters at a law firm or legal aid office (as many often do). There is no reason why that status and function should not be formalized systematically, as has been done in the medical profession. Many technical jobs now performed by lawyers must be broken down and analyzed to determine whether they can be done more efficiently by less extensively trained persons. New legal technicians roles should have their own career lines, training programs, and system of accreditation. There are no justifiable, functional barriers to developing such legal technician roles except the profession's own self-serving notion of the intrinsic mystery of legal tasks. Freeing lawyers from routine tasks—drafting form documents, tedious shepardizing, negotiating with welfare caseworkers—might, indeed, free them to contribute more profoundly to both their client's and the rule of law's welfare (Cahn & Cahn, 1970, p. 1019).

The Training of Paralegal Workers

One way of asserting dominance over other occupations is to control their training; physicians, for example, supervise not only the activities, but also the education, of paramedical workers. Historically preoccupied with competition rather than control, lawyers have had little to do with the training of other occupations. Insurance adjusters, realtors, and accountants emerged independently. These careers are often unplanned, and training for them usually takes place informally and on the job rather than through formal schooling.

In 1968 the ABA resolved that the legal profession should encourage not only the employment, but also the training, of "nonlawyer assistants." Reformers are urging the profession (and law schools) to assume responsibility for educating not only attorneys, but also those who work in paralegal capacities. Formal training programs have begun to appear, primarily at the educational margins of the law school world. Some are proprietary ventures—for example, the Institute for Paralegal Training in Philadelphia, Pennsylvania, which offers college graduates three months of formal preparation for the role of legal assistant. The University of West Los Angeles School of Law in Culver City, California, an unaccredited law school, offers a special paralegal course "to those women and men desiring to work as legal 'assistants,' a potentially highly profitable field." Graduates of unaccredited law schools (and some from accredited schools as well) may follow paralegal careers, for example, in insurance adjusting or realty.

Community colleges, which have expanded along with the paraprofessional ranks of large work systems, are often mentioned as a location appropriate for paralegal training. Yegge et al. (1971, p. 196) note that "community colleges are new and not burdened by tradition or aspirations to classicism. As a result they have often been more receptive both to vocationally oriented courses, and to new teaching methods." In a proposal for legal education in Hawaii, Ehrlich and Manning (1971, p. 34) urge that paraprofessional training be introduced into the curricula of community colleges:

As we envisage the community college training, law would become one of the subjects in which a student could gain either an Associate in Science degree or a Certificate of Achievement, following the basic scheme now in operation at the community colleges. Indeed, one of the occupational curricula now offered at the Honolulu Community College—police science—is closely related in substance to some elements of the paraprofessional program that we have in mind. Further, the paraprofessional programs for health services at the Kapiolani Community College—dental assisting, medical assisting, practical nursing, and radiological technician—are all, in their classroom components, similar in design to the classroom components of a paraprofessional program in law.

Casting about for appropriate settings for the training of paralegal workers, some have turned to law schools (unless bar admissions requirements are changed, the two-year law degree at Stanford is, in effect, a paralegal degree). Schools of social work, urban affairs, engineering, and business administration have also been suggested. All these proposals involve a shift from on-the-job to college-based training—a familiar trend in the world of occupations.

Parenthetically, it should be noted that lawyers are not now trained to delegate work; Johnstone and Hopson (1967, p. 155) have observed, "It is surprising how many competent lawyers are unable to delegate effectively any of their work. They are skilled journeymen but untrained and unwilling to act as foremen." If the paralegal movement succeeds, the training of lawyers may have to change to take account of problems of delegation and referral.

The movement to set up formal schooling for paralegal occupations raises questions not only of location, but also of length. A shift into community colleges would settle at least some kinds of paralegal training at the two-year, post-high school level. The Philadelphia program (which is not affiliated with a college) consists of three months after a B.A. The two-year Stanford degree is also post-B.A. As yet, there is no stable pattern, but one can predict that if formal programs are established, the length of training for each type of paralegal worker will be reflected in a difference in income and prestige.

There is already some indication that, at least in the paralegal occupations developing in law firms (e.g., legal secretaries and legal assistants), the recruits will largely be women (Selinger, 1969; Johnstone & Hopson, 1967). Some are also arguing that these roles could provide employment for nonwhite minorities. A parallel with the medical work system again appears—a hierarchy of status reinforced by a stratifying of sex and ethnicity.

These speculations about a changing division of labor in law have run far ahead of the present reality. There is a trend to specialization, and law firms and legal aid offices are hiring more subprofessionals. There is widespread talk of formalizing specialties, including advanced degree programs; of drawing law-related occupations into a cohesive work system under the control of lawyers; and of establishing formal schooling for paralegal occupations. There are scattered programs along these lines. But there is also resistance—from lawyers who fear they will lose clients and income if tasks are reallocated, from those who still cherish the myth of a homogeneous profession, and perhaps from law-related occupations with little intention of being drawn under the thumb of the legal profession. It is tempting to claim that the division of labor in law is in a state of flux similar to that of medicine in the nineteenth century, and that the end result will resemble the elaborate and hierarchical work system and the pattern of professional dominance now so clear among the healing occupations. Like other professions, law often turns to medicine as a model. But the characteristics and problems peculiar to the work of law may shape its future in unique and unforeseen ways.

WHOM DOES THE LAW SERVE? Lawyers, being professional, claim an ideal of service, a concern with the public welfare. But the values and organization of the legal profession favor some clients over others. Lawyers, as do physicians, regard the ideal professional relationship as a private transaction with an individual client (which, in law, may be a business or a corporation, but is still regarded in individualistic terms). This tends to turn professional responsibility away from concern with the overall distribution of legal services and toward a more individualistic conception of needs and services.

Not all clients are equal in the eyes of the legal profession. The fee-for-service system favors those who can pay, and the poor often go without the help of lawyers. "Surveys conducted in several states indicate that about two out of three lower class families have *never* employed a lawyer, compared with about one out of three upper class families" (Carlin et al., 1967, p. 47). In the late sixties approximately $6.4 billion was spent annually for private legal services, while the Office of Economic Opportunities Legal Services division, set up to serve 35 million poor, has a budget of around $56 million (Van Loon, 1970).

The poor are penalized not only because they lack income, but also because they lack knowledge about how to assert their legal rights. Compared with the rich, the poor are relatively lacking in "legal competence," a term which Carlin et al. (1967) use to cover the ability and willingness to take initiative to protect one's interest, knowledge of how to use legal machinery, and a sense of oneself as a possessor of rights. Although they suffer many legal wrongs—and perhaps more than an equal share, since "poverty creates an abrasive interface with society; poor people are always bumping into sharp legal things" (Wexler, 1970, p. 1049)—the poor are unlikely to redress their grievances through law. "[T]heir narrow world, powerlessness, lack of organizational participation and negative legal experience tend to give the poor a conception of themselves and the legal system that is incompatible with effective use of law" (Carlin et al., 1967, p. 75).

When they do seek private legal services, the poor usually end up with lawyers who are at the lower end of the profession in quality of training, and who, because of insecure practices, are most likely to exploit clients (Carlin et al., 1967; Carlin, 1966). In law, as in medicine, the success of a professional is gauged by his income and the status of his clientele. The poor are seen as undesirable clients, and their problems as the dirty work of the profession. The legal problems of the poor are often described as "repetitive," "uninteresting," and "unchallenging." "Interesting" problems seem to be a class privilege. According to the traditional values of the profession, a lower-class clientele is a mark of a failure.

Implicit in the foregoing is a philosophy of distribution—an assumption within the legal profession that the rich have a more legitimate claim to services than do clients from lower socioeconomic strata. This assumption runs deep, shaping the very definition of legal services. The law is not a neutral instrument; it is oriented in favor of the propertied, "those groups or classes in society having the power to bend the legal order to their advantage"

(Carlin et al., 1967, p. 4). The law, for example, favors landlords over tenants and those who lend over those who borrow money. A four-year study of consumer credit found that debtors did not get a fair hearing in court (*New York Times*, July 19, 1971). Both procedural and substantive law are biased in favor of landlords, a point which Carlin et al. (1967) document in some detail.

In addition to favoring certain parties in legal relationships, the law embodies a double standard, in some cases denying the poor and nonwhites the protection and benefits which it provides for middle- and upper-class whites. For example, there are two separate systems of family law, one for the poor and the other for the more affluent. "The rules differ with respect to property and support relations of husband and wife, creation and termination of the marital relationship and responsibility for the support of relatives" (Carlin et al., 1967, p. 10). Welfare law and de jure discrimination against nonwhite minorities also involve dual and discriminatory systems of law.

Other sources of bias in the law are de facto: in written form the law treats everyone alike, but correlates of poverty (such as indigence, ignorance, or insecurity) make equality impossible. Carlin et al. (1967, p. 20) conclude:

[T]he problem of remedying bias in the law shades into the problem of remedying poverty itself. Effecting *legal* equality becomes at some point a problem of effecting *social* equality.

Law Schools and the Bias toward the Propertied The implicit goal of law schools is to create successful lawyers, not to provide an equitable distribution of legal services. The biases of the practicing profession are reflected in the law school curricula, in the methods of teaching, and in the career models implicit in the course of training itself.

Law school curricula are oriented to the interests of the rich and propertied.

In the first year, criminal and personal injury law, affecting great numbers of citizens, receive less thorough treatment than contracts or commercial property transactions; the course on legal procedure draws chiefly on business examples. The second-year law student is advised he is not a real lawyer without the three business-oriented courses known popularly as Making Money, Counting Money, and Keeping It from the Government (Corporations, Accounting, and Taxation). While these three are nominally optional at Harvard, for example, 94 percent of the student body follows faculty urgings to elect them. Courses on estate planning abound, but few schools teach environmental planning; consumer law is only beginning to receive attention (Van Loon, 1970, p. 336).

Law students are rarely introduced to the economic and legal institutions which shape the experiences of the poor — for example, welfare agencies, local police departments, and credit unions. The training of lawyers may make them reluctant to even define the problems of the poor in legal terms; there is a tendency in the legal profession to ignore the legal dimensions of the problems of the poor, to regard these problems as "basically social or psychological, calling for therapy rather than justice" (Carlin et al., 1967, p. 58).

The legal profession tends to define service to the propertied as its central or true work, and law schools orient their students toward profitable clients and problems. The role of the corporate lawyers lies behind much of law school training, especially in the elite stratum of schools; schools with more state or local orientations also prepare their graduates to serve paying customers. Erwin Griswold (1968, p. 151), former dean of the Harvard Law School, comments upon the commercial flavor of legal education:

Almost inevitably our students are led to feel that it is in [business and finance] that the great work of the lawyer is to be found. By methods of teaching, by subtle and often unconscious innuendo, we indicate to our students that their future success and happiness will be found in the traditional areas of the law. . . .

Challenges to the Traditional Mandate In law, as in medicine, the unequal distribution of professional services has become a public issue and a focus of organized movements both within and outside the profession. Clients bypassed or given second-class treatment under the traditional forms of law practice have gained increased recognition of their right to counsel, and the federal government, social movements, and an emerging segment of the legal profession have begun to support these rights.

Edgar S. Cahn and Jean Comper Cahn, pioneers of the poverty law movement, write of an "institutional crisis which is threatening to overwhelm the traditional adjudicative machinery of the legal system" (Cahn & Cahn, 1970, p. 1008). The crisis is in part the result of an explosion of rights and grievances. In recent years court decisions and statutes have expanded the legal rights of juveniles, public housing tenants, persons accused of crimes, welfare recipients, and members of minority groups. This "rights explosion," if honored in practice, threatens to overwhelm the already strained capacity of the legal system. In the criminal field alone "the newly expanded rights to counsel for those charged with a crime will require, conservatively estimated, a fivefold increase in the number of public defenders" (Cahn & Cahn, 1970, pp. 1008–1009). There is also pressure for legal scrutiny of administrative bodies in the fields of poverty, welfare, housing, transportation, urban renewal, and pollution control. Challenges to previously unreviewable discretionary decisions will further intensify the caseload of the courts and the demand for legal services.

In 1965 the federal government began to intervene in the distribution of legal services. In spite of initial, and some continued, resistance from the bar (which fears a loss of business and the threat of outside control), the government established the Office of Economic Opportunity Legal Services Program to distribute legal services to the poor. Although it still embodies elements of charity (the style in which the legal profession has traditionally approached the needs of clients unable to pay), the OEO program in many ways represents a break with the philosophy of traditional legal aid societies. This break is indicated by:

. . . (1) the importance placed upon the establishment of neighborhood law offices to increase the accessibility of legal services to the poor; (2) the requirement that the poor be represented on the governing board of the legal service agency to enhance responsiveness to client needs; (3) the adoption of a more aggressive stance in promoting the collective as well as individual interests of the poor, including the use of legal advocacy as an instrument of social change; and (4) concern for insuring the independence of the legal service organization from those vested interests that might be threatened by more vigorous representation of the poor (Carlin et al., 1967, p. 59).

OEO legal resources have gone far beyond those of traditional legal aid organizations, which in 1963 had a total budget of less than $4 million and were processing about the same number of new cases per thousand population as in 1916 (Carlin et al., 1967). When the OEO Legal Services Program opened in the fall of 1965, it had a budget of almost $25 million. By 1970 the budget had more than doubled (reaching about $60 million), and supported 2,000 attorneys working in every state except North Dakota (*New York Times*, May 18, 1966, p. 16; *New York Times*, Dec. 15, 1970).

Challenges to the mandate and orientation of the legal profession have come from political and social movements as well as from government programs. The civil rights, environmental, and welfare rights movements have dramatized the problems of the unrepresented and the need for law reform. The public interest and consumer advocacy movements (represented most visibly by Ralph Nader and the Center for Responsive Law) have been vocal in challenging the traditional organization and values of the legal profession.

Law students have been active in these movements, sometimes in a quasi-legal capacity. The Law Students Civil Rights Research Council set up summer internships for law students to work with civil rights lawyers. In the last few years hundreds of law students have spent their summers as "Nader's Raiders," investigating federal agencies and corporate structures from a public interest perspective. Nader has encouraged this involvement, noting that students are less invested in the status quo, they are relatively free to take risks, and they represent a large manpower reserve. They may be in a unique position to investigate the American economic system in a way which universities and professional groups have failed to do ("Nader Urges Student Investigations," 1969).

Some law students have publicly challenged the legal profession. At Harvard Law School in December 1969, 40 students picketed recruiters from Cravath, Swaine & Moore, a New York firm, to protest the firm's representation of clients with interests in South Africa. Earlier that fall there was a similar demonstration against recruiters from Ropes & Gray, a Boston law firm which represents coal producers in West Virginia (referring to black-lung disease among miners, the picketers chanted, "Ropes, Ropes, Ropes & Gray. How many lungs did you ruin today?") In both cases, the protesters tried to raise the issue of accountability, to confront the "hired gun" theory of legal representation (the notion that the legal profession is neutral) with questions of public interest, and to encourage graduating law students to boycott firms tied to politically or ethically questionable activities. The same year law students sent out a questionnaire to firms using the Harvard Law School Placement Office, asking for detailed information about firm activities, public service (or *pro bono*) work, the ethics of their corporate representations, and hiring practices (especially regarding nonwhites and women). Of the firms receiving questionnaires, three-quarters refused to reply (Van Loon, 1970).

These pressures have had some impact on private law firms, partly because students from elite law schools (where most of the activism has developed) have threatened to look elsewhere for employment. Writing about the late sixties Smigel (1969) describes the recruitment problems of large law firms. The number of these firms has increased, and students from the "national" schools (where the firms prefer to recruit) now have more alternatives (government work, judicial clerkships, teaching, and public service jobs with the OEO and Vista). Students who have asked for paid time off to work in public service projects have been in a good bargaining position, and some firms have responded.

In recent months, there has been much soul-searching among the larger firms. Memos suggesting various opportunities for *pro bono* work by younger associates have been circulating between partners. A few decisions have been made. Some New York and San Francisco firms are considering or have instituted time off allowances ranging from a few weeks a year to a sabbatical. Piper & Marbury, a large Baltimore firm, has announced its intention to establish a branch office in the slums to service the needs of poor people, without charging fees if there is an inability to pay anything. Arnold and Porter, the second largest Washington, D.C., firm, has appointed a full time *pro bono* lawyer and is permitting all firm members to spend, if they wish, an average of 15 percent of their working hours on public service activities. Hogan and Hartson, the third largest D.C. firm, is setting up a "Community Service Department" to "take on public interest representation on a non-chargeable or, where appropriate, a discounted fee basis," according to the firm's memorandum on the subject (Nader, 1969, p. 22).

Many of these firms have admitted that they regard *pro bono* ventures primarily as a recruitment device.

The executive committee of Hogan and Hartson concedes that "there is a tendency among younger lawyers, particularly those with the highest academic qualifications, to seek out public-service oriented legal careers as an alternative to practice in the larger metropolitan law firms." In its internal firm statement, the committee notes that it "regards the relative disfavor into which the major law firms have fallen to be attributable, at least in part, to the feeling among recent law school graduates *that these firms have failed to respond to the larger problems of contemporary society"* (their emphasis) (Nader, 1969, p. 22).

Changing Career Choices? Large law firms—and the media, which have made much of the "new breed of lawyer"—have been impressed with an apparent shift in the career choices of graduates from elite law schools. In the late sixties, statistics from schools such as Harvard, the University of Michigan, and Columbia indicated a turn away from corporate and private law and a growth in public service work. Of the 1969 graduates from the University of Michigan Law School, 26 entered Wall Street firms, compared with an average of 75 in preceding years (Nader, 1969). A year after graduation, 50 percent of the 1964 Harvard Law School graduates were in private law practice; for the class of 1967 the figure had dropped to 44 percent. The remaining 1967 graduates who responded to the survey were distributed as follows: business and commercial jobs, 6 percent; government, 8 percent; judicial clerkships, 12 percent; teaching, research, and study, 5 percent; fellowships, 2 percent; legal aid work, 2 percent; and Peace Corps, 1 percent (*Harvard Law Record,* Oct. 29, 1971).

However, after 1967 and 1968 (when again 44 percent had entered private practice) the drop away from private practice began to reverse. A year after graduation 49 percent of the 1969 graduates of Harvard Law School were in private practice (although 4 percent were working in Legal Services and 2 percent in Vista, a rise over 1967). Statistics for the class of 1970 indicate a rise to 61 percent in private practice (a record high since 1960, when the figure was also 61 percent): 3 percent were in Legal Services and 1 percent in public interest jobs (ibid.). Surveying his fellow 1970 graduates from Columbia Law School, Andrew Dolan (1971, p. 32) also found continued interest in traditional jobs:

Of the 187 students who indicated where they were working or of whose plans I had personal knowledge (40 remain unaccounted for, but I assume the trend among them will be substantially similar to that of the others), 141 noted that they would be engaged in corporate practice. Another 12 accepted judicial clerkships and indicated they would enter corporate practice upon completion. Nine others were undecided on their plans after clerking. Five more became criminal prosecutors. Of the remaining 20, about two-thirds said they would be engaged in some form of poverty work. Significantly, none indicated that he would be serving the needs of the lower middle class, and how many of that dozen or so in poverty work will resist the lure of corporate practice and for how long is an open question. In short, at least three-quarters of my classmates, by their career choice, have decided to dedicate their skills and efforts to the rich, and I believe, work either directly or indirectly against the poor and working classes.

Reports of a "new breed of lawyer," of elite law students massively deserting corporate and private practice for careers in poverty and public interest law, have apparently been exaggerated. Some argue that the most recent statistics prove that the "new mood" among law students (as Smigel labeled the spirit of activism, protest, and idealism) was a fleeting phenomenon, a product of the late sixties. Reflecting on the job choices of the 1970 Harvard Law School graduates, the director of the placement office stated:

They put up a big fuss that they are different now, but they're not. . . . Students are much more serious about interviewing this year. And they seem to be doing more of it. Perhaps it is a reflection of their worry that firms may not be hiring as readily as before (*Harvard Law Record*, Oct. 29, 1970, pp. 4–5).

Although private practice still holds appeal for the bulk of law school graduates, there has been an increase in alternative kinds of work. The OEO Legal Services Program and Vista have provided increased employment opportunities for poverty lawyers; the number of public defender offices nearly doubled between 1964 and 1967, going from 139 to 266 (Bellow, 1968). Foundations and private contributions have supported new enterprises in public interest law—for example, the Center of Responsive Law, founded by Ralph Nader, and the National Resources Defense Council, organized by a group of recent law school graduates and funded by the Ford Foundation to "protect our natural resources and human environment by legal action through the courts." As the number of lawyers working in public interest and poverty law has increased, new circles of colleagueship, career lines, ideologies, and definitions of priorities, problems, and clients have evolved. In short, public interest lawyers have become an emerging professional segment (Bucher & Strauss, 1961).

Poverty and Public Interest Law

Those engaged in poverty and public interest law share a mission: to represent the unrepresented and thereby provide a more equitable distribution of professional services. Charles Halpern (1970,

p. A-18), director of a Washington-based public interest firm, summarizes this sense of purpose:

We are called public interest lawyers, . . . but less pompously we're just lawyers for unrepresented people, the ones who are getting clobbered but with no one there to protect them. These people are all over the place — not just the poor, but also the victims of pollution, the victims of corporate arrogance or maybe just the odd guy who wants to eat his pickles without DDT in them.

Serving clients considered undesirable or illegitimate under the traditional focus of the legal profession has involved establishing new forms of payment and practice and breaking orthodox assumptions about who initiates and determines professional relationships.

Since their clients are not in a position to pay for legal services, poverty and public interest lawyers rely on third-party payment. This outside financial support has come from the federal government (especially OEO and Vista), foundations, and law firms (both large private firms with *pro bono* arrangements and public-oriented firms founded by young lawyers) which use fee-generating work to support public interest activity.

Dependence on outside sources of payment makes these enterprises inherently unstable.

The current crop of public interest law firms are essentially hothouse flowers. They are the product of limited, short-term foundation largesse. A major and as yet unanswered question for these new public interest law firms is that of economic viability. . . . It remains to be seen whether government or private law firms will be willing to underwrite public advocacy (with integrity) on a massive scale and, if so, in what fields other than poverty law. The question of economic viability makes it critically important to ask whether it is possible to institutionalize career lines which permit lawyers who desire to live on a better than subsistence level to engage substantially or exclusively in work on behalf of clients who pay little or nothing (Cahn & Cahn, 1970, pp. 1007–1008).

Third-party support for poverty and public interest law may be a product of "a national affluence which may prove to be temporary" ("The New Public Interest Lawyer," 1970, p. 1448). Such support has already begun to decline; in March 1972, Columbia University Law School reported that "the job market for graduating law students had changed dramatically within the last year," including a tightening of the public service sector, which forced more to go into private practice (*New York Times*, Mar. 14, 1972).

Third-party support may also be withdrawn when advocates for the poor and the public interest come into conflict with established institutions. The resistance of the organized bar and some government officials to the funding of the California Rural Legal Assistance illustrates the kind of conflict which can shake the financial underpinnings of public interest law. *Pro bono* ventures may create conflicts of interest within private law firms—for example, when, in its public interest role, a firm is called upon to litigate against the very corporate clients it represents as part of its regular business.

The role of public interest and poverty lawyers departs from the orthodoxies of the legal profession not only in form of payment, but also in style of practice. Lawyers in OEO neighborhood legal services offices do not pick and choose their clients; in theory, they provide free legal services to every person who can prove himself "eligible" by low-income criteria who walks through the door. According to the OEO mandate, responsibility extends beyond individual clients to include the concept of delivering professional services to a total population—which marks a departure from the traditional philosophy of the legal profession.

The professional rule against advertising services works to the special disadvantage of the poor, who tend to be outside informal networks of referral and to have less knowledge and initiative in asserting legal rights. Rather than waiting for clients to request their services, poverty and public interest lawyers have attempted to create wants, to educate various publics about legal rights and the availability of professional services. This involves enlarging the lawyer's role to include a teaching and, in effect, an advertising function. Poverty and public interest lawyers have gained some support from the bar in their claim that the rule against soliciting business discriminates against the poor and disadvantaged. The ethics committee of the District of Columbia Bar ruled that public interest law firms, and, by implication, legal aid offices, may advertise to clients in publications and over the air (*New York Times*, Mar. 10, 1971; Freedman, 1971).

Public interest and poverty lawyers have moved in other directions in rethinking and changing the lawyer's role, sometimes in ways which violate basic tenets of the legal profession. Some poverty lawyers regard themselves as community organizers. Wexler (1970, p. 1053) argues that "the lawyer who wants to serve poor people must put his skill to the task of helping poor people organize themselves"; organizing rather than solving legal problems should be the ultimate goal. This entails dealing with organized groups, which may mean refusing services to clients who are not in the organization. Wexler (1970, p. 1054) also urges poverty lawyers to demystify the law and to help poor people acquire new skills rather than new dependencies: "The hallmark of an effective poor people's practice is that the lawyer does not do anything for his clients that they can do or be taught to do for themselves." These proposals run up against two professional traditions: primary obligation to individual clients, and the guarding of professional mysteries and expertise from the hands of laymen.

In seeking legal and social reform, poverty and public interest lawyers have begun to press class suits, which means directing attention "away from a particular claim or grievance to the broader interests and policies at stake, and away from the individual client to a class of clients, in order to challenge more directly and with greater impact certain structural sources of injustice" (Carlin et al., 1967, p. 57). The shift diverts resources away from serving individual clients and creates conflicts between the goals of individual service and collective reform. Tracing the history of the OEO-funded San Francisco Neighborhood Legal Assistance agency, Carlin (1970*a*) describes a basic tension between the goals of serving a mass clientele on a case-by-case basis and of pushing for legal and institutional reform through class suits and other forms of advocacy.

Some critics charge that the class-suit approach is in part a retreat from the dirty work of serving individual clients:

There are definite indications . . . that the onerous and oft-times monotonous business of serving individuals—and poor ones at that—is repelling to many of the products of the antiseptic and aridly intellectual process called higher and professional education. There is enough evidence to produce worry among some observers that this retreat to test cases and law reform is the O.E.O. counterpart syndrome to the hitherto existing tendency to seek out the so-called Wall Street or corporate law firm where there is little if any direct contact with the dirty, little problems of the ordinary men (Pincus, 1969, p. 5).

Few lawyers come from poverty backgrounds, and the code and etiquette of the profession are firmly middle and upper-middle class. Thus poverty lawyers find that "there are important problems of style, differences in income and education, frustrations and anger about failures, and a host of social, cultural and psychological differences that tend to divide rather than unite poor people with their lawyers" (Wexler, 1970, p. 1052).

The legal problems of the poor involve matters which the legal profession regards as routine and uninteresting. For example, in the San Francisco Legal Assistance neighborhood offices about 30 percent of the clients came for help with a family problem (half were seeking a divorce); the next biggest group sought help in dealing with administrative agencies (welfare, unemployment insurance, social security, immigration and naturalization, and the draft); about 15 percent of the clients had problems with landlords; and another 15 percent with merchants (Carlin, 1970*a*). The orientation of law schools to business and corporate matters implicitly defines this type of practice as unimportant and unworthy of any but the lower reaches of the profession. This is especially true of elite law schools, whose graduates have been most drawn to the poverty law movement. (Some graduates of lower-stratum law schools have always ended up with clients from lower socioeconomic groups, but these practices have been marginal, *faute de mieux,* marked with a sense of failure, and have not shared the sense of mission of the current movement to provide legal services to the poor.

The poverty and public interest law movement has not found it easy to rearrange the profession's hierarchy of legitimate and favored clients, to side with the poor rather than the rich, and to emphasize redistributing legal services over service to paying clients. The movement lacks stable supporting institutions — finances depend on the government and foundations and are highly vulnerable to political and economic pressures. Compared with other career options, lawyers who undertake this kind of work have to settle for low pay, low status (except within their own circles of colleagueship), and heavy, sometimes overwhelming, caseloads.

The large turnover among lawyers working in OEO Legal Services offices is not surprising. Some observers of the recent wave of interest in poverty and public interest law chalk it up as a fad or at best a trend which will crystallize into a career stage or part-time charity effort, rather than into full-fledged specialties and legitimate career lines within the legal profession. A lawyer in a Wall Street firm expressed this point of view:

We have people in legal aid, but our young men will be disillusioned with this kind of practice after a while. They think they will be developing new law, but most of their work will be landlord and tenant disagreements. Our lawyers will finally say, "Someone has to do it, but are we the ones?" (Smigel, 1969, p. 368).

Thus far, public interest and poverty law has been the special province of the young. Although there are exceptions, public interest advocates and OEO Legal Services attorneys have not been older, established members of the profession. The high turnover rate does suggest that this kind of work is now a youthful career stage (some law students call it "the public service bit") rather than a long-term commitment. In recent years a period of exploration—as an appellate clerk, Reginald Heber Fellow, legal aid attorney, public defender, or member of Vista or the Peace Corps—has become relatively common among graduates of national and some state law schools. Such opportunities (including "the public service bit") offer a period of experimentation before committing oneself to a long-term, higher paying, and more legitimate career.

Can legal services be redistributed and the unrepresented gain adequate legal counsel if this work is relegated to a career stage or a part-time effort? Those working for these goals would certainly say no. In law, as in medicine, the issue of distributive justice has become a subject of increasing debate and an organizing point for new kinds of careers. But the goals far exceed the current achievements.

CLINICAL LEGAL EDUCATION Criticism of the traditional mandate of the legal profession, growing support for poverty and public interest law, and student demands for "relevance" have affected law school curricula. Many law schools have added courses which suggest a more balanced perspective—for example, Race, Racism and American Law (Harvard), Law for the Poor in an Affluent Society (Columbia), Consumer Protection (Stanford), Natural Resources (California), and Urban Public School Systems (Chicago) (*New York Times,* Nov. 19, 1969. pp. 37, 39).

Such courses, however, represent additions to, rather than transformations of, the core curriculum. They are typically electives offered during the third year, perhaps too late to influence career choices. The fare of required courses has remained substantially unchanged in its commercial and business orientation, although "[c]atalogue descriptions of these courses have been changed recently to suggest that the subject matter of these courses can be adapted to the needs of the poor or the nonbusiness clients" (Rock-well, 1971, p. 97).

In addition to new courses, many law schools have begun to establish clinical programs which bring students into contact with real clients and problems and combine education with service. Most commonly this involves assigning law students to a legal aid clinic or neighborhood legal assistance office, where their work is supervised by an attorney (in some cases a faculty member). In another, "farming-out" type of arrangement, law students receive academic credit for a period of work in outside offices such as private or public interest firms or government agencies.

Clinical programs offered for credit, considered a legitimate part of the curriculum and supervised by the law school, gained strength in the late 1960s. Most accredited law schools now have some kind of clinical program, although these programs range widely in structure and size and are usually elective rather than required.

The addition of clinical programs represents a departure from the traditional isolation of law schools from the practicing profession. Advocates of clinical legal education carefully use the word *clinical* rather than *apprenticeship,* emphasizing the integration of theory and practice and of practical and classroom experience, as well as supervision by trained educators. But some legal educators fear that these programs involve "giving back the hard-won academic base of legal education to some not-so-thinly disguised office training" (Stevens, 1970, p. 37). There are echoes here of the old battle between the schoolmen and proponents of practice-based training.

Pressure for clinical legal education has come from a variety of sources. In many law schools, students have demanded contact with actual clients and cases, and faculty members concerned with student unrest and malaise have turned to clinical programs as an antidote. Some law school teachers who are critical of the traditional methods and content of legal education regard clinical programs as a means of reform. Some practicing attorneys favor clinical education as a way to teach students the "nuts and bolts" of being a lawyer.

The movement for clinical legal education has also received encouragement from outside the profession. In expanding legal services for the poor, the Office of Economic Opportunities also expanded opportunities and clients available for clinical instruction.

In some cases the OEO made direct grants to law schools to run neighborhood law offices; more frequently law schools have developed clinical arrangements with independent OEO and legal aid offices. Title XI of the Higher Education Act promises direct federal support for clinical legal education, although the funds have not been, and may never be, appropriated. In 1968 the Ford Foundation established a philanthropy, the Council on Legal Education for Professional Responsibility (CLEPR), with the mission of "encouraging a profound examination of existing instruction in law schools, challenging law schools to become professional schools involved in legal process, legal services and practice skills, and expanding the schools' activities beyond theorizing about legal doctrine" (Pincus, 1971, p. 1). By the fall of 1971, CLEPR had made grants totaling about $3.75 million to support clinical experiments in 85 accredited law schools (Pincus, 1971).

Justification for Clinical Legal Education

Advocates of clinical legal education criticize the isolated and narrow focus which has characterized law schools since the consolidation of Langdell's model. Reichert (1968, p. 172) points to the wide gap between law school training and the requirements of practice:

A fairly well-kept secret of the profession is that most law schools teach a student practically nothing about how to practice law. Sidney Post Simpson's statement of two decades ago is still true today: "A law school graduate who passes his bar examination is not a lawyer. No one knows it better than he, unless it be his law office or his prospective clients." Or, as Judge Jerome Frank put it, law schools are "library law schools" rather than "lawyer schools." To him, law students were "like future horticulturists studying solely cut flowers" or "prospective dog breeders who never see anything but stuffed dogs."

National law schools emphasize theory and analysis and cherish the goal of teaching students to "think like lawyers," which is not the same thing as practicing like lawyers. A Yale law professor said in an interview: "We very consciously *don't* fit somebody to hang out a shingle and try a case" (Mayer, 1966, p. 117). Ferren (1970, p. 97) summarizes this point of view:

The faculty of a so-called "big firm" law school may downgrade the practical skills goal because of its alleged lack of intellectual content. Such professors are likely to take the position that such skills come quickly in practice, and that a law school should accordingly devote full time to nurturing analytical skills.

Ferren notes that this view assumes that students will get practical training from sources other than the law school. They apparently do. Within the last 10 years it has become common for private law firms and some government agencies to hire law students to work during the summers [an example of the growth of this practice: in 1957, 22 students from Columbia Law School had summer positions with law firms; in 1967 the number had risen to 222 (Smigel, 1969)]. These programs are mainly recruitment devices, but they also give students a sort of apprenticeship which is interspersed (though rarely integrated) with classroom training. Large law firms and government agencies assume that recent law school graduates will not be trained in the practical aspects of legal work; in effect they provide a structured apprenticeship period for new recruits. Law schools whose graduates enter these kinds of careers can assume that practical skills will be taught by someone else, usually on the job, and outside of the law school setting.

The movement from law school to first job is probably more difficult for those entering small firms, solo practice, and the new careers in poverty and public interest law, careers whose structure and resources preclude a regular or easy apprenticeship. In a study of solo practitioners in Chicago, Carlin (1962) found they had typically graduated from a proprietary or Catholic night law school and had attached themselves to another lawyer as a kind of apprentice during the first few years out of law school. Although it provided some kind of bridge between school and practice, this arrangement was full of conflict and largely symbiotic. The employer wanted cheap labor, and the young lawyer wanted to learn his way around courts, local agencies, and practical procedures. In a study of law students in Chicago, Lortie (1959, p. 367) found that graduates of independent local law schools tended to favor more practical law school training, while "university men are more likely to defend a strictly theoretical curriculum, but this association is reversed where they enter private practice rather than firms."

Those urging more practical instruction argue that this sort of training should not be left to the vicissitudes of one's career, for "clients suffer from the inexperience of the young but licensed lawyer, the experience is not available to all, it is poorly organized, [and] it is conducive to bad habits" (Kitch, 1970, p. 5). Traditional law school methods and courses cover only a narrow range of the skills used by practicing lawyers. The case study method ignores the skills of interviewing, negotiating, and counseling; of making decisions about alternative strategies, and of applying ethical canons to specific cases. Law school courses usually deal with appellate decisions, that is, with cases already at some distance from raw facts. Rather than exploring the process of gathering and sifting facts and building a case, "the quest for fact moves backward from a legal conclusion contained in an appellate decision, through a mythical reconstruction of the past (as filtered through restrictive laws of evidence) and finally ends in assessing the grievances of parties possessing all the animation implicit in their classic names—Richard Roe and John Doe" (Cahn & Cahn, 1970, p. 1026). Clinical programs, it is argued, will draw law school learning closer to the skills of the practicing lawyer.

The goals of service as well as education are used to justify clinical programs. Law students represent a reserve of manpower which can be used to expand the delivery of legal service; "if all law students were to spend the equivalent of one semester in clinical work, then every year approximately 10,000 supervised law students would be available for service" (Carlin, 1970*b*, p. 1). The bulk of clinical programs involve the poor as clients, most often in poverty law offices, but also in public defenders' offices and prisons. The link between the learners of a profession and poor clients—the trade-off between receiving free services in return for being learned upon—is presented in law as well as in medicine.

This is true partly because of bar restrictions. The model student practice rule adopted by the ABA in 1969 and the rules of many states limit students to indigent or legal aid clients—a limitation which is probably rooted in the bar's fear of loss of paying business (Ridberg, 1970). The poor and their problems rank low in the legal profession's hierarchy of legitimate and desired work, and by this definition, the stakes involved in leaving poor clients in the hands of novices seem lower than for paying clients.

Law students and legal reformers also favor centering clinical legal education on poor clients, but for somewhat different reasons. Those critical of the bias of legal education toward paying clients welcome a chance to focus on the poor and their problems, and some argue that experience in clinical programs will draw students closer to the needs of the unrepresented and encourage them to choose careers in poverty and public interest law. [On the contrary, one observer argues, familiarity may breed contempt, "as witness the frequent callousness of those who now man the systems the students so readily condemn" (Kitch, 1970, p. 17)].

The use of students to expand legal services to the poor fits with the general mission of providing a more equal distribution of legal services—a mission also used to justify the development of paralegal occupations. While increasing the number of clinical students and paralegal workers may increase manpower, if these less-trained workers are relegated primarily to poor clients, the result may be a double standard of service. Some argue that the problems of the poor can be handled as well, or better, by less-trained practitioners, but the claim is open to debate.

In all professions when learners are part of the work system, they tend to be delegated the less desired chores and to be regarded, implicitly if not explicitly, as a source of cheap labor. At least one observer of a poverty law office (Cohen, 1970) has noted that students were assigned to the more routine chores and that practicing attorneys saw them more as employees than students. Recognizing their contribution of labor, some students resent working for nothing or for a meager wage, especially if they have had regular employment in a law office at a higher rate of pay. For example, it has been the custom for senior law students at Washburn University in Topeka, Kansas, to work in downtown law firms as paid law clerks. "Students rely heavily on this source of income and have accordingly resisted the institution of a clinical program that has attempted to substitute academic credit for financial remuneration. Faced with this situation, Washburn has opted for designating the private practitioners who employ senior students as supervisors" (*CLEPR Newsletter,* January 1971, p. 6).

Service versus Education

How much educational value is there in clinical programs? The goals of service and those of education do not always mesh, and in practical settings, with the pressure of actual cases and clients, service functions may predominate. A director of a clinical program which placed students from six New York City Law schools in Legal Aid Society offices drew conclusions about the program:

As service to clients it was a substantial success. As an educational experience for its participating students, it was a substantial failure. . . . If anything, students were taught poor habits such as mechanical handling of clients, shunting of the poor, lack of privacy, glibness, failure of complete dedication to the individual clients and representation without proper preparation. The basic premise was that students were a good resource to assist in the overwhelming problem of caseload, and all attempts to use the program as a method for teaching the proper practice of law through representation of the poor were of secondary value to the primary goal of service (Cohen, 1970, pp. 204, 209).

It is as possible to learn bad as it is good habits from experience. In the absence of careful supervision and without close integration with the rest of the law school curriculum, clinical programs may be no better for learning skills than is practice itself. Critics have suggested that the import of some clinical programs may simply be to advance by a year an experience a student would have anyway. In rejoinder, advocates of clinical instruction stress the importance of supervision, of structuring clinical arrangements in a careful way. They point out that after graduation from law school students may not go into positions where they can get the kind of supervision that good clinical programs can offer, and that, if properly planned, clinical programs can expose the student to a greater variety of experience than he would acquire on the job.

Clinical Programs: Problems and Issues The debate over clinical legal education involves a number of issues, starting with the question of how much time students should spend in clinical settings, how many students should participate, and how much credit should be given for the course. At one extreme are a few law schools with a thoroughly clinical orientation. Northeastern University School of Law in Boston reopened in 1968 after having been closed for almost 15 years. Following the "work-study" philosophy of the university, the law school program alternates periods of full-time academic study with periods of paid, full-time employment in private law firms, corporations, government offices, and legal aid clinics. All students participate. Along similar lines, Antioch College has announced plans to open a new law school in Washington, D.C., which will be based not in classrooms but in a public interest law firm (*New York Times,* Dec. 5, 1971).

These two programs represent an exceptional commitment to clinical training. In most law schools clinical courses are optional and involve relatively few students—according to one estimate, an average of 8 to 30 students (*CLEPR Newsletter,* January 1971).

Law schools have only recently begun to grant credit for clinical experience. The significance of credit in advancing the status of clinical programs is illustrated by the history of clinical training at the University of Minnesota Law School. In 1957 a voluntary student legal aid clinic was organized on an extracurricular, and rather limited, basis. The clients were university students, mostly involved in landlord-tenant disputes. During the 1965–66 school year, at the urging of the student body and the clinic's student directors, the law school granted three academic credits to students who had successfully completed 90 hours of clinic work over a two-year period. In 1967, as a result of pressure from the clinic, the State Supreme Court established a student practice rule, allowing supervised third-year students to appear in court on behalf of indigent clients. The legal aid clinic expanded to serve the neighborhood poor as well as university students, and the school developed clinical ties with the Minnesota Public Defender. By 1969 more than half of the student body participated in clinical programs, and the school hired a clinical professor of legal education to become a full-time adviser to the clinic (Oliphant, 1970).

Debate over the merits of clinical education centers not only on the issue of credit, but also on the question of how to integrate such programs with the rest of the curriculum, expecially with classroom work. Few law schools have reorganized their curricula around a clinical approach; in most schools clinical courses (and the new courses in urban, poverty, and public interest subjects) are tacked on to the traditional curriculum and have little impact on the content or teaching methods of regular courses.

A sense of division between classroom and clinic is reinforced not only by different settings, problems, and educational methods, but also by separate faculties. In the "farming-out" type of arrangement, where law students leave the school to get clinical experience with outside firms or agencies, supervision often lies in the hands of practicing attorneys (the analog of part-time clinical teachers associated with medical schools). Such supervision is often felt to be inadequate, and some law schools have added a new slot—clinical law school professor—to the faculty roster.

In the fall of 1971, the Council on Legal Education for Professional Responsibility sponsored a workshop on "the life and times of clinical law teachers." The participants, clinical faculty from a range of schools, spoke of the strains of "being in both the academic and practicing camps," the burden of being simultaneously responsible for running a law office and serving clients and for teaching law students. The clinical professors also complained of being relegated to second-class citizenship with the law school (*CLEPR*

Newsletter, November 1971). This conflict between teachers based almost wholly in the academic world and those with an ongoing tie to the practicing profession and clients is familiar in medicine as well as in law.

Although the movement for clinical legal education has gained a foothold in the nation's law schools, with the tangible achievement of credited courses and clinical faculty, there are many strains, conflicts, and problems involved. Many faculty are not sold on the value of clinical courses, regarding them as an ill-considered fad and even a backsliding from hard-won academic gains. Conflicts between the clinical approach and traditional highly theoretical concepts of law school teaching and learning involve the general tension between theory and its application.

Cost is often cited as the most serious drawback of clinical programs. With a high student-faculty ratio (at Harvard, for instance, there are 60 faculty members for more than 1,700 students), and with a minimal amount of capital equipment, law schools have traditionally provided a relatively cheap form of professional education. Some unaccredited law schools are still run for profit, and some academic law schools have a reputation as money-makers for the rest of the university. Since supervision of students working with clients requires a substantially lower student-faculty ratio and an increase in administrative expenses, clinical instruction costs much more than traditional classroom methods. According to one estimate, clinical programs cost at least three times as much per student as a medium-sized law school class (Wilson, 1970, p. 176).

The addition of a clinical dimension to formal legal education involves changing the relation of the law school to the practicing profession and the delivery system. Through teaching hospitals, medical schools have always had contact with clients and the delivery of services — a role which has increased in recent years. In contrast, law schools have no tradition as delivery institutions, and some legal educators and practitioners prefer to keep it that way. Debate over clinical legal education raises larger questions about the mission and responsibilities of the law school, which leads to the next topic: the institutional ecology of legal education.

THE INSTITUTIONAL ECOLOGY OF THE LAW SCHOOL Like other professional schools which have become part of the world of higher education but which still have as a goal the training of practitioners, law schools balance demands from the university, the practicing profession, and the state. However, the institutional context of law schools is less complicated than that of medical schools, mainly because law schools have not traditionally functioned as delivery institutions.

[The early law school] was in a sense created by an act of withdrawal. As compared to the apprenticeship system that had preceded it, the turn of the century law school withdrew from the courts, withdrew from the practitioner, withdrew from the community, and withdrew from working context and withdrew from any effort to teach law students how to do (Manning, 1969, p. 4).

Pulling away from institutions of practice did not, however, entail full integration with institutions of education. Although most law schools are attached to universities, by and large they have been relatively self-contained, with their own faculties and body of knowledge and only minimal ties to other disciplines or educational programs.

The history of reform in legal education is in part a history of efforts to break down the isolation of law school — on the one hand, to draw the law school closer to the delivery system and the practicing profession, and on the other hand, to bring a fuller integration of the law school with the university. This section sketches the institutional context of the law school and various directions of change.

The Law School, the Practicing Profession, and the State Although the early schoolmen fought to make attendance at a law school the only qualification for entry into the profession, they were not successful. In all but a few states, final admission to the profession is based on passing a bar examination, controlled not by the law school establishment but by the state government and the practicing profession. An implicit goal of law school training has always been to prepare students to pass the bar examination, although some schools emphasize this objective more than others. The more local, or "black letter," law schools, including those that are unaccredited, offer a curriculum directly geared to the state bar examination. In contrast, national law schools have a more abstract and theoretical focus, and their graduates sometimes have a poorer record on state bar examinations than do graduates of the more "local" schools.

The cram course, a marginal and highly expedient enterprise, has long filled the gap between law school training and the content of state bar examinations. Left over from the commercial era of professional education, these institutions are on the outskirts of the educacational establishment; anxiety about the bar examination provides them with a steady stream of clients.

In New York State almost two thousand people a year take the cram course offered in five cities by the non-profit Practicing Law Institute; in California there are fifteen hundred students a year in the "Wicks Course" started by USC Professor G. Richard Wicks, and definitely for profit; the name will stay, though Professor Wicks died in late 1966. These are lecture courses supplemented by study outlines to be memorized, with very little of the question-and-answer routine of the law school . . . (Mayer, 1966, pp. 105–106).

Bayless Manning (1968, p. 6), former dean of the Stanford Law School, laments the poor educational value of the cram course.

It is revolting to contemplate the cram courses that have sprung up through the country as the by-product of the present system for qualifying young lawyers. In preparation for local bar examinations, a vast proportion of the graduates of our law schools—even the ablest students trained at our most distinguished schools—sit through six hours of daily lectures for six to twelve solid weeks memorizing in Chinese fashion endless outlines and gimmicks of local examinationship—outlines and gimmicks that will be erased from their minds within a month after the examination date. Whatever improvement is made in law schools greatly increases the necessity for this kind of cramming unless the bar examinations change too.

Manning's last point indicates a recurring frustration of legal educators: bar requirements ultimately constrain some lines of innovation in law schools. This is true, for example, of the proposal to move to a two-year basic law degree, which can succeed only if state bars change their admissions requirements from three to two years of law school. (Incidentally, one result of shortening legal education might be an increase in the power of the profession over the education of the lawyer, since the time spent in an academic setting would be decreased.) Formal specialization in law, which would include licensing and certification procedures, would also require the cooperation of the bar. Thus far the bar has made little accommodation to the reality of specialization. The expansion of clinical programs also depends on help from the bar, mainly in the form of student practice rules to allow students to defend clients in court.

The movement for clinical legal education has drawn some law schools into the delivery of legal services and closer to the practicing profession, although with nothing approaching the delivery function of medical schools. Some law schools now staff and run their own legal aid clinics. For example, the University of Connecticut School of Law runs a legal clinic with 2 directors and from 16 to 32 second-year students *(CLEPR Newsletter,* April 1969). Northwestern University Law School coordinates a legal services clinic with medical and dental clinics (run by the medical and dental schools) to form a university complex serving around 25,000 poor people *(CLEPR Newsletter,* January 1969).

A more common pattern, and one which keeps the law school at a distance from delivery functions, is the farming out of clinical students to outside agencies.

A wide variety of agencies, both public and private, are involved in one clinical project or another. For example, the students at the Valparaiso University School of Law, in northern Indiana, work with the State Mental Hospital and the Model Cities Agency; students at the University of Cincinnati College of Law work with lawyers from the Legal Aid Society in that city. At the Howard University School of Law, students have clinical experience with either the Washington, D.C., Legal Aid Agency; the Office of Economic Opportunity (OEO); the legal aid service office at Howard; or a selected private attorney (Council on Legal Education . . . , 1970, p. 23).

As law schools enter the business of providing legal services, they are more likely to come into conflict with practitioners. As mentioned earlier, clinical programs are usually limited to clients who cannot pay for regular legal services, a division of labor which keeps law schools from taking business away from the practicing bar. Nonetheless, some clinical programs have had difficulty establishing satisfactory relationships with local bar associations. In setting up a clinical program with ties to legal aid and public defender agencies, the University of Wyoming Law School had to overcome initial opposition from a group of local lawyers. This involved working out compromises in the areas of eligibility and excluded cases and giving local members of the bar a substantial role in determining the general policy of the clinical program *(CLEPR Newsletter,* January 1971).

Conflict with the practicing profession has also developed when clinical programs have turned to the mission of law reform. Sensitive to this possibility, the clinic at the University of Toledo Law School tries to avoid test cases and law reform efforts, which "can often impede the programs accepted by judges and practicing attorneys" *(CLEPR Newsletter,* March 1971). George Washington Law School pulled back from a role in the delivery of services and legal reform by severing ties with the Urban Law Institute, a federally funded service and legal reform agency. The dean of the law school explained the action:

We never contemplated that the university would operate a large law firm and engage directly in the practice of law. . . . Although George Washington would be happy to cooperate with some of the Institute's activities, it was "not willing . . . to take responsibility for a public interest law firm" *(New York Times,* May 16, 1971).

In the aftermath of this academic dispute, Antioch College and the Urban Law Institute agreed to establish a new kind of law school, based in the firm and organized almost entirely on a clinical basis. This would move away from the traditional conception of a law school and toward a teaching law firm, on the analogy of a teaching hospital.

Since the time of Flexner, medical schools have accepted a role in the delivery of services, and involvement in patient care has been a core activity in the training of physicians. Law schools have yet to accept contact with clients as a part of the educational experience or the delivery of services as a regular institutional function. The movement for clinical legal education is pushing in these directions and is forcing a reconsideration of the purposes and goals of legal education and the position of the law school in relation to the practicing profession, the community, and the university.

Legal Educators The composition and recruitment of law school faculties have changed along with the institution itself. The first specialists in teaching law were practitioners who took on apprentices and initiated lecture courses for cohorts of students. When full-time law schools developed, the typical professors were successful attorneys and judges who had proved themselves in legal practice. This tradition began to change at Harvard under Langdell, who initiated the practice of hiring recent law school graduates; Ames, who succeeded Langdell as dean, was the first to be hired as a teacher without practical experience as a lawyer (Stolz, 1970). Recruitment to law school faculties has increasingly moved away from practice-based criteria.

Many law schools appear to have a supercilious attitude toward the practice of the law. As a result, comparatively few really experienced practitioners are found as full-time faculty members in many leading law schools. The reluctance to hire experienced practioners cannot be based on the practicing lawyer's lack of teaching experience—few, if any, law professors have any background in teaching when they are first hired. Rather, faculty recruitment policy shows a discernible preference for specific types—law review at a leading law school, clerkship with an appellate court judge, then a year or two with a government agency or a large law firm. Irving M. Mehler, then Assistant Professor of Law at the University of Denver, reported [in 1958] the results of an ABA section study which showed that, of teachers listed on 15 consecutive pages of the Association of American Law School's Teacher's Directory, 34 had no experience in practice (Reichert, 1968, p. 174).

Law school teaching has emerged as a separate career line, in some respects one of the most elite careers in the legal profession since recruitment is highly selective (although the pay is considerably lower than that received by the most successful practitioners). Some observers have noted an increase in the number of students planning ahead to teaching careers, in contrast with the past when teachers often "fell in" to that type of work rather than specifically preparing for it. Some students who regard the role of practitioners as confining favor the autonomy (and some, the opportunity of being a critic and reformer) that teaching can afford. Law school teaching can be added to the list of new careers which have grown in popularity with recent graduates.

The pattern of selective, highly academic recruitment, and career lines which are often aloof from practice, is more typical of teachers in national and state law schools. The lower stratum of schools—some of them lacking university ties, some unaccredited, and some with students who attend part time—often rely on practitioners who teach on the side. For example, in 1971 the John Marshall Law School in Chicago, a large independent school with both full- and part-time divisions, had 25 part-time and 20 full-time faculty. William Mitchell College of Law in St. Paul, Minnesota, an independent night school, had 32 part-time and 13 full-time faculty. In contrast, the University of Chicago Law School, a national school, had 4 part-time and 34 full-time faculty; a state school, the University of Minnesota Law School, had 4 part-time and 32 full-time faculty (*Annual Review of Legal Education,* 1971).

Law schools in all orbits draw on part-time teachers to give courses in which professional experience is of special value, a trend which may pick up with the institution of sabbaticals in law firms and the growth of clinical programs. The clinical movement is creating a segment of practitioners with law school ties who, in the way they combine teaching with practice, resemble the part-time clinical staff of medical schools. Although full-time faculty predominate, part-time teachers still play a significant role in legal education; in 1971 in the accredited law schools there were a total of 3,139 full-time and 1,691 part-time faculty (ibid.).

The division between full- and part-time faculty may go deeper than the amount of time spent in teaching. The problems of clinical law professors—balancing competing demands of classroom and clinic, and finding themselves less than full colleagues in the eyes of more academic teachers—indicate conflicts within law school faculties which resemble the tension between basic science and clinical faculty in medical schools.

Individual law school faculties are much smaller than those of medical schools, and there is no subdivision into departments. In their younger years, teachers may be shifted from course to course, and even among older teachers there is less specialization than in the teaching of other fields.

[L]aw schools retain a quality of colleagueship more characteristic of the small liberal arts college than of a major university with its bony departmental structure. Even the largest law faculty works together, talks together, eats together. Even the largest, quite in contrast to the graduate schools of arts and sciences, remains remarkably devoted to teaching (Riesman, 1968, p. 71).

Teaching is firmly established as the core activity of law professors, with few of the competing demands of research or practice which characterize careers in medical school faculties.

Men can become professors in major law schools without any publications (other than their student work on the law review); and they can lead a life as capable teachers and consultants (for example, as arbitrators) with very little writing, none of it "research," or at any rate none of it regarded as a contribution to cumulative scientific endeavor. There is seldom anyone around a law school (unless it be a social scientist on a temporary project) who brings another model of the scholarly career than this—anyone with a degree other than an LL.B. (Riesman, 1962, p. 34).

In 1971 all but 10 of the 147 ABA-approved law schools had some kind of university affiliation *(Annual Review of Legal Education, 1971).* This relatively standard pattern contrasts with the diversity of the turn of the century, when legal education took place in law offices as well as in schools and when the schools ranged from those with university connections to those connected with the YMCA, the Knights of Columbus, or schools of business or to those run as independent, profit-making enterprises. By the late 1920s there had already been a major shift toward university affiliation, but according to the 1928 *Annual Review of Legal Education,* of the 176 degree-conferring law schools (66 of them approved), 12 were connected with schools of business or commerce, 17 were maintained by the YMCA or the Knights of Columbus, 36 were "frankly independent," and 111 were "in contact, more or less, with a college of liberal arts." Of these colleges or universities, 38 were owned by states, 2 were owned by municipal governments, 21 were Catholic, and 50 were Protestant or nonsectarian private *(Annual Review of Legal Education,* 1928).

Why has affiliation between law schools and universities become nearly universal? The search for status is one important motive. Throughout the history of American legal education, the most prestigious law schools have been university-connected. A university tie may also be associated with quality. In his survey of legal education in the 1920s, Reed observed, much as his contemporary, Flexner, had done in medicine, that the better law schools were university schools (Reed, 1921). As an institutional base, the university helped the schoolmen separate training from practice, buttressed the profession's claims to a unique body of theory and abstract knowledge, and thereby gave the profession greater bargaining power in establishing a monopoly over a sphere of work.

Universities also gain prestige from having an affiliated law school, which helps establish an institution as a "real" university.

An institution like Princeton, for example, which has a first-rank graduate school of arts and sciences but no medical school or law school, is still widely regarded as a slightly overgrown liberal arts college (Jencks & Riesman, 1969, p. 215).

Furthermore, having a law or medical school is often an asset in university fund-raising, suggesting a "practical" focus and giving the university "the appearance of public utility, offsetting the widespread assumption that universities are purely self-serving and parasitic" (ibid.). Since legal training often serves as a prelude to political careers, a university may choose to add a law school for possible long-range influence in legislatures (Mayhew, 1970).

Law schools vary in extent and type of university affiliation. Like medical schools, law schools are sometimes located miles away from the main university campus. Northwestern University School of Law is located near the Chicago Loop, while the main university campus is several miles away, in Evanston. Cleveland-Marshall College of Law is located in downtown Cleveland, about a mile from the main campus of Cleveland State University, with which it affiliated in 1969. Cleveland-Marshall was for years prior to that time an independent law school; its location in the heart of a city and near various courts is typical of many independent (or previously independent) urban law schools. For example, Detroit College of Law, which has no university affiliation, is located in downtown Detroit near federal, state, and city courts. Seton Hall University School of Law is also located in an urban business center—Newark, New Jersey; the principal campus of the university is at some distance—South Orange.

Another pattern is for the law school to be located on the same campus as the university, although even then law schools are typically set somewhat apart, with their own buildings and even quadrangles. This is true, for example, of the University of Michigan Law School, Baylor University School of Law, Yale Law School, and Boston College Law School.

The physical separation of the law school from the rest of the university reflects a tradition of academic distance. The original pattern, set by Harvard, Columbia, and other early university-affiliated law schools, was one of academic and administrative isolation rather than integration. This isolation was part of Langdell's vision. While he favored a university base for legal education, he also regarded law as a self-contained discipline based on doctrinal analysis of appellate court opinions. This view encouraged aloofness rather than a turn toward other disciplines or departments of the university.

[T]he law school . . . did not truly enter into the rest of the university or inter-relate with it. Law faculties were isolated; law courses were open only to those who were taking the full three year law curriculum; law students took no courses except in the law school; and the law faculties were made up exclusively of men who had been trained in law schools. As a by-product of its withdrawal, the law school . . . became a closed system. Vis-à-vis the legal profession, law school became academic; vis-à-vis the Academy, law school was set apart as a professional, vocational school (Manning, 1969, p. 5).

In the 1930s the legal realism movement began to challenge the intellectual self-containment of the law school. The legal realists were particularly interested in relating the social sciences to law teaching and research, for example, developing the connection between the field of criminal law and the work of penologists, psychiatrists, and sociologists. Since that time there have been varied movements to draw the law school closer to the university. These movements have typically centered in elite schools, which, in contrast with local schools, do not operate so much under the constraint of the bar examination and therefore have more room to experiment.

Yale Law School has long been known for its interdisciplinary focus. Starting in the early 1930s, specialists in other disciplines (economists, psychologists, psychiatrists, philosophers, sociologists) have had regular appointments on the law school faculty. The practice of hiring its own set of nonlawyers rather than becoming dependent on other departments or sending its students outside for nonlaw courses has allowed the law school to retain autonomy while drawing on other fields. The arrangement, it should be noted, is rarely reciprocal; socal science faculties do not include lawyers. "Little effort has been made to introduce into social science curricula the contribution legal scholars might make to understanding those aspects of American society to which they have particular access" (Riesman, 1968, p. 70).

In addition to appointing faculty from other disciplines, or in some cases arranging joint appointments, an increasing number of law schools have established joint degree programs. At Stanford University joint graduate degrees are offered in law and business and in law and economics. New York University offers joint degrees in law and sociology, law and public administration, and law and business. The University of Denver has joint degree programs in law and sociology, law and psychology, law and geography (natural resources), and law and business.

While efforts to integrate the law school with the rest of the university are widely advertised, the reality is still one of relative isolation. Few students are registered in joint degree programs, and only a small minority of law schools offer such arrangements. Most law students do not take courses outside of the law school, and only rarely do law school classes have students from other parts of the university. Some law schools have a separate academic calendar; at Yale, for example, the law school year begins about 10 days ahead of the rest of the university, and the exam period is also at a different time.

Strong forces hold the law school at a distance from the rest of the university. The goal of training professionals, of inducting recruits into an exclusive club, encourages separation from other aims, functions, and types of students. There has always been an uneasy balance between the graduate model of legal education, which would maximize ties to the university, and the more self-contained professional model, which looks toward the practicing bar. Some current reform movements—especially the push for clinical legal education and the proposed move from three-to two-year J.D. programs—may tip the balance even further in the direction of the practicing profession.

There is finally a financial dimension to the relationship between law schools and universities. Historically the move toward university affiliation helped counter openly commercial ventures in legal education. Since 1922, to gain ABA approval a law school cannot be operated as a commercial enterprise, nor can the compensation of the staff depend on the number of students or fees received. Some unaccredited law schools and cram schools, however, are still proprietary.

While not run for profit, university-connected law schools have a reputation for being at least financially self-sufficient and in some cases for providing subsidies to the rest of the university. Financial considerations may have encouraged some universities to add law schools. After the Civil War, experiences at Columbia and Harvard "showed that a law school could pay its way in tuition as well as prestige and there followed a rapid increase in the number of University law schools" (Stolz, 1970, p. 66).

Law schools tend to be "run on the cheap" (Stevens, 1970, p. 40). Classes are large, traditional teaching methods require relatively little capital equipment (especially in contrast with medical schools), and the ratio of students to faculty is notoriously high (at Boalt Law School, for example, there are about 850 students and a faculty of 35). These students all pay regular university tuition, and hence the cost per law student is less than in other divisions of the university.

Many law school reforms, for example the introduction of clinical courses, the reduction of class sizes, and minority recruitment programs, entail increased expense, and law schools have begun to feel short-changed. In contrast with medical schools, which are at the opposite extreme, law schools have received relatively little federal money. Foundation support has also been slim. Some law schools get subsidies from the university (for example, when Cleveland-Marshall Law School merged with Cleveland State University, state subsidy reduced the level of tuition fees), but many universities follow the policy, "each tub stands on its own bottom"; i.e., each professional school must be self-supporting. This often makes the law school highly dependent on alumni contributions. Stevens (1970, p. 40) summarizes this dilemma:

> Some new sources of funding . . . must be found if the law schools are to escape the trap in which they seem to be caught; but it is perhaps significant that the law schools have realized they are under-funded at the very moment the universities—especially the private ones—appear to be nearing financial crisis.

Differences and Relationships among Law Schools

This chapter has already alluded to a basic paradox in United States legal education: in courses, teaching methods, and case materials, law schools are remarkably homogeneous; but in the origins and destinations of their student bodies, law schools vary tremendously, much more than medical schools and graduate schools of arts and sciences. A huge gap separates national law schools, whose students come from elite undergraduate schools and head for jobs in large law firms, corporations, and the federal government, from independent night law schools, whose students are often from lower-income backgrounds, work full time while going through law school, and end up in solo practice and in jobs like bill collecting and insurance adjusting. The stratification of the legal profession parallels the stratification of law schools.

A number of efforts have been made to classify the differences among law schools. In a study of a sample of 1,103 students who entered law school in 1961, Warkov and Zelan (1965) used measures of academic quality to divide the 124 schools their respondents entered into three categories. Eight "Stratum I" schools had students—51 percent of them graduates of prestigious undergraduate schools—with the highest median Law School Admission Test scores; Stratum II included 16 schools with the next highest median LSAT scores and 16 percent from prestigious undergraduate schools; and Stratum III, including the remaining 100 schools, had students with the lowest scores and 7 percent from prestigious undergraduate backgrounds.

Another better-known scheme classifies law schools as "national," "state," and "local," according to the dominant origins and future careers of their student bodies. Referring to similar criteria, Cavers (1968) writes of "big-firm schools," "state university law schools," and "small-firm schools."

The national or big-firm schools, which Cavers puts at 15 to 20 in number, have student bodies with high academic credentials and from a wide geographic area; offer curricula aimed at national problems; prepare their graduates for national corporate practice; and are located in universities of some prestige. Another 40 to 45 schools are affiliated with state universities and tend to serve a regional territory. The University of Idaho College of Law, for example, is the only school in Idaho, and two-thirds of its students come from within the state. The curricula of such schools are often geared to legal practice within the state. (Unlike medicine, in which the body of knowledge is relatively homogeneous, there are state variations in the system of law.) Graduates of state-supported schools enter careers ranging from national, corporate work to smaller firms and state politics. Several state-supported law schools, for example the University of Michigan and Boalt of the University of California, are "more 'national' in purpose and market than others that dominate their locale (for example, the University of Washington)" (Riesman, 1962, p. 13).

Local or small-firm schools, which Cavers numbers at 70 or 80, range from those which resemble state schools in quality and focus to those which do not meet accreditation standards. Cavers (1968, p. 146) describes this latter extreme:

Among the law schools in, say, the lower half of this stratum are many which, with limited faculties and facilities, are offering a basic curriculum aimed primarily at the state bar examinations to students who, in comparison with the students in [national or state] schools, have attended inferior colleges, compiled much poorer college records, and received far lower scores in the nationally administered test for aptitude in law study, if indeed they have troubled to take it.

Many of the local schools have unique missions and clientele. Some are located near state and local centers of government and provide part-time legal education for those seeking to upgrade their employment. Others are in large urban areas and have historically provided mobility for immigrants. Some, such as those which are Catholic-supported, serve students from particular ethnic backgrounds. Some of the graduates of these schools enter business or local politics; others become solo practitioners or enter small firms. The criminal defendants' bar, traditionally held in low esteem by the profession, is drawn largely from local law schools, and many municipal and county judges are also graduates of these schools.

There is an obvious division of labor among these various kinds of schools. They draw their students from different sources; their graduates go into different kinds of work. While nominally members of the same profession, the two extremes—the graduate of a local law school who works mainly at settling insurance claims and the graduate of a national law school who is in a Wall Street firm— never meet. They have different functions and circles of colleague-ship and, in effect, exist in distant professional worlds.

Those critical of the homogeneity of legal education urge law schools to recognize this factual division of labor and to realize it more fully in specialized programs. Cavers (1968) urges state schools to create "institutes of government" to study and teach about problems of state and local government and administration. Some big-firm law schools, he suggests, could move in an applied social science direction. He calls on local schools to recognize the special careers of their graduates (in criminal defense, state and local judgeships, solo and small-firm practice) and to structure their curricula accordingly. This might include specializing in urban law and criminal law and procedure. Cavers notes the example of the University of Detroit School of Law which, aided by an OEO grant, has initiated a program in urban law.

How are enrollments distributed among the various types of law schools? From 1890 to 1938 there was a greater increase in part-time and mixed schools (offering full- and part-time programs), which would both fall in the local orbit, than in full-time schools. Part-time schools were strongly hit by the Depression, and since that time there has been a steady movement to full-time or mixed programs. In 1961 around 29 percent of students in approved schools were in part-time programs; by 1971 the figure had gone down to 20 percent (*Annual Review of Legal Education,* 1961; 1971).

Apart from the general division between part-time (all local schools) and full-time (which would include schools in all three strata), Cavers notes general trends in enrollments in the three types of law schools. In the period 1961–1965, law school enrollments increased by 46 percent, and the bulk of the increase was absorbed by the state and local schools, which rose to 23 percent and 66 percent of the total law school enrollment, respectively; national schools accounted for 11 percent of the total enrollment in 1965. During that period national schools expanded enrollments at one-fourth the rate of law schools taken as a whole (Cavers, 1966). In a later and related study, Cavers notes that between 1968 and 1970 law school enrollments increased 25 percent. Sampling enrollment increases in national, state, and large urban schools with mixed divisions, he found that expanding enrollments were widely and unevenly distributed, with the greatest increase among day students in the large urban schools (Cavers, 1971).

STUDENT
EXPERIENCE
IN LAW
SCHOOLS

Law schools have developed a distinctive subculture, a set of rituals and experiences which serve as much to initiate and haze as to teach recruits the skills and knowledge of the profession. "Learning to think like a lawyer" is often cited as the purpose of law school training; it resembles the value medical students come to place on "clinical experience" (Becker et al., 1961, pp. 242–254). Used to justify more concrete aspects of training, "thinking like a lawyer" and "gaining clinical experience" are general goals which contain elements of mystique and style as well as expertise.

"Thinking like a lawyer" points to form and approach more than to substance. This focus dominates standard law school teaching: the use of appellate cases to extract principles of reasoning, and the Socratic method of contact between teacher and students. Classes are large; law school teachers are almost legendary for their virtuoso style, skill at performance, and ability to put students on the defensive. The Socratic questioning sequence gives law school classrooms an adversary, hostile atmosphere which is sometimes justified as preparation for litigation, although the majority of lawyers do not work in courtrooms. Savoy (1970, p. 457) calls the method "an initiation rite of public humiliation, sarcasm, and ridicule," a theme elaborated by a Yale Law School student:

A great many students, of all levels of academic competence and of many varieties of personality, feel the socratic method (the basic question and answer, suggestion and criticism, approach, rather than the stricter version once popular and now practiced by only a few teachers) is an assault. The observation that students often respond physically and emotionally to questioning as though they were in the presence of a profound danger is simply *true*. A participant or observer not blinded by his own fear or by his involvement in practicing the technique notices the student response almost immediately. Few will deny that the atmosphere of the first year classroom is as heavy with fear as it is tense with intellectual excitement (Kennedy, 1970, pp. 72–73).

As well as fearing ridicule in class, first-year students often have difficulty managing the amount of study expected (Patton, 1968), become uncertain about whether they will make it through to graduation, and find the law school atmosphere condescending and paternalistic:

Law schools do little to encourage students to use initiative in educating themselves. Students are not really treated as adults. They are made to feel that they are beginning their education all over again, and the classes put very little emphasis upon individual work and thinking. The students get caught up in examinations, grades, and class ranking. In many ways the LL.B. program is undergraduate, not graduate education (Reich, 1965, p. 1403).

Law schools have a reputation for being highly competitive. Students who enter a law school of high or moderate prestige have already been through "what amounts to a prolonged nation-wide competition of intimidating rigor" (Kennedy, 1970, p. 75), a competition which has grown tougher with the upsurge of applications in recent years. Within the law school, competition among students is encouraged by aggressive and adversary teaching methods and by ranking, grading, and job recruitment procedures.

Many law students believe, with some degree of truth, that one's career as a law student and possibly as a lawyer can be made or broken in the first year. Ranking in class is directly linked with career choices; careers in law school teaching, for example, are rarely open to those who have not been on law review. (Incidentally, in being student-run, law reviews are unique among professional periodicals.) Law firms emphasize grades and honors in seeking recruits for summer jobs and later for regular employment. This sorting begins well before graduation since law review staffs have traditionally been picked on the basis of first-year grades, and job recruitment increasingly begins during the second year.

The stratification of law school classes affects present experience as well as future opportunities. Those on law review have a better chance of getting to know faculty members and often become an elite society unto themselves. At the other extreme, "many students whose first-year grades have been disappointing tend to lose zest for their work" (Cavers, 1971, p. 40); some withdraw from active participation in the law school world and adopt an attitude of passivity and cynicism.

According to a time-worn law school expression, "the first year they scare you to death, the second year they work you to death, and the third year they bore you to death." As law students learn the ropes, master classroom procedures, and become accustomed to the style of "legal reasoning," attitudes of boredom, resignation, and cynicism become relatively common (Vargas, 1969). These attitudes are also a way of coping ("most of us see law school as a hurdle which is not too relevant to practice," "law schools are supposed to be harassing;" "law school is just something I have to get through to get a union card").

Unrest among Law Students　In recent years law students have expressed "growing distaste for competition and for the divisive, unpleasant effects of any system of social organization that makes the success of some dependent on the failure of others" (Bok, 1969, p. 4). This distaste can be found among those who have done well as well as among those who have not. And it has had tangible effects; for example, law reviews at many of the national schools have begun to shift to new criteria for membership. In 1969 the *Stanford Law Review* opened membership to any second-year student who attends a brief training program; if a student's work during the first semester measures up to *Review* standards, he or she automatically becomes an editor. This move was justified as "a significant advance to abolish the law school's track system of education and to enable students to make their own choices" (*Harvard Law Record,* Nov. 29, 1969). Law reviews at Yale, UCLA, Harvard, and the University of Chicago now take a few members each year on the basis of a written competition rather than grades. In some schools, a growing number of eligible students decline to compete for law review, moot court, and other competitive honors.

Grading reform has become a central issue in the law school

world and a focus for student discontent with the ranking system. Northeastern University Law School recently moved to a total pass-fail system. Stanford added a voluntary pass-fail option. Yale Law School moved to a four-category basis (honors, pass, low pass, and flunk) and eliminated mathematical averaging and class ranking. Boalt Hall, at the University of California, Berkeley, moved to three categories (top, middle, and low), although students agitated for pass-fail. Harvard Law School offers first-year students a choice among three grading systems; the standard nine-category system (still used for the second-and third-year classes); straight pass-fail; and a system of high, satisfactory, low, or fail.

These new systems have their own drawbacks. Those which continue with several categories (for example, top, middle, and low) still involve ranking, and some see them as little more than a shift in nomenclature. Pass-fail systems may encourage employers to put greater emphasis on "personality," social background, "contacts," and other ascriptive criteria in their hiring practices. As long as the profession is stratified and law schools function to sort recruits into the various strata, problems of ranking and competition are almost inevitable.

Other aspects of law student unrest have already been mentioned: "third-year malaise," or widespread apathy and disengagement by students nearing graduation; and along more activist lines, student protests and demands for reform in the profession as well as in law schools. The issues which have focused law student activism are similar to the issues which medical students have taken up in recent years. Some concern the role of the legal profession in society; the bias toward the propertied; the neglect of the poor, minorities, and consumers. This activism has been organized on a nationwide basis (for example, by the National Lawyers Guild and the Law Student Civil Rights Research Council) and also by more local enterprises, like the Environmental Law Society at Stanford.

Like their counterparts in medicine, law students have criticized law schools and the practicing profession for narrow and discriminatory recruitment practices (a trend discussed in the next section). They have also demanded a role in the governing of law schools, and in many places, students have been added to faculty committees. Looking at legal education as a whole, Stevens (1970, p. 38) argues that student activism and protest, which are largely centered in the elite schools, may have the ironic effect of widening the gap between different types of law schools:

Roughly speaking, the most radical demands are being made at the best-known (i.e. elitist) schools. Yet the bulk of the demands — closer faculty cooperation, work in the ghetto, individual research projects, and the abolition of the large class (once the prize of the law school and now thought to be abrasive and distortingly competitive) — would not only call for greater funds but would widen still more the gulf which would be further muddied, not bridged, by less competitive admissions. In short, the reforms being demanded could, ironically enough, make the profession and the law school both more hierarchical and more elitist.

CHANGING PATTERNS OF RECRUITMENT

Although it shares the "gentlemen's club" aura of the other ancient professions, law, in some respects, is less exclusive than medicine. This may partly be a question of size, since there are more than twice as many law students as medical students. In 1970–71 there were a total of 86,028 law students attending 146 accredited law schools and less than half that many medical students (40,487 students) enrolled in 103 medical schools (*Annual Review of Legal Education*, 1971; *Journal of the American Medical Association*, 1971). Law schools range more widely in admissions requirements, including part-time schools, those willing to accept older students, some with low admissions standards (often coupled with the flunking out of large numbers of students), and a fringe of unaccredited schools with entry based mainly on ability to pay.

The variation in law schools is partly rooted in the belief that legal education, and hence access to public service, should be widely available. Compared with the medical profession, the legal profession has fewer sanctions over training programs. The entrepreneurial spirit, both academic and commercial, has freer play in law, since law schools require little capital equipment.

The legal profession, which has provided mobility for wave after wave of immigrant groups, has a stronger ethnic tradition than medicine. In his study of the New York City bar, Carlin (1966, pp. 20–21) notes a steady increase in the percentage of ethnic, non-Protestant lawyers:

In 1900, a little more than half the lawyers in the New York City bar were "Old Americans" (that is, at least third generation). The remainder were newer Americans, primarily of German or Irish descent. In 1960, only about one-third of the lawyers were Old Americans, and the newer Americans were now primarily of eastern European, Jewish origin. . . . During this same period (1900 to 1960), the percentage of Catholic lawyers admitted to the bar remained relatively constant. The proportion of

Protestants declined from more than 25 percent before 1920 to 10 percent of those admitted since 1955. The proportion of Negro lawyers in the bar increased only slightly—from 0.3 percent in 1900, to 0.6 percent in 1930, to 1 percent in 1960.

Law is more accessible than medicine, but within narrow limits. Barely 1 percent of the members of the legal profession are black, although blacks constitute 11 or 12 percent of the national population; "only seventeen percent of all black lawyers practice in the South, where about half the nation's black population live" (O'Neil, 1970, p. 295). There are five million Chicanos in the United States, but only around 400 Chicano lawyers (*Conference of California Law Schools . . .*, 1968). In the city and county of Denver, about 9 percent of the population is of Spanish-American descent, yet only 10 of the 2,000 attorneys practicing in the area (that is, ½ of 1 percent) have Spanish surnames (O'Neil, 1970). There are about 1 million American Indians in the United States, but in the late 1960s, only 20 Indian lawyers (*Conference of California Law Schools . . .*, 1968).

Related to the underrepresentation of nonwhite minorities is the fact that the legal profession draws its recruits from a relatively narrow socioeconomic base. In the mid-sixties about two-thirds of United States law students were from families in which the father was a professional, proprietor, or manager (nationwide, 15 percent of all families were in that category), and two-fifths of the law students were from families with an annual income of over $15,000 (as against one-twentieth of families nationwide) (Mayer, 1966).

Law is even more a male profession than medicine; less than 3 percent of all lawyers are women compared with 9 percent of physicians. The percentage of women lawyers remained fairly steady during the last two decades; it was 2.5 percent in 1951, 2.7 percent in 1957, 2.7 percent in 1963, and 2.8 percent in 1971 (Hankin & Drohnke, 1965; Shanahan, 1971, pp. 1, 25). In 1968 ten of the approved law schools had no women students (Association of American Law Schools, 1968). Some law schools remained closed to women until recently; Harvard Law School admitted its first women in 1950, and Notre Dame in the fall of 1969.

That the legal profession is over 96 percent white and male and that a disproportionate number of its members come from affluent backgrounds have shaped the occupational culture, career assumptions, values, and etiquette of the profession. Women and nonwhite lawyers have not been accepted as equal colleagues and have often ended up in specialties of low status and low income. For example, trusts, estates, and domestic relations (all specialties of low prestige) have been "sex-typed" as women's work in law. Until recently, large, prestigious firms have been reluctant to hire either women or blacks for their legal staffs and within the profession there has been

. . . condescension toward black solo practitioners, characterizing them as legal hacks. The profession views graduates of black law schools as presumptively incompetent and further compounds the insult by viewing older black lawyers as "out of touch" with the black revolution. Younger black (brown and red) lawyers who take militant stances are presumed to be poor craftsmen, concerned with radical rhetoric rather than qualified as true professionals. The more pernicious criticism denigrates them as unprofessional in manner, irresponsible, psychologically scarred, unsound in judgment because of racial loyalties and, thus, regrettably unacceptable to the select inner circles of law firms, policy making bodies or collegial social gatherings (Cahn & Cahn, 1970, p. 1040).

Minority Recruitment Programs

In recent years the exclusive composition of the legal profession has been widely criticized. As in medicine, recruiting practices are tied to the unequal distribution of professional services. There is a critical shortage of lawyers serving poor people, of whom minority groups constitute a disproportionate share, and nonwhite minorities often feel that white lawyers are simply not accessible to them. Furthermore, "the white or Anglo lawyer is far less likely than the man who comes from the ghetto or the *barrio* to understand the background of the case, to be able to locate and interview witnesses, to gather material evidence within the community, and so on" (O'Neil, 1970, p. 297).

Movement for change in the basic structure and orientation of the legal profession has included pressure for broadening the composition of the practicing bar. In addition to the special minority recruitment programs formed by many law schools in recent years, there has been a nationwide program with outside financial support. With the help of OEO and foundation money, the Council on Legal Education Opportunity (CLEO) was formed in 1967 by the American Association of Law Schools, the National Bar Association (a black professional group), the American Bar Association, and the Law School Admission Test Council.

Since 1968 CLEO has sponsored summer study programs for minority students who do not meet regular law school admissions requirements (Law School Aptitude Test scores and undergraduate grades). These students are given a free six-week course in writing and legal reasoning, and at the end they apply to whatever law school they choose. By the end of 1970, CLEO had sponsored 22 Regional Summer Institutes, enrolling more than 800 students. More than 50 law schools had been directly involved in running the institutes, and the alumni of these programs gained admission to more than 100 law schools. In addition, at least 20 law schools have operated their own substantial preparatory programs either in the summer or during the school year. For example, the University of New Mexico runs a summer prelaw program for American Indians, and the University of Denver, a program open primarily to Chicanos (O'Neil, 1970).

Some of these prelaw training programs are voluntary; in other cases participation is required for admission to the host law school. Some minority students have complained that these programs stigmatize them, marking them off as a special case even before admission. In other cases the programs have not been sufficiently useful and have been discontinued. But in general, minority recruitment efforts are on the upswing and have already had an impact on the number of blacks, Chicanos, Indians, and other nonwhite students enrolled in law school.

By the fall of 1968, there were 1,122 (nonwhite) minority students in the nation's law schools (not including enrollments in all but one of the predominantly black law schools). More than half of these students were then in the first year. A 1969 survey of 136 accredited law schools revealed a total of 3,038 black, Chicano, Puerto Rican, American Indian, and other students from minority or disadvantaged backgrounds (O'Neil, 1970). Even with this increase, the number of nonwhite law students has not climbed beyond 2 percent, and some observers wonder if a saturation point has been reached, above which minority enrollment is not likely to increase substantially.

Understandably, Harvard and Yale have been deluged with applications from minority students who show reasonable promise of success in law school. Meanwhile, many other schools — Berkeley, UCLA and Illinois, for example — have begun to receive more applications from "qualified" minority students than their resources enable them to accept. Only a few years ago the supply of minority prospects for law study fell far below even the meager demand that then existed. Now the situation has reversed; although demand has increased sharply, supply seems to have increased at an even faster rate and to have out-stripped the supporting capacity of the system (O'Neil, 1970, p. 302).

The "supporting capacity of the system" in part refers to financial aid. Like medical schools, law schools have few financial resources for students, many of whom incur substantial debts in order to finish their training. Students from poor backgrounds have fewer financial resources to begin with. They often find it difficult to obtain loans. They are less likely than middle-class students to want to take on large debts, especially when they can go into business or other occupations and earn money without further schooling.

In a 1965 survey of minority students and law school deans, the AALS Minority Groups Committee found that financial problems were the most serious barrier to legal education for college graduates from minority groups (O'Neil, 1970). Many law schools have provided scholarships for minority students, but money for these purposes is very slim and often dependent on foundation grants.

O'Neil (1970) notes that the most impressive increases in minority enrollments have been at elite schools like Harvard, Yale, Columbia, UCLA, NYU, Berkeley, and Michigan, and should not be taken as representative of legal education as a whole. These schools have drawn top minority students away from other schools, "so that the black student who once went to John Marshall or Chicago-Kent now goes to Northwestern or Illinois, taking the place of a student newly eligible for Harvard or Yale, while minority enrollment in the marginal schools may actually decline" (O'Neil, 1970, p. 306). On the other hand, this "moving up" process may make room for students previously excluded from the system, since the student who ends up at a lower orbit, John Marshall or Chicago-Kent, might previously have not gone to law school at all.

It should be noted that the increase in minority student enrollments since 1965 is about equal to the increase in the number of students preferentially admitted and is also buttressed by the number of students recruited and given financial aid by CLEO (a program with limited resources which may not continue indefinitely) (O'Neil, 1970). The imminent phasing out of several predominantly black law schools may also affect the recruitment and training of minority students. Florida A & M was recently phased out, and Texas Southern has been very near to closing its operation. The law schools at North Carolina Central University and Southern University (in Baton Rouge) remain alive, although with small enrollments. Howard is far larger than the other predominantly black law schools and has a steadily growing enrollment, but "the gradual equalization of the racial mix in its student body has restricted the number of places available for black students" (O'Neil, 1970, p. 308).

Some schools have dramatically increased the number of their minority students. Between 1965 and 1969 Harvard Law School increased its black enrollment from 20 to 81. In 1969 Yale Law School had 50 blacks in its 550-member student body, UCLA had 95 blacks, Chicanos, and American Indians in a student body of around 600, and blacks constituted one-fourth of the entering class at Rutgers Law School in Newark. In many of these schools black and Chicano students have formed their own associations, and in some schools they have pressed for changes in the curriculum. At Rutgers, for example, the Association of Black Law Students proposed a curriculum which would train "'People's Lawyers' on behalf of the oppressed and the emerging forces for change" (Hinds, 1971, p. 235). In response to the lead of the black law students, in 1970 the entire Rutgers Law School community approved a plan to restructure the curriculum to train not only those "who would practice law on behalf of the traditional interests of society," but also a new breed, characterized as "people's lawyers" ("Strategy for Change . . . ," 1971). The proposal calls for more courses in poverty and urban law, the use of more case materials related to contemporary urban problems, and a clinical program focused on the legal needs of poor and black communities.

Both students and faculty in schools with increased minority enrollments have noticed an effect on the daily world of the law school. As one law professor put it, "a criminal law teacher can't help but be affected by the experience of teaching students with a different experience of law enforcement." Leon Letwin (1969, p. 2), who helped organize the special minorities program at UCLA, suggests that the educational process works both ways:

The infusion of minority students into law schools is increasingly seen as a way to improve the quality of education for the entire student body. Recognition is developing that there are values to be served by making it possible for students — and faculty as well — to come to grips with the sharply divergent attitudes and perceptions of minority students, and with the problems generated by racism. So viewed, a change in student composition is not merely a way of helping "disadvantaged" black and brown students. It is a way of helping combat a severe form of educational disadvantage suffered by the predominantly white, middle-class student body and faculty that constitute the principal constituencies of the law schools.

Edgar S. and Jean Camper Cahn (1970, pp. 1028–1029) write in a somewhat more pessimistic vein about the challenge which increased minority enrollments pose for the predominantly middle-class world of the law school:

Unfortunately, descriptions of reality (such as the conduct of officials) drawn from personal experience fail to comport with the neat logical reality assumed by many professors and casebooks. At considerable personal cost, black law students in predominantly white schools vainly seek to destroy the myths of white students and professors — to propound the reality of the world they know and to challenge the reality of the parchment world of the judicial opinion. We have seen representations of this nonsanitized world rejected — partly because it comes with that raw emotionalism and strident absolutism which offends the decorum of the law and the equanimity of the law school universe. All too often, black law students are forced to play jester in the king's court — cast in the role of the law school's own "house militants." If black law students get attention and even win some acknowledgment and semblance of authority, they also are secretly derided as not "real" legal craftsmen.

Recruitment of Women

Women are vastly underrepresented in the legal profession as a whole, and even more so in the upper levels of practice. According to one survey, in 1968, a year when women were 51 percent of the population and almost 40 percent of the work force, only 186 of the 2,700 lawyers employed by 40 top law firms in six major cities were women. Of the 3,000 firms rated as "leading" by the 1957 bar register, only 32 reported a woman law partner. Of almost 10,000 judges, less than 200 are women, of whom all but a few sit in courts of limited jurisdiction. In a study of the relative income of male and female lawyers, White (1967) found that in the first year of legal practice there was a $1,500 income differential in favor of males. With each year, men increased their lead in income, to the point of earning from $9,000 to $18,000 more than their female colleagues.

Discrimination against women begins even before they enroll in law school.

Although no law school uses either a formal or informal quota system to limit the number of females enrolled, they do admit to scrutinizing female applicants more closely for ability and motivation. Some schools give close consideration to the marital status of women before granting admission, and other schools take into account the possibility that a female student might not graduate and continue to practice. It follows that a male applicant is often chosen over an equally qualified female (Dinerman, 1969, p. 951).

Like their counterparts in medical schools, women law students often experience social isolation, ridicule, and other attitudes which imply that they don't belong in a male-dominated profession. The most open discrimination often comes upon graduation, when women seek jobs. Even those who make law review have had difficulty obtaining clerkships, and many law firms (especially those of high prestige) have openly admitted that they do not hire women.

The plight of women lawyers has recently gained some acknowledgment both within and outside the profession. In 1969 the AALS passed a resolution urging law schools to take steps against sex discrimination in hiring practices. Some law schools have barred firms with a record of sex discrimination from using school placement facilities. Some women students have begun to take the issue to the courts. Recently women law students from Columbia and New York University filed complaints of discrimination with the New York City Commission on Human Rights against 10 prominent New York law firms. Like minority law students, women students have formed their own associations, with some national coordination, partly to combine efforts in fighting discrimination.

After remaining at less than 3 percent of the overall law school enrollment for decades, the number of women law students has lately increased. In 1968 women constituted about 5 percent of law school student bodies; the figure rose to 8 percent in 1970 and 9 percent in 1971 (Cavers, 1971, *Annual Review of Legal Education,* 1970; 1971). The percentage of women students varies a great deal from school to school. In 1970 Boston University Law School had 16 percent women; Boston College Law School, 7.5 percent women; Harvard Law School, less than 8 percent women; and Northeastern University Law School, over 25 percent women—one of the highest percentages in the country (*Boston Herald Traveler,* Jan. 18, 1970).

The increase in female admissions in the late 1960s was partly attributable to the draft; faced with the prospect of losing many of their male students, some law schools began admitting more women. The general thrust toward recruitment of nonwhite minorities helped call attention to the generally exclusive qualities of the profession, and the feminist movement has pushed for a more equitable representation of women in law. The number of women applying to law schools has increased greatly in recent years, which leads to the final topic: the overall increase in law school applications and enrollment.

The Boom in Law School Applications

Many members of the legal profession are still trying to assess the dramatic increase in the number of people applying and being admitted to accredited law schools. After World War II, law school enrollments boomed, reaching a peak of 57,759 in 1949. Enrollments then declined and remained fairly stable (at around 35,000) through the 1950s. In 1962 there was a sharp increase, and law school enrollments continued to grow until they had expanded 51 percent between 1961 and 1966 (from 41,499 to 62,556). In 1968 there was a slight drop, and then a jump of almost 25 percent between 1968 (62,779 students) and 1970 (82,041). In 1971 there was another large increase, to 93,118 (Cavers, 1971; *Annual Review of Legal Education,* 1971). Analyzing recent enrollment figures, Cavers concludes that they have been distributed "rather widely and somewhat unevenly among the many smaller law schools in our legal educational system" (Cavers, 1971, p. 9).

An increase in law school applications has paralleled the upsurge in enrollments. In 1970 about 75,000 people took the LSAT examinations, and in 1971 the number exceeded 100,000. In Congressional hearings in February 1971, "an A.B.A. spokesman indicated the rise in applications may reach 45 percent" ("On the Rise," 1971, p. 44).

Why the heightened attraction of legal careers? Russell Simpson, assistant dean of Harvard Law School, suggests two factors: the new activist generation of undergraduates are attracted to new public interest careers which have the image of providing a powerful tool for social change; and other options seem less favorable due to diminished employment prospects in fields such as the natural and social sciences and the humanities (Cavers, 1971). Cavers suggests yet a third factor; law can lead to a variety of careers. "The wide range of career options that training for the profession of law offers may be exerting an important influence in attracting college graduates to the law schools as other doors appear to be closing or to be revealing less inviting vistas" (Cavers, 1971, p. 9).

What will be the long-range result? More stringent admissions requirements and increased competition among applicants are already evident. Although many schools have expanded enrollments and six new law schools have gained ABA approval since 1968, it is doubtful that law schools will expand enough to meet the rising demand for places. If law schools do continue to expand, the legal profession will swell rapidly in size. There is already indication that the job market in law is tightening. In theory the need for more lawyers is there, but the clients whose needs are unfilled are precisely those who are "legally indigent," who cannot pay for services as they are currently organized.

4. Systems of Theological Education in the United States

by Everett C. Hughes and Agostino DeBaggis

The early European colonies in North America were enterprises, each of one nation and religion. The religion was often a sectarian dissent from the established church in the homeland. Many of the later settlements on the Western frontier were also of this kind. As the settlements touched each other and merged, we became a people strongly religious, but of many faiths. By the time our fathers founded "the first new nation," they felt it necessary to write it into our Constitution (Amendment I) that "Congress shall make no law respecting an establishment of religion or prohibiting the free exercise thereof."

The later immigration to cities added Roman Catholics of many nations, but one faith, as well as people of other races and non-Christian religions. The resulting new secular order was one of what is now called denominational pluralism.

This pluralism and the complete separation of church and state are reflected in the great number and variety of institutions established to train religious leaders and clergymen.

A recent *Guide to Religious Education* (White, 1965) lists well over 1,350 schools in the United States and Canada that teach theology, divinity, religious education, church music, sacred literature, pastoral psychology, church administration, and related topics. They range from famous and sophisticated graduate schools of theology affiliated with the old private universities to small proprietary schools and schools offering correspondence courses. All offer courses to prepare individuals for ministry or church work of some sort. We will focus on the mainline professional theological schools, with little attention to others.

For analytical purposes let us divide institutions offering training for the clergy into three categories:

1   *Graduate Professional Schools* These most prestigious seminaries or schools of theology will be at the core of this study.

2 *Undergraduate Professional Schools* These are the Bible colleges, generally fundamentalist.

3 *Proprietary Schools* They are owned and operated by one or several individuals or by small religious groups which are cultic in character.

In the university system of medieval Europe, the general model of education for the learned professions was a broad program of studies in liberal arts followed by an apprenticeship with an experienced professional; thus, theory followed by practice.

Such a course, which brought the Cambridge student to his Bachelor's degree, while perhaps designed primarily as a foundation for clerical education, by no means fully prepared a clergyman for his office. Strictly professional preparation began with the study for the M.A. degree, which was rarely taken except by those who planned to enter holy orders; hence, its requirements were of a professional character. To qualify for this degree the candidate studied Hebrew, probably continued the study of Greek and read theology; he might, or not, as he chose, remain in residence for the required three years between the first and second degrees (Gambrell, 1937, p. 18).

Generally the candidate for the professional theological degree continued his studies with a practicing clergyman. The more popular of these gathered a large number of candidates into assemblies which came to be called "schools of the prophets."

In the late eighteenth and early nineteenth centuries came the first effort to reform theological education significantly. Two principal factors gave momentum to this movement. One was increasing concern for the quality of professional education in general, an awareness of the need to upgrade the quality of the training not only of clergymen but of other professionals as well. The second was the need of denominations to establish separate schools in order to conserve purity of doctrine. All who sought entrance into one of the established professions mingled together as students at the university. There was constant interaction of students and faculties. One of the first professional groups to establish a separate, isolated system of education was the Catholic clergy. In reaction to the trauma of the Protestant Reformation, the Catholic hierarchy instituted a rigidly regulated system of seminaries. In them, aspirants to the priesthood could be insulated from the contagion of revolutionary spirit and unorthodox doctrine. This system did, in fact, ensure a better educated clergy than existed before the Reformation. The education of European Protestant ministers generally continued at the university.

Each of the churches brought to the new world its accustomed method of training clergymen. The colleges established in seventeenth- and eighteenth-century Protestant New England were intended primarily for the training of future clergymen. They incorporated the traditional curriculum which was in vogue at the English universities such as Cambridge. The programs included undergraduate studies in logic, rhetoric, Latin and Greek, the philosophies (natural, moral, mental), and one quarter of divinity in the senior year.

Conservative leaders of the organized churches, wishing to forestall any tampering with traditional doctrine or any novel method of interpreting the sacred scriptures, eventually established separate institutions for the education of their future clergymen. The opening of these theological seminaries gradually separated theological education from the intellectual mainstream of American society which continued to expand with the universities.

The great time in ministerial education is the period of the enlightenment, or, in America, the Revolutionary Epoch (roughly 1775 to 1800). Before that time, learning as such was all of a piece. With that period came the beginnings of the general estrangement of Protestant christianity from the dominant intellectual currents of the modern age, during which the churches relinquished the control of education, which previously had been their prerogative. Consequently, from the beginning of the nineteenth century, the education sponsored directly by the denominations has been on the defensive. Meanwhile, the fragmentation into denominations meant that not only were all the groups thrown in common on the defensive against the rising "secular" learning, but each was in effect thrown on the defensive against the education sponsored by all the others (Niebuhr & Williams, 1956, p. 236).

As denominational Protestantism became increasingly fragmented, the number of theological schools multiplied; each denomination and sect established its own network of institutions for the training of ministers. These institutions tended to be enclaves for specific religious subcultures and led to a cloistering of ministerial students.

A much more extensive cloistering of theological students had long since occurred within Catholicism. One of the major complaints of reformers during the late Middle Ages was the inefficiency of training offered to prospective parish priests. At the time of the Reformation, the bishops of the Roman Catholic Church in the Ecumenical Council of Trent enacted a decree, the purpose of which was to reform Roman Catholic theological education. The French Vincentian Fathers and the Sulpician Fathers were largely responsible for the development of the strong Roman Catholic seminary system. The Counter-Reformation spirit—conservative, legalistic, and isolationist—prevailed in these post-Reformation seminaries. American Catholic seminaries, the first of which was established in Baltimore in 1791, manifested this same conservative characteristic.

The American diocesan seminary, as we have said, is primarily a cultural, intellectual, and organizational transplant. It is not only European in its background and traditions, but its establishment in this country, from the beginning was usually by Europeans. Of all the aspects of the Catholic church's life in this country, it is probably the one that for most of its history was least affected by the American environment (Poole, 1965, p. 49).

Thus, although they arrived at it by different historical paths, the situation of the Roman Catholic and Protestant churches regarding theological training was quite similar during the nineteenth century: an ever increasing number of student enrollments; multiplication in the numbers of institutions which, with few notable exceptions, functioned in isolation from the university centers of secular learning; antagonisms among the schools—on the one hand, those established by various Protestant denominations, and on the other, those established by various Catholic orders. This situation prevailed until the early twentieth century when a new ecumenism emerged to breach some of the ideological and organizational gaps within denominational Protestantism, and much more recently between Protestantism and Roman Catholicism.

The phenomenal growth of theological schools in the United States occurred without assistance from government. Religion and religious organizations in the United States have had to be enterprises largely as a result of the separation of church and state.

The withdrawal of government support from religion made American Protestantism unique in the christian world. The United States became the first nation in which religious groups were viewed as purely voluntary associations. To exist, American churches had to compete in the marketplace for support. And conversely, membership in a given religious denomination was a voluntary act (Lipset, 1963, p. 160).

Voluntary support of the faithful in an age of faith and conservative religion has been more than adequate to build a strong system of theological schools and seminaries. Support of these institutions may become precarious in a time of liberalism and secularism. Each of the many religious organizations has its own definition of proper theological training for its ministers. In an ecumenical and secular period the various organizations will compete for the same dollar and even for the same theological students. This may lead to mergers in the cause of survival.

DENOMINA-TIONAL DIFFERENCES Sociologists have distinguished three major types of Christian religious organizations. The church is the dominant religious organization in a national society. The countries of Europe characteristically have had such an established church in the past. Dissenters from the theology and practices of such a church may cut themselves off to follow what they consider the true teachings of the founder. They found sects which are at war with mores, the church, and the world. European sects, and new ones founded here, have flourished in America; they have also changed their form.

An entirely new conception of church and church institutions has emerged in America. Pluralism of religions and churches is something quite axiomatic to the American. This means that outside the old world distinction of church and sect, America has given birth to a new type of religious structure—the denomination. The denomination as we know it is a stable, settled church, enjoying a legitimate and recognized place in a larger aggregate of churches, each recognizing the proper states of others. The denomination is the non-conformist sect become central and normative (Herberg, 1960).

In the United States we have no established church. We have some which were established in Europe and which do not take kindly to being considered one denomination among many. They are yielding the point in practice recently. Other religious bodies are too sectarian to accept the notion of being a denomination, of being one of many branches of the church. Religious organizations in our society either are denominations or are more or less aloof of the church or sectarian frontier. Their ministerial training and the career patterns of their ministers vary according to their place on this scale and their place among the social strata.

Each type of religious organization has developed its own system for training men to serve in its ministry. The educational system is correlative to particular conceptualizations of the ministerial role within the overall social organization, and more particularly to the concept of vocation or "divine calling." Here we arrive at the fundamental question as to the source of authority for preaching the word of God.

Sociologists of religion have developed several typologies of religious personages and their roles. Weber (1968, p. 439), in his discussion of ideal types, contrasts the priest with the prophet.

We shall understand "prophet" to mean a purely individual bearer of charisma, who, by virtue of his mission, proclaims a religious doctrine or divine commandment. The personal call is the decisive element distinguishing the prophet from the priest. The latter lays claim to authority by virtue of his service in a sacred position, while the prophet's claim is based on personal revelation and charisma. It is no accident that almost no prophets have emerged from the priestly class. The priest dispenses salvation by virtue of his office. Even in cases in which personal charisma may be involved, it is the hierarchical office that confers legitimate authority upon the priest as a member of a corporate enterprise of salvation.

Each religious organization must come to terms with the question of mandate. It must establish ways of discerning whether a prospective candidate has a divine calling. The method varies from group to group. Substantially, however, it may be said that there is direct correlation between the interpretation of vocation or calling and the level of formal education required of candidates to the ministry.

Generally, those religious groups which are designated as sects require some charismatic expression of divine power in the candidate, whereas those religious groups whose theology is more highly rationalized and accommodated to the norms of secular culture demand higher educational achievement and increased professionalization. Johnson (1961) has presented a developmental model for the study of the process by which the clergy become professionalized.

Wilson (1959, pp. 494–504) observed the same phenomenon in certain sectarian groups:

The movement had ceased to be simply a revival campaign but had become an established sect, with revivalism as the technique of recruitment. Ideally, the movement still had a "called ministry" but increasingly the real criterion determining who would actually minister was not that of Spirit-leading but that of Bible School training.

As religious groups move from the sectarian model of social organization, the concept of vocation tends to become more highly rationalized and more emphasis is laid on formal education as a prerequisite for ministry. Most religious organizations in the United States, apart from the sectarian or cultic groups which were alluded to above, require a certain minimum of formal theological education of its prospective ministers. As clergy become more professionalized, the training programs tend to move into the more open milieu of interdenominational and interdisciplinary study within university settings.

We now look at the traditional models and systems of theological education in order to understand the ferment of the 1960s and recent trends.

TRADITIONAL MODELS AND SYSTEMS

The Protestant system

The major Protestant denominations train their ministers in seminaries, usually sponsored by the denomination, to which students are admitted after gaining a bachelor's degree in a liberal arts college. As an undergraduate, the candidate is not cloistered. He will probably have had some informal practice in the pastoral role by working with some minister of his acquaintance. He need not have made any formal declaration of his intent to study theology.

Only in the seminary does formal training in theology and the work of the ministry begin. At the end of three years of study, sometimes interrupted, the candidate is awarded the bachelor of divinity. He is then eligible, in most denominations, for full ordination and for the pastorage of a parish or congregation of his denomination. He becomes a full colleague of ministers of his own denomination and, indeed, of other denominations of similar standing and character.

This inner group of Protestant denominations is in some measure heir to social movements and institutions of the Anglo-Saxon and northern European region. It includes the Anglican, Presbyterian, Congregational, Methodist, Baptist, Lutheran, and Reformed traditions. Once divided to the point of bitter conflict, these denominations have formed a variety of bodies in America; the tendency now is for them to merge. Many lay members move from one to another for convenience and other reasons of circumstance or mild conviction. Many clergy are ordained in one denomination and move to another with or without a second ordination. Congregations often find their pastors outside their own denomination.

The majority of ministerial students terminate their studies when they have the bachelor of divinity and move into parish ministries.

However, there has been a significant increase in the number who pursue postgraduate studies. Some work for master's degrees in some special branch. Others work for a doctorate in some field related to theology or the professional work of the clergy.

Specialized two-year courses now prepare people for religious education and community service; with a master's degree, but without ordination, such people become the paraprofessionals of religion.

Statistics of the American Association of Theological Schools show that, in 1960, of the total numbers of students enrolled in its member schools, 12.7 percent were enrolled in postgraduate programs. By 1967 the number had increased to 17.9 percent. Enrollment in doctoral programs continues to rise at an amazing rate. Between 1969–70 and 1970–71 there was an overall increase of 24.45 percent; enrollment in professional doctoral programs during that year increased by 63.01 percent, and for the academic doctorates (Ph.D.) enrollment increased by 31.39 percent. This significant increase in the number of students enrolled in postgraduate programs suggests that increasing numbers of theological students have career goals other than the traditional ministry. Higher education and administration are common alternatives.

The Bible colleges
The Bible colleges, of which there are about 200 with more than 30,000 students, are the second great group of Protestant schools which prepare for the ministry. They are generally sponsored by denominations that are not quite in the mainstream of American Protestantism—by people who have protested yet again—the Assembly of God, the Church of God (there are several so called), Holiness Churches, Christian and Missionary Alliance. These fervent groups are just now graduating from gospel halls to more churchly buildings. They form what is perhaps the most vigorously growing wing of American Protestantism. The Accrediting Association of Bible Colleges reports 50 accredited members and 14 associate members. The enrollment in their affiliate schools has increased by 100 percent in the last decade.

These colleges generally claim to stick to the letter of the Bible —the letter is the authorized King James version. Their founders reacted against the very implications of the historical linguistic and historical archaeological studies of biblical documents and of the "Holy Land" and its environs. The conservative theological position has been preserved, along with some antipathy to modern science:

Such mistrust of any education tinged with "modern" influences resulted in the creation of scores of Bible Colleges and training schools for ministers. In many instances, the level of training in these institutions has been of rather doubtful quality. On the other hand, leaders of the Bible School movement have been developing a theory of liberal arts education with the Bible at its center, and through an accrediting association have moved toward standardization and steady improvement of a program which seeks to synthesize conservative Evangelical christianity with a valid educational ideal (Neibuhr & Williams, 1956, p. 276).

Many who enter the ministry in these Bible churches do so without academic preparation. They may then enter a Bible college, but without the preparation or the time to take a full sequence of college and seminary study. A few Bible colleges still grant a three-year diploma in pastoral studies; the great majority offer a four-year program, with Bible studies at the center, for a baccalaureate degree. Traditionally, four or five years of study have been considered adequate preparation. But apparently the Bible schools are on the usual American road to longer general training followed by longer professional training.

While terminal ministerial programs continue to prevail in the typical Bible College curriculum, pre-seminary programs are increasingly finding their place. . . . One reason for this is that the Bible College has as its primary objective the preparation of students for christian ministries and therefore naturally directs its attention toward ministerial education whether terminal or preparatory. Furthermore, the Bible College has sought to keep abreast of the needs of its students for a broader experience in general education—as is true in many other specialized fields (Accrediting Association . . . , 1968, p. 9f).

The Roman Catholic system
The Roman Catholic system of training candidates for the priesthood is vaster and more complex than the Protestant. A recent survey (Center for Applied Research . . . , 1969) compiled a list of 625 institutions. Fifty-five had closed, moved to another location, or ceased to engage in the training of candidates. A total of 528 (92.7 percent of 570) institutions responded to the questionnaire.

The seminaries were classified according to the following categories:

1 *Major Seminaries* — those institutions which train students exclusively at the philosophy and theology levels, as they are called. Major seminary programs typically offer a six-year program beginning with the junior year of undergraduate work; the program comprises the equivalent of the last two years of undergraduate study plus four years of graduate work.

2 *Minor Seminaries* — those institutions whose programs include work at the high school and/or junior college level. This type of program in its fullest development comprises six years of study.

3 *Major-Minor Seminaries* — those institutions which train prospective priests from the first year of high school through graduate theological study. It should be emphasized at this point that Catholic seminary training has traditionally been structured on this six-six, or more precisely, four-two-two-four pattern. These levels have been referred to as high school, junior college, philosophy, and theology, respectively.

The data indicate that a total of 439 institutions could be characterized as major seminaries, minor seminaries, or major-minor seminaries. However, of that number, only 7 offered programs covering every level of the 12-year training cycle. The major seminaries number 134, minor seminaries 183, and mixed (major-minor) 122. High school programs in operation number 171. The high school seminary has been criticized by many within the Catholic church as being alien to American culture. Moreover, it has been found that the greatest decrease in seminary enrollment occurred at the high school level — a decrease of 4,316, or 21.4 percent, from 1966–67 to 1967–68.

A young Catholic may enter formal training for the ministry at a much earlier age than his Protestant counterpart. Upon entry into the system he is clearly "set apart" from his peers and is rewarded by the honorific status of being a future priest. The process by which he is socialized into the priestly role is longer and much more intensive than that in the Protestant system.

The control of Catholic seminaries still rests almost exclusively with the church itself. It should be noted that of the total of 570 institutions, only 197, or 37.3 percent, are accredited by either the regional accrediting agency or the professional accrediting agency. This reflects the general tendency of Catholic seminaries to be withdrawn from the marketplace and from the mainstream of intellectual life. It reflects the tendency of certain religious groups to treat their own ministers as special cases who need not conform to norms of secular society when they demonstrate sufficient proof of a divine calling.

The vast system of parochial schools feeds the Catholic seminaries. While all religious groups foster vocations through cultic religious socialization in Sunday school programs and through other methods, the parochial school has been the most effective milieu in which to develop the seeds of a calling to the ministry (Fichter, 1961). The continuing decline of the parochial school system will aggravate the already serious problem of recruiting candidates for the Catholic clergy.

THE SIXTIES: REVALUATION AND REFORM Profound changes in the existing pattern of seminary education in North America must quickly be effected; these changes are likely to be even more profound and more continuing than many seminaries and churches currently perceive; and the pace of change at all levels in theologic education must be accelerated if seminaries are to retain their historic position in Roman Catholicism and in major Protestant denominations as the primary source from which the churches secure new clergy (American Association . . . , 1968*b*, p. 757).

These words are from the report of the Resources Planning Commission appointed by the American Association of Theological Schools in 1966.

The report of the commission then presented what it considered to be the reasons compelling the reform of theological education.

1 The growing demands from the laity that traditional formulations of the christian message be reinterpreted in ways which speak directly and intelligibly to the ethos of our secular culture.

2 The need for the churches to challenge many of the values of our society and times and to minister more effectively to ills which beset the society and world in which we live.

3 The emergence and development of new types of ecumenical education and the changes which they are producing, both in the spirit of the christian community and in the organization of the institutional church.

4 The need, not only for better communication among christians, but also for a new type of communication with judaism and non-christian religions (American Association . . . , 1968*b*, p. 758).

The adequacy of the traditional seminary training has long been questioned. The criticism has become more acute as the church endeavors to minister to contemporary secular American society.

The seminary is expected to meet the same problems as all professional schools. Every profession must define the area of its competency and thus the boundaries of other professions. Each must define its particular skills for meeting particular problems. It must evaluate the performance of its practitioners. It must recruit candidates of good quality in sufficient numbers to carry on its work. This has become an acute problem, especially in recruiting clergy from the lower socioeconomic classes. There is also the problem of specialization, and consequently of relating the work of the specialties to one another. Even in religion, professional practice is concentrated in large organizations with hierarchies of personnel. Finally, every profession has to find its proper measure of integration of professional training with the mainstream of higher learning in the universities. Every profession to some extent cloisters its students physically, psychologically, and philosophically from the rest of the intellectual world. The balance is often delicate; certainly, at present, it is changing in most professions.

The Role of the Clergyman

During the sixties a great deal was written both in the popular press and in learned journals regarding the role of a clergyman in contemporary society. There was a prevalent sense of dissatisfaction among clergymen because of their perception that many of the traditional functions for which they had been trained were irrelevant to contemporary needs. At the same time there was considerable experimenting with new forms of ministry. Some clergymen were leaders in the civil rights movement of the early sixties and later in the antiwar movement. The participation of clergymen in marches and demonstrations proved to be offensive and scandalous to many conservative laymen and clergy. Those who participated in these activities thought it their responsibility to take a clear stand on the moral issue of racial injustice. Their participation in these activities was not required of them and was often clearly discouraged by their superiors. These ministers, on their own, were adding a new facet to their role.

James M. Gustafson commented thus:

The American clergy extend their areas of responsibility in part because they are no longer certain what their unique function is. To be sure, they maintain the traditional religious activities, but in the secularization of modern life God is very remote to most men. Indeed, it is difficult to be a clergyman in an age in which the death of God is one of the basic principles of life. . . . The dilemma of the modern clergyman is that he represents a historical tradition which in many respects is dissonant with contemporary knowledge and with the principles of practical life in the age of technology. He is no longer clear about his authority. In this uncertainty he seeks out those activities which secure for his profession some legitimacy (Lynn, 1967).

The unique function of any denominational clergyman can be identified easily enough. It is the transmission of a sacred tradition which consists of three essential elements:

1 *An Ideology:* a corpus of theological doctrines contained in sacred books, traditions, and theological writings.

2 *A Moral Code:* a set of moral norms as seen from the perspective of theology. The moral code is the yardstick which is used to measure the extent to which individual and collective human behavior conforms to the ideals of the group.

3 *A Pastoral Role:* The pastoral function includes two major components. One is the cultic process whereby a clergyman transmits theological doctrines and celebrates them by means of rituals. The rituals of any religious group reflect its interpretation of the teachings of the sacred books and traditions. There is great contrast between the ritual forms utilized by hierarchically organized churches with their highly regulated systematized liturgies and the ritual forms of the more democratically organized congregation-oriented denominations. In all cases, however, the cultic component of the pastoral role includes preaching the word and celebrating the sacred rituals.

Counseling is the second major component of the pastoral role. The clergyman is expected to guide his parishioners in all those aspects of their lives which have theological dimensions according to the ideology of the group. He educates his parishioners in a wide range of matters affecting human and religious behavior. He socializes both the young and adults; he serves as premarital and marriage counselor; he counsels the troubled, the bereaved, the sick, the dying, the imprisoned, the handicapped, and the poor. Since, theoretically, there is no human situation or problem which does not come under the purview of the ideology and the code of the denomination, his counseling functions are virtually limitless. He is expected to be capable of interpreting the meaning and validity of all human behaviors in the light of doctrinal theology. In the course of this pastoral work he is likely to meet the lawyer, the physician, the undertaker, and the social worker on the doorstep.

The core activity or unique function of any clergyman may be summarized briefly then as that of a *transmitter, celebrator, interpreter, and perpetuator of a creed, a code, and a cult.* All three elements of the sacred tradition are subject to change and reinterpretation since theology grows and develops through its own internal dynamic and through interaction with other sciences and a changing society.

Thus while it is possible to identify the core activity or function of the clergyman, the specific ways of exercising it are subject to historical change. In our era the clergyman's role is being extensively studied, evaluated, and redefined, a creative process which is leading to new ways of exercising ministry. The process is having a significant impact on theological education.

The clergyman is ordained for service in a particular denomination, except for a few who found a new sect or great independent congregation. A few go from study to teaching and research in theological or other schools. An increasing percentage eventually become administrators in religious establishments. But the traditional career begins with assignment to pastoral duties in a local parish or a congregation; most careers continue and end in pastoral office. Of the approximately 135,000 ministers in 17 Protestant communions recently surveyed, approximately 85 percent were in parish work (Scherer, 1965).

American Priests shows that 75 percent of priests under 35 years of age report that parish work is their main job; it goes downward with age to 63 percent of those over 55. Nearly half of the priests under 35 are associate pastors (*American Priests,* 1971, p. 200). It is a position very low in autonomy and satisfaction. The highest level of satisfaction among priests is found among those who work in the chancery (diocesan) office or those who do some special work. The parish may be the main job for most, but it is not the most prized kind of work.

In a typical American parish the clergy must be entrepreneurs in order to assure the parish's financial and social viability. The pastor must engage in a wide range of activities which do not constitute his unique function as a professional and for which, in many instances, he does not feel adequately prepared.

In a 1964 survey Protestant clergymen were asked to rank a number of ministerial activities by level of importance and by amount of time spent in each activity. The clearest and most significant deviations in the rank ordering were in the entrepreneurial aspect of their work. Church administration was ranked twelfth in importance and second in consumption of time. Office work ranked twenty-first in importance but seventh in amount of time spent. Conversely, officiating at weddings, baptisms, and funerals, while ranked ninth in importance, was ranked nineteenth in terms of the amount of time involved (National Council of Churches, 1964).

In a discussion of data which reveal the ministers' low estimation of the executive role, the authors conclude as follows:

This seems to indicate that either the denominations must get someone to handle these tasks in the local church (e.g., a church business administrator, perhaps even on a multi-parish basis); or they must *train* the pastors in administration and group dynamics (Scherer & Wedel, 1966, p. 56).

A similar survey of Catholic priests was conducted by Joseph H. Fichter and the results published in 1965. The priests were asked to rank nine activities on three dimensions; first, how time-consuming they were; second, the degree of satisfaction obtained from the activity; third, the adequacy of their training for the particular activity. The results of the survey reveal significant inversions of the rank orderings and bear striking resemblance to the data for Protestant ministers in that administrative activities were ranked second, third, and fourth in terms of their time consumption, but were ranked lowest on the dimensions of satisfaction and adequacy of training. From these and other data, Fichter (1965, p. 187) draws the following conclusion:

These findings imply a two-fold distortion of the parish priest's pastoral image. In the first place, the parishioners see the priest spending a great deal of time on tasks that are essentially non-sacramental. Except for counseling, he is largely serving his people in tasks that are subsidiary to his priesthood. It is no wonder then that the parishioners have a central image of the priest as the organizer or executive of an enterprise. This is an image too that the priest by instinct and training would like to repudiate.

A more serious distortion is that which exists between the training and interests of the clergy on the one hand, and the tasks they must perform on the other. They rate executive and financial activities as those for which they are least prepared in the seminary, and which are most distasteful for them. Yet, these essentially secular tasks consume an excessive amount of energy and time.

A number of surveys confirm the findings that Catholic priests believe that their theoretical training is better than the practical and that discontent with their training is stronger among young priests (Fichter, 1961; 1968; *American Priests,* 1971). But even the older priests thought that too little attention had been given to professional-client relationships and that the seminary had isolated them overmuch from the mainstream of social and intellectual life.

Students and young clergy do not oppose scholarship, but look for a more relevant and vital scholarship. Some seminaries, they say, are not where the world is, either in location or thought; their methods are antiquated, their concern circumscribed, their scholarship time, remote, and unreal, fitting the student "at best for an outmoded world that is no longer the real world at society's growing edge" (Pusey & Taylor, 1967, p. 118).

Many young clergy believe their seminary training did not prepare them for the experiments in ministry required to make their work effective. While the core activity of the clergyman may remain the same, the auxiliary activities change from situation to situation. The young men want the seminaries to prepare them for new roles.

Until now, about 80 percent of the non-retired Episcopal clergy have continued in parish life; new roles found among the remaining 20 percent include: teaching at all levels; chaplain services in hospitals, armed services, schools and colleges, penal institutions, and the like; work in various kinds of industry, urban centers, or the reconciliation of races; professional posts on newspapers, magazines, and in radio and television; administrative work in the interdenominational or Episcopal offices; and overseas service. New varieties of experimental ministry are appearing monthly (ibid., p. 40).

Most denominational churches require candidates for ordination to complete a basic course in theology leading to the first professional degree. The program is of three or four years' duration at the graduate level. Upon successful completion the student is awarded a bachelor of divinity degree. Some schools provide opportunities for doctoral and postdoctoral studies.

Traditionally, this training program has comprised four major areas of study: (1) *Bible*—biblical languages, biblical texts and their interpretation, biblical archaeology. (2) *History*—the study of the Judeo-Christian religion in all of its major historical phases.

(3) *Systematic theology*—the study of theology in its principles, doctrines, and derivations, comprising both doctrinal theology and ethics (moral theology). (4) *Professional studies*—or pastoral the-ology, in which the candidate is trained to transmit and perpetuate the sacred tradition through the acquisition of certain technical skills required to fulfill this ministry, e.g., homiletics, which is the study of preaching (how to prepare and deliver an effective sermon); liturgies (the study of ritual celebrations); and pastoral counseling (techniques for guiding the faithful according to the tenets of the faith). The curricula of all theological schools include all four areas of study, although the relative weight given to each component varies from school to school. The general criticism which seemed to prevail in the sixties indicated that the curriculum was too heav-ily weighted with theoretical courses and that even the professional-technical courses were presented from a theoretical perspective.

In theological education, our question has usually been put in this way: we have learned pretty well how to teach Bible, doctrine, ethics, and the other "content" (that is, specialist) materials; but how can we teach the men to use these properly in practice? The one thing I am sure of about theological education is that it will never answer this question so long as "practice" is considered as an addendum (Hiltner, 1954, p. 249).

One of the principal solutions to the problem was seen in the widespread introduction of clinical-pastoral training through super-vised field experience. The second breakthrough during the sixties was the move to provide opportunities for increased specialization and the emergence of experimental approaches to ministry.

There is talk of ongoing close dialogue between administrators and faculties of theological schools on the one hand and practicing clergymen on the other hand. The American Association of The-ological Schools has emerged as perhaps the most powerful instru-mentality for fostering this dialogue and guiding the reform move-ment.

The Clergy as a Profession

A profession claims to possess a body of knowledge and a reper-tory of skills not shared by others. Thus equipped, it claims a monopoly over the performance of certain services. The clergy profess as their peculiar services the transmitting of a set of beliefs, the celebration of the rituals of their cult, and the proclaiming and support of a moral code. In our society, the clergyman competes with those of other denominations. They may convert his followers to another creed or simply offer them more attractive services, more compatible fellow worshipers, or a more convenient place of worship. Preachers of exotic doctrines and open opponents of church and religion are numerous but not threatening; their followers are few in comparison with the multitudes who are active members or lukewarm followers of the standard denominations.

A more severe competition to the professional clergy comes from the large number of other professions which now perform specialized personal services. The clergyman, the lawyer, and the physician were once the chief counselors of people with problems; the clergyman was perhaps called upon for a wider range of problems than the lawyer and the physician. Many problems brought all three into action. The psychiatrist, the clinical psychologist, the social worker, the marriage and family counselor, and the guidance counselor are among those who perform personal services which the minister might have been called upon to perform. He may find such professionals more highly trained than himself to perform these services.

Members of his own congregation are not likely to compete with the minister in his core activities. But they may have more skill in finance, administration, communication, and community organization. The minister is not always sure what to do himself, and what to delegate and how to delegate to others. In the past, the clergyman has been a generalist by default, taking on all the tasks of operating parishes and congregations. The division of labor and authority between him and his laity varied greatly from the congregational churches to the hierarchical ones. In all, the minister—the pastor—was expected to take initiative to keep the enterprise alive and healthy. Some believe the solution to the problems of the clergyman's role is to delegate all administrative matters to qualified laymen. He could then devote his time and efforts to his core activities. Another proposal is to make clergymen double specialists by obtaining degrees in some other field as well as in theology: theology and counseling, theology and law, theology and communication, theology and medicine.

These other professions tend to be skeptical of candidates not fully committed to them. The training is long and expensive. It is doubtful whether the man with license to practice two professions would, in such a time as ours, devote himself fully to the one which is in doubt about its mission.

Still another proposal is that of group practice. The clergy of a given community would each specialize in some aspect of service; they would operate as a team rather than as general practitioners each for his own body of laymen. In order to do this they would have to recognize each other as full colleagues, each acceptable to a wide variety of laymen (Scherer & Wedel, 1966, p. 24).

Whatever solutions are proposed to the problem of multiple roles and services required of clergymen, they will require innovations in the curricula of seminaries, experiment in local settings, and acceptance of new role definitions of the clergy by the laity. The trend seems to be toward making the clergyman a specialist by design rather than a generalist by default.

Theory and Practice in Theological Education

Theology is the systematic statement of belief in God and of the relation of God to nature, including man. Before the word *science* took on its present limited meaning, theology was called the queen of the sciences. The great body of learning developed by the medieval universities was called theology. The name theology persists in the modern seminaries which train priests and ministers, although there is no consensus among the religious bodies as to the true theology, at least no consensus comparable to that achieved among scientists concerning many of the phenomena they investigate.

Ministers and priests consider theology the theoretical base of their calling. In the theological seminary there is the same difficulty as in all professional schools to establish a balance between theory and practice. There is the additional problem that even accepting similar theological assumptions, the churches and the clergy do not agree as to what social actions are proper. Still another circumstance is that even churches which disagree on points of theology agree on many of the functions which should be performed by the clergy. The theological seminaries find many areas of agreement and cooperation. All have to find the balance between pursuing theological scholarship and teaching men how to serve people effectively. As in other professions, in theology practical training is postponed. This order was criticized thus in 1924.

The seminaries as a class of educational institutions do not offer clinical training to their students. Their programs have to do largely with the minister's acquaintance with the historical background and the roots of his religion. They teach a modicum of facts about the four traditional fields of theological study. In the general field of practical theology they spend most of the time on the building of the sermon — with a smaller amount of attention on its delivery. The instruction in pastoral methods and practices is usually treated academically and theoretically. It is rare to find a case where the student is really trained in actual parish work; especially as an "intern" — as assistant to an experienced minister. The assignment to "student churches," with perhaps an occasional visit by the more favored to the city institutions, is in many instances looked upon as constituting sufficient training in this aspect of the minister's work. In most schools a member of the faculty has supervision of securing employment for students, which is considered field work. Inspections are not usually made nor are reports called for (Kelley, 1924, p. 145).

Since the time of that criticism nearly all seminaries have introduced some field training into their curricula. It has often consisted simply of having the students spend some time as substitute or assistant pastors in churches not far away. In fact, many Protestant seminarians have depended upon such work for their livings; in turn, many smaller churches have depended upon the seminaries to provide them with cheap ministerial labor. In the course of the usual three-year theological education, today's student must typically spend four to six semesters in a field placement. The supervised work in the field might be in social service agencies, mental hospitals, prisons or juvenile detention homes, poverty programs, homes for the aged, urban or suburban parishes, or schools and colleges. Ordinarily the theological school requires supervision by a faculty member and by a qualified person in the field.

The denominations apparently agree on the social problems with which their clergy should know how to deal. One Catholic order, which used to have its aspirants spend their first year of training cloistered, contemplating the death that lies in wait for all mankind, now has them in the hearts of the city engaged in settings very like those listed above. Field experiences and internships are perhaps the most open, the most ecumenical, and the most experimental aspect of theological training.

An example of this kind of openness is found in the program of field education sponsored by the Boston Theological Institute (a consortium of seven Catholic and Protestant theological schools in the Boston area: Andover Newton Theological School, Boston College Department of Theology, Boston University School of Theology, Episcopal Theological School, Harvard University Divinity School, St. John's Seminary, and Weston College). In addition to the field education programs of the individual participating schools, the standing committee on field education of the Boston Theological Institute operates the following programs available to students of all seven schools on a cross-registration basis.

1   Supervised work with alcoholic patients at a nearby state hospital and their families both on the ward and in the community.

2   Supervised experience in a cluster of churches in a nearby suburban community. Within this supra-parish setting, opportunities are afforded for study, research, and experimentation in ecumenical ministry (Catholic and Protestant).

3   Supervised experience in a local rehabilitation program for criminal offenders.

4   Supervised ministry in a major military hospital under the direction of Roman Catholic and Protestant Navy chaplains.

5   Supervised experience and research in the field of communications, with special concentration on the media of radio and television, and visual education.

6   Ecumenical tutorial programs for seventh- and eighth-grade boys in the inner city.

7   Supervised experience in working with teen-age runaways and in drug counseling within a program initiated and sponsored by seminary students with interprofessional consultants.

8   Supervised ministry in a local suburban community, with special focus on adult education and experiments in ecumenical encounters.

Each of these programs is under the supervision of a project director and a faculty representative, and most of them are assisted by a "project theologian" whose role is to assist participants to glean the theological implications and dimensions of the experience.

The overall expectation of any well-supervised program of field education in ministry is not only that the candidate will learn certain specific technical skills but, more importantly, that he will conceptualize a personal-professional identity model constructed from theological sources and experiences in contemporary society and that thus he will achieve a theological integration of his personal-professional identity.

A student who enters a theological school to prepare for ordination in the ministry of a denomination is ordinarily required to study all four areas of theology—Bible, systematic theology, history, and pastoral theology. The relative emphasis on the several areas varies. The American Protestant denominations place great emphasis on knowledge of the Bible. For some sects the preferred Bible is the English version authorized by the Church of England early in the seventeenth century. Some think it the only Bible and believe theological knowledge and much other knowledge is contained in it, although Galileo some centuries ago suggested to ecclesiastical authorities "that the Bible tells us how to go to heaven and not how the heavens go" (O'Dea, 1972). A more common Protestant view is that the theologian should know the Hebrew and Greek sources and be aware of the problems and pitfalls of translation, while still clinging to the Bible as the main source of religious inspiration. The study of Latin, Greek, and Hebrew, once generally required of candidates for ministry in the standard denominational colleges and seminaries, has gradually fallen off. Those who do study those languages do so as academic specialists on the history and development of the Bible rather than as theologians. They are as much (or more) members of the community of scholars as of the church.

The Catholic seminary was until recently centered much more on study of systematic theology and on the traditions of the Roman Catholic Church. The aspirant to the priesthood learned Latin both as the language of liturgy and as the official language of Catholic theology, canon law, and the communications of the Pope with his bishops, clergy, and people. Since the Second Vatican Council the emphasis on systematic theology has been much reduced as has also the place of Latin in liturgy and Catholic learning. Theology itself has become more concerned with modern social philosophies and problems. The disparity between what the seminarian learns in order to practice his profession of ministry and what the scholarly specialist learns appears to have become greater in both the Protestant and Catholic seminaries. At the same time, Catholics and mainstream Protestants appear to approach each other in what they teach and learn. The Catholic scholar may find a closer colleague in a Protestant who specializes in the same line of theological or biblical research than in a Catholic pastor. The Catholics and Protestants who serve slum parishes, missions, or social agencies may be close colleagues, understanding each other perfectly. The pastors of thriving suburban Catholic parishes and Protestant parishes or congregations may learn techniques from each other to better compete for the souls and the support of the local families. Implicit in their competition is a recognition of colleagueship; they play by the rules of middle-class Christianity. The rabbi of a prosperous temple is part of the team. They can all trade pulpits or, at least, lecterns from time to time.

Students who enter theological school with the intention of seeking advanced theological or academic degrees are, in some seminaries, not required to take the practical courses described above. The trend toward specialization has thus entered the seminaries themselves. At the same time, they seek to upgrade themselves by giving master's and doctor's degrees, both for professional work and for the more purely scholarly work.

Thus there appears in seminaries a variety of courses of study, varying in length of time and in the nature of the study, and in the prestige accorded to the people who take them and in the careers which they may follow.

In the standard seminary course which gives an aspirant the credentials for ordination, there lingers the expectation that he will become a pastor of a territorial parish or congregation of his denomination. This is the equivalent of the general practice of medicine. In both professions aspirants are encouraged to prepare for this general practice, but in both this is far from being the most prestigious and profitable. The aspirant is not taught by people who have been general practitioners. There is also a good deal of doubt whether such practice will flourish or even hold its own. Young men entering the seminaries may see preparation for general ministry as a course which will limit their career opportunities; it is the old story of Martha versus Mary.

The Seminary and the University
At any rate, denominational officials and theological educators appear to be under pressure to develop closer relations between seminaries and universities. But of the 179 schools affiliated with the American Association of Theological Schools (1971) only 16 are integral parts of universities: the remaining 163 are classified as independent, although some of them are attached to an undergraduate college. It can still be said that:

Theological education, to an uncomfortable degree within Protestantism and to a shocking degree within Catholicism, is the only major professional field largely separated from an organic and living relationship to the graduate faculties of great universities (Wagoner, 1966, p. 92).

In those schools which are part of universities, a large and rising proportion of the students are enrolled in programs leading to some higher degree, such as doctor of theology or doctor of philosophy; 1,047, or 30 percent, of the 3,699 students in these schools are in such programs. In the independent schools, 3,703, or 15 percent, of a total enrollment of 27,267 are in postgraduate programs. But it is in the university schools that the greater number of students in Ph.D. programs are found (American Association . . . , 1971).

The university school provides programs for training a cadre of theologians and ministers who are qualified to assume highly specialized roles, e.g., on theological faculties and university faculties, especially in departments of religion; in denominational offices; in positions in administrative bodies; and in assignments in elite parishes.

This type of integral relationship permits specialized programs sponsored jointly by the theological faculty and other graduate faculties. Thus, for example, advanced degrees in Christian education may be offered jointly by the theological faculty and the school of education. Proximity to liberal arts colleges and universities, then, affords opportunities for increased collaboration and the development of new programs for advanced specialization. It affords the opportunity for sharing perspectives and insights from many disciplines.

Seminary-university relationships also have an ecumenical effect, for the seminaries affiliated with the major universities generally have students and staff of a number of denominations. In addition, a cluster of theological schools may gather around a university and in some cases may form an organized consortium. Such a consortium allows theological schools to share facilities, curricula, staff, and students. It is cheaper to operate than would be a number of separate seminaries. The liberal and highly academic Baptist Divinity School of the University of Chicago has long gathered about it seminaries of several denominations. Boston Theological Institute includes Catholic, Episcopal, Methodist, and Unitarian member schools. At least 32 member schools of the American Association of Theological Schools have formal relationships with other theological schools. The association itself includes schools of Roman Catholic, Eastern Orthodox, and Protestant denominations. It would be an interesting result if some young persons were to decide to study theology and only later pick the denomination in which they would serve. It might well be that when the churches become as ecumenical as that, there will be no "vocations" to the ministry. The vocation to the ministry has historically been a call to the ministry of a particular denomination. It is feared that many will lose their sense of vocation if they are integrated with non-seminarians and even with seminarians of other denominations. This fear is perhaps greatest in the Roman Catholic Church, in which celibacy is still mandatory for the clergy.

Many men in seminary work are convinced that to bring any normal seminarian into contact with women is automatically to jeopardize or destroy his vocation. This argument cannot be dismissed arbitrarily because there is always enough evidence to support it in fact as well as in theory. It is not an imaginary danger. Thus, the problem is fundamentally a question of two conflicting views of the best method of preparing the priest. The one would isolate him until he is strong enough in his vocation to withstand the sexual temptations after ordination. According to this view, clerical celibacy is not a normal or ordinary way of life and so cannot be prepared for in the conventional way. The ordinary activities and associations of university life may be a good preparation for persons planning to marry, but they are hardly suitable to those entering the celibate life. Rather, they contribute to worldliness, and may force the future priest into the impossible position of trying to reconcile two conflicting ways of life. The opposing point of view is that such a situation tests a student's vocation far better than the tests of isolated seminary life. This view is usually summarized as "better that he leave before ordination than after," a statement that is often made in its oversimplified sense (Poole, 1965, p. 90).

Underlying this is the eternal question of the dangers of contact with people of other faiths and of the point in one's career when one becomes immune to such danger. There was a famous controversy, in the time of Pope Leo XIII, between the Bishop of Trier and the Bishop of Cologne over this. The Bishop of Cologne wanted his clergy to go to university before ordination, so that they would understand the new industrial world in which they would have to serve. The Bishop of Trier wanted his young men to go straight to seminary and to be ordained, thus committed, before contact with the world. It is an issue that does not die.

The American Association of Theological Schools recommends broad undergraduate education so that young people will have more time in which to make a choice of vocation.

Today, however, because of the wide range of undergraduate programs and majors offered by a great diversity of institutions of higher education, it is no longer feasible nor realistic to demand one particular type of undergraduate preparation as a prerequisite for theological studies. Some of the ablest students in our theological schools have made their decision to prepare for the ministry after their undergraduate study was completed, or even after a period of time in an occupation apparently unconnected with the church's ministry (American Association . . . , 1968*a,* p. 55).

Specialization and the Paraprofessionals

This problem is related also to the age of commitment to the ministry and to the depth of commitment. These are, in turn, related to specialization of religious services. The Catholic church, for long ages, solved all these problems by mandatory celibacy and by the multiplicity of religious orders. The priests are still sworn to life-long celibacy; those in special orders, such as the Jesuits, Dominicans, and Oblates, are doubly committed—to celibacy as priests and to some line of service emphasized by the order, such as teaching, preaching, or working in missions. The brothers and sisters of religious orders were committed to celibacy and to some specialized service either for a period of time or for life. Celibacy as a commitment has no meaning unless it is made before or at least not after the usual age of marriage. One who has thus set himself or herself apart is a marked person, spoiled for later return to ordinary life. The general secularization of life has been accompanied by a remarkable increase in the number of people who do return to the world—both priests and other "religious" including many nuns. This relative ease of leaving "religion" is evidently bringing about efforts to allow people to enter some branch of professional religion at later ages and with as firm a commitment.

Here again comes the question of specialization. The Catholic religious orders were traditionally all specialists of some sort. They were also, informally and in part formally, part of a system of ranks and prestige. The ordained priest in the Catholic church has a mandate and an authority superior to others in the church, even to others better educated than he. The minister ordained in a Protestant denomination is in a similar position, but less emphatically so. Both the priest and the Protestant minister are part of a complex system in which there is constant interplay between generalist and specialist, some of whom might be called paraprofessionals. As vocations to the priesthood fall, the priest has need of an increasing number and variety of helpers. One solution is the restoration of the permanent diaconate. Until modern times the diaconate was a phase in the training and career of the priest. All deacons were young and on their way to the priesthood. Regulations for the newly restored permanent diaconate require that men under 35 who seek ordination as deacons must still observe the law of celibacy. However, men of 35 or over, either married or celibate, may now be ordained deacons. With the restoration of the order of deacons, some of whom will be married men, we have the first instance in the modern history of the Roman Catholic Church in which some of its duly ordained clergymen will be married. The long-range implications of this change cannot be predicted, but it might be viewed as a crack in the rigid, centuries-old tradition of celibacy for its clergy.

Following a papal decree of 1967, the deacon is to assist the bishop and priests at liturgical actions; to administer the sacrament of baptism in solemn ceremony; to reserve and administer the sacrament of Eucharist; in the absence of a priest, to assist at and bless marriages in the name of the church; to officiate at funeral and burial ceremonies; to read the sacred scriptures and instruct the faithful; to preside at worship when a priest is not present; and to administer works of charity in the name of the hierarchy. Thus, the new deacon will be able to exercise authoritatively many new functions within the local Catholic congregation.

The decree sets out specific regulations for the selection and training of deacons. The bishops of the United States have petitioned Rome and have received permission to restore the diaconate in the United States. They have established guidelines for the development of programs for training permanent deacons. By October 1970, 11 training centers had been established in the United States and a total of 275 candidates were in training. Of this number, 89 percent were married men, 9 percent were single men, and 2 percent were widowers. Most of the men were in their thirties and forties. Of the 275, 60 percent were college graduates and all but a few of the remaining 40 percent were high school graduates. The training program for these deacons will be three years, as a rule. The curriculum includes studies in the four major fields of Bible, systematic theology, history, and pastoral (practical) theology. Deacons are required to have supervised field experience.

We have a special reason for dwelling on this case. The priesthood, as other professions, has counted on its own aspirants, its colleagues of tomorrow, to do its more routine and less prestigious work. It can no longer get enough aspirants to do such work as part of initiation into the final and highest rank. It has created a permanent lower rank accessible to candidates of greater age and less education—and accessible without the supreme cost of separation from the world by lifelong celibacy. It may be symptomatic of late twentieth-century America that there will be a supply of people who, after their first youth, will accept a second chance at limited social mobility and a professional career, albeit of less than top rank. It is perhaps not by chance that this should also be a period in which there is strong pressure to break down the barriers which isolate the sexes in various social roles. It is also a time in which the role of religion and the nature of religious institutions are in question.

Recruitment and the Future

The professional age has come. Professional services of many kinds are much in demand. Seeing individuals and families through the turning points of the life cycle is surely a service that will be in demand as long as the human generations turn. There will be troubled people and people in trouble. People will seek moral guidance and others will be more than willing to give it. Yet the historic profession that has performed these functions, and sometimes others, is in a crisis. Its future is in question.

Each of the others (professions) is increasing or at least sustaining its great importance in society, whereas the church and the ministry are at best holding their own, or perhaps declining in significance. . . . The other professions, while under self-criticism, and in the case of education under public scrutiny, are not being subjected to the radical questions about their validity that the church and ministry are. This radical questioning has many roots: the uncertainties of the functions of the churches in modern society, the conflicts between those who view its function in moral and social reforming terms and those who view it in more therapeutic terms, the crisis in credibility about religious doctrines and dogmas, the sense of being fated by historical developments to a position of obscurity if not oblivion, and the problems of communication through the traditional language of the community. Ministers, theology students, and theological educators often demonstrate a crisis of self-confidence that in my judgment is not equalled in other professions (Gustafson, 1969, p. 244).

Gustafson's comments are particularly applicable to clergymen of those denominational churches which may be characterized as liberal and accommodating in their theological perspectives on the role of religion in the social order. Clergymen of the more conservative, evangelical sects and denominations, because of their radical commitment to traditional interpretations of the scriptures, are perhaps less susceptible to this sense of anomie. A clergyman's sense of "rightness" about his theological position would seem to be a major factor determining both his level of satisfaction in his professional work and his willingness to urge others to enter the profession.

Enrollment in professional theological schools has not kept pace with increases in other institutions of higher learning. Data compiled by the U.S. Department of Health, Education and Welfare indicate that in the period from 1960 to 1965 enrollment in all institutions of higher education, public and private, increased by 54.3 percent, whereas during this same period, enrollment in professional theological schools increased by only 18.6 percent. Moreover, it should be noted that theological schools had the lowest rate of increase among all the independently organized professional schools (e.g., teachers colleges, technological schools, schools of art, and other professional schools) in the public and private sector combined. Even among those institutions which are in the private sector of higher education, with the sole exception of technological schools (an increase rate of 10.6 percent), the professional theological schools had the lowest rate of increase (18.6 percent).

It should be noted that all professional theological schools are privately owned and administered. Overall increase of enrollment in the public institutions far outstripped the rate of increase in private institutions (71.1 percent increase in public institutions as against 29.9 percent increase in the private institutions). Since the theological schools cannot rely on government support, they will have to rely increasingly on denominational support and other private sources to meet mounting educational costs.

Denominational seminaries and Bible colleges have long since sought and, in most instances, received accreditation by the Regional Association of Colleges and Secondary Schools. There is in the United States, however, only one accrediting agency for graduate theological schools, the American Association of Theological Schools. The association has experienced phenomenal growth in recent years, with a major breakthrough in 1966 when the first Roman Catholic schools were admitted into the association. Membership in the association has increased from 95 schools in 1968 to 179 schools in 1971. Since 1956, when it was incorporated, the association has published data regularly on various characteristics of its member schools.

In the base year of 1956, there were 20,720 students enrolled in 122 member schools of the association. In 1960, there were 19,976 students enrolled in 122 schools; in 1965, there were 21,529 students in 127 schools; by 1970 this number had increased to 30,966 students in 179 schools. While it is clear that there has been a substantial and impressive increase in absolute numbers, a closer look is necessary in order to refine the data and to establish certain trends and shifts.

Enrollment in the schools experienced a decline in the early sixties and reached its lowest in 1964, at which time it was 7 percent lower than the base year of 1956. Thereafter totals began to rise again but leveled off and reached a new plateau in the late sixties.

Enrollments in professional programs dropped from 24,809 in 1969–70 to 23,950 in 1970–71, a decrease of *3.46* percent (American Association . . . , 1971). Conversely, enrollment in graduate programs beyond the first professional degree expanded from 3,865 to 4,734 in the same period, a sizable *22.48* percent increase. Thus, while there is no significant change ($+$ .03 percent) in the absolute number of student enrollments, a significantly higher percentage of the seminarians are seeking graduate degrees. (This represents the continuation of the trend established earlier; in 1960, 12.7 percent of all students were enrolled in graduate programs; by 1965, this had increased to 17.1 percent of total enrollment.) The constantly rising graduate enrollments suggest the possibility that many seminarians are seeking advanced specialization and perhaps careers alternative to the typical parish model.

Apart from the data for the schools of the AATS, the data on the larger Roman Catholic seminary system reveal even more significant changes within that church. Both the number of institutions and their total enrollment increased consistently during the fifties. The reversal of this trend set in during the mid-1960s. The number of seminarians belonging to Catholic religious orders peaked in 1963 and since then has decreased by a full 50 percent from 22,327 in 1964 to 11,589 in 1970. The enrollment in diocesan seminaries peaked two years later and has dropped consistently since. The total number of Catholic seminarians has decreased from 48,992 in 1965 to 28,819 in 1970. During this same period a large number of seminaries have closed altogether or consolidated with other seminaries. All of this has major implications for the church's future allocation of its manpower and for the future of the church itself. It is difficult as yet to say whether the substantial loss of priests and seminarians is a short-term reaction to the anxieties and upheavals of the sixties or is a long-range trend. One thing is clear; over and above the uncertainty and unrest which many Catholic clergymen share with the Protestant clergy, there are specific issues which confront the Catholic clergy: the theological question of birth control, divorce, and sexuality; the canonical question of celibacy; and the ecclesiological question of hierarchy and authority.

Until such time as the clergy of both the Protestant and Catholic churches are able to resolve their "crisis of self-confidence" and regain a strong sense of professional identity and a firmer footing in new forms of professional practice, it seems unlikely that they will be able to attract greater numbers to the theological schools and seminaries. There is also a question of the quality of people who offer themselves.

Not enough men of first class ability are being attracted to the ministry to meet the existing needs. Competition from other professions and occupations has become more acute over the last century. At one time the ministry was at the top of the professions in terms of status and prestige. This is no longer the case, and the churches face a difficult and constant task in recruiting and training men (Neibuhr & Williams, 1956, p. 275).

The problem might be relieved in some measure by the development of a new informal hierarchy, with the academic clergy possessing higher degrees at the top along with the administrators and statesmen of the church, followed by the parish ministers of the more prestigious local parishes, and they in turn being assisted by the paraprofessional permanent deacons and specialists in religious education, social services, and other activities. Each of these ranks might attract its own kind of people.

In any case the future of theological education will depend upon both the actual careers offered and the conception which people preparing for their life's work have of the mission of the churches and of the opportunities in it.

In this essay we have said nothing either of non-Christian theological training or of the education of the ministers of the black American Christians. The Jewish rabbi is educated in schools completely separated from universities, although he is usually a man of university education, often a man with higher degrees. Jews don't fear that higher education will weaken a man's sense of calling;

nor does there seem to be a crisis of self-confidence in Jewish theological education. It does appear that the more liberal reform seminary in Cincinnati depends for its staff on scholars of conservative training.

Whatever universal qualities the Christian religion may have, the communion cup is not one of them. The Protestant churches have separated the races at the baptismal font, at the marriage altar, at the graveside, and even at Sunday services. Yet American Negroes became ardent Christians and were very enterprising in establishing and maintaining churches. They founded colleges, very religious and financially very poor. Northern Protestant denominations also established colleges for Negroes in the South. These colleges produced many ministers for the Negro churches. But the churches have not developed theological seminaries. A handful of black men—Martin Luther King was one—entered seminaries and graduate schools of the larger, predominantly white denominations and universities. In the main, the Negro church has flourished without formal theological education. One can well ask whether the ministry is a true profession when so arbitrary a criterion as race plays a part in determining full colleagueship, either in the eyes of ministers or in the eyes of those who seek ministry.

Of course, one can ask whether the ministry is a true profession until all recognize the same faith and follow the same practices. That would be true, probably, only in a totalitarian state or in a state without religion. Since we are neither, it is likely that we will for a long time develop, in a pragmatic way, a good deal of theological consensus, with perhaps increasing areas of agreement but also with new sects and religious experiments arising from time to time. Theology educators had better keep their eye on the religious weather.

5. Social Work Education

by Arnold Gurin and David Williams

Social work education, like education for any profession, is dependent for many aspects of its development upon changes within the profession that it serves. At different times in different professions, education may be in the forefront of innovation in the field; at others it may simply be following and adapting itself to new trends in the world of practice. At all times, however, the professional school is involved in a system of interrelationships not only with the university community of which it is a part but with the professional field of practice for which its products are being prepared.

It is, therefore, appropriate to begin this discussion of education for social work with some comments on the current state of affairs in the social work profession. The present period is one of great ferment both in practice and in education for practice. Although our own analysis is not adequate to determine the matter precisely, it would seem that neither education nor practice is clearly leader or follower in this process. Rather, they are interacting with each other and with the world around in response to much larger forces that affect them both. In the literature that has grown up on the subject of social work as a profession, it is popular to describe social work as a "new," "young," or "emerging" profession (Kahn, 1959; Wilensky & Lebaux, 1965). The sense of not yet having arrived fully as a profession continues to pervade the field in spite of the fact that social work can identify a history of professionalization that goes back three-quarters of a century. As early as 1915, Abraham Flexner declared that social work lacked the attributes of a profession. Less surprising than that statement is the frequency and immediacy with which it has been quoted ever since, either to indicate the peculiar limitations of social work in the family of professions or to argue that Flexner was wrong and that social work is indeed a profession (Meyer, 1971).

In justifying his negative evaluation, Flexner pointed out that social work was lacking in several of the crucial attributes of a profession. He found social work deficient in professional attributes in the areas of intellectual knowledge and technique. One of the points that he stressed which continues to have relevance in a somewhat different context today is that social work, unlike professions that met his criteria, was not based on standards of *individual* responsibility of the practitioner.

The latter criticism points to one of the continuing characteristics of social work, which is its identification with organizational structures and institutions.[1] It has always been difficult to separate social work as a profession from the problems, policies, and commitments of the wide variety of organizations in which social workers practice. Such organizations touch many different segments of the society and do not by any means constitute a cohesive field of activity. They include governmental and voluntary structures and encompass multiple functions such as income maintenance, paramedical services, provision of institutional care for many different kinds of conditions, protective services for various handicapped and dependent groups, correctional measures to deal with deviant behavior, and counseling and therapeutic services to deal with interpersonal and intrapersonal problems, to mention but a few of the categories. Obviously, such diversity of functions has as one of its concomitants a broad spectrum of value commitments, some of which will inevitably contradict one another. One thus finds, for example, within a program such as public assistance, policies set by legislation and governmental officials that call for the imposition of sometimes harsh conditions to control the behavior of recipients, while professional social workers administering such programs are committed to the professional ethic of self-determination for their clients.

The crucial problem in this situation is that the social work profession does not control most of the organizations which employ social workers. In that respect, social work is different even from other professions that are embedded within institutions, such as the ministry and, at least to some extent, teaching. Social work, over

---

[1] It was estimated in 1967 that, of 42,000 practicing professional social workers, about 8 to 10 percent were in private practice and that the vast majority of these were practicing only part time (Golton, 1971, p. 952). In 1971, membership in the National Association of Social Workers was about 52,000, but there is no estimate of the numbers of private practitioners.

the past three-quarters of a century, has been able to establish hegemony in only a relatively small portion of the broad and diversified fields that it serves.

A few figures will suffice to document the character of social work manpower problems.

In 1960, it was estimated that there were some 105,000 persons in the United States occupying positions defined as social work. Of these, only some 20,000, or less than one-fifth, were completely professional in the sense that they had completed two full years of graduate education (U.S. Department of HEW, 1965, p. 34).

Equally significant is the uneven distribution of professional personnel among the different types of organizational programs. Thus, only 5.3 percent of all professional social workers with two years of graduate education were found in public assistance agencies, a drop from the comparable figure of 10.4 percent in 1950. In contrast, over one-fourth of all the fully trained professionals were in child-welfare work and almost one-fifth in psychiatric social work.

Even more graphic are the contrasts revealed by the figures indicating the ratio of trained to untrained social workers in the different fields. In 1960, only 3 percent of all the social workers in public assistance agencies had two years of professional education. On the other hand, 36 percent of social workers in other family services (primarily voluntary) had such training. The comparable figures were 41 percent for child welfare, 55 percent for medical social work, and 72 percent for psychiatric social work.

It is clear that there has been a strong tendency for the most fully trained and, therefore, the most professionalized social workers to gravitate toward specialized types of functions in which the distinctive professional techniques and values have become more firmly established than in the mass services dominated by governmental policies and particularly in the public assistance system. A special paradox reflected in these figures is the high proportion of professionals in medical and psychiatric settings where the dominant profession has tended to be medicine rather than social work. Except for rather small and limited areas, professional social workers have thus been largely ancillary to either politically dominated mass service systems or medically dominated professional systems.

The above figures describe the situation that existed in regard to the deployment of social work manpower at the beginning of the decade of the 1960s, prior to the very substantial expansion of all human service programs that occurred during the Kennedy and Johnson administrations. Unfortunately, there is no body of data available that would make it possible to analyze in quantitative terms how that expansion influenced the manpower situation in social work.[2] It is obvious, however, that the governmental programs of the 1960s had a profound effect both on the social work profession and on social work education.

A task force of the Department of Health, Education and Welfare was set up in the mid-1960s to look into the problem of social work manpower. Its report, submitted in November 1965, reviewed demand and supply in various areas of governmental activity and cataloged the serious shortages found in almost every category. The report reflected the gap between the heightened demand generated by new and expanded governmental programs in public welfare, mental health, medical care, antipoverty, and others and the numbers receiving professional training in schools of social work at that time. Its recommendations stressed the need for rapid expansion of social work education at both the graduate and undergraduate levels to "close the gap."

It is interesting to review the report of the task force in the light of subsequent events. All of the issues that face the profession today were envisaged in the report, but the recommendations tended to emphasize the traditional reliance of the profession upon graduate training as the major solution to its manpower problems. While the nature of the problem was identified with reasonable accuracy, the suggested solutions have proved to be quite unrealistic.

The report pointed to the lack of adequate data on the actual supply and demand factors affecting manpower in the human services and, therefore, the difficulty of dealing with the problem in precise terms. Perhaps even more serious was the lack of adequate information about what the job requirements in the various fields served by social workers actually were and what levels and types of training were necessary to perform different categories of tasks. For some time prior to this task force, it had been recognized that not all tasks carried out by social agencies required graduate training. The task force agreed, but lacked information on which to determine what level of education should be required for particular tasks or responsibilities.

The task force concluded that large numbers of additional social

[2] An ambitious program of manpower studies is now under way. See U.S. Department of HEW, 1971.

workers would be needed in the coming years, even if the necessary goal of "reorganization of social welfare services and more effective utilization of available manpower" (U.S. Department of HEW, 1965, p. 82) were to be achieved. The report set forth a number of projections of the likely demand for social workers in various fields. It called for a tripling of graduate enrollment in graduate schools of social work within the next five years, supporting that recommendation with listings of demands from various public services. The projections reflected the commitment of these services to the goal of greater professionalization, since they called for increasing not only the numbers of trained workers but also the *ratio* of trained to untrained personnel. Thus, the projected demand in the public assistance system involved increasing the proportion of trained staff to 33 percent in 1970. In the public child-welfare services, trained personnel were to constitute fully 92 percent of the total by 1970 (U.S. Department of HEW, November 1965, p. 39).

The report clearly carried water on both shoulders. In addition to these very large (and obviously unrealistic) projections of the numbers of social workers with complete graduate training, the report called for substantial expansion as well in undergraduate training. It was forward-looking in recommending that graduates of a baccalaureate degree program in social work be accorded professional status—a recommendation that was implemented five years later. The report also called for other categories of nonprofessional personnel such as aides and technicians without spelling out their functions or training requirements. On the other hand, considerable stress was placed on the need for greater professionalization through licensing provisions for those accorded professional status, as well as for higher salary levels and better status for professional social workers.

In the period since the issuance of the task force report, the profession has grown substantially. Graduate enrollment in schools of social work in the United States rose from 7,196 in 1964 to 12,821 in 1970, a growth of 78 percent. This rate of growth represented an average annual increase of 13 percent, compared with an annual average rate of 8 percent in the previous decade (U.S. Department of HEW, November 1965, p. 80). Significant though this expansion was, it failed by far to reach the target of the task force, which had called for tripling the numbers—the actual increase resulted in less than a doubling of the number of graduates per year.

It must be concluded that the task force lacked realism in its projection and that it was continuing to rely more heavily than warranted on the traditional standard of professionalism. That is to say, it was anticipating that a larger proportion of social welfare positions would be filled by professionals with graduate training than is now the case or than is likely to be the case in the future. Only fragmentary data are available for the period since 1965. It seems likely, however, that social workers with graduate training constitute a smaller proportion of the total supply of social work manpower than they did in 1965. For example, an analysis of the membership of the National Association of Social Workers (NASW) in 1969 (with membership at that time limited to those who held at least a master's degree) indicated that only 36.5 percent were in positions that involved rendering direct services to clients, as compared with 51 percent in 1961 (Meyer, 1971, p. 964).

In addition, the intervening years have brought about a change in thinking as to the validity of the earlier assumptions concerning the actual need for full professional training in regard to at least some of the positions in social welfare and, more generally, in all the emerging human service fields. The antipoverty and related programs of the middle and late 1960s stressed the desirability of improving the social and economic opportunities of disadvantaged segments of the population by offering them training and employment opportunities in the human service programs. Supporting that objective though for other reasons was the allegation that all human service professions are deficient in meeting the needs of the disadvantaged elements who made up their clientele. It became widely accepted that "indigenous" personnel, drawn from the client population itself, were necessary at many points in the direct service activities to give more adequate, understanding, and empathic service to the people who needed it.

All these factors served to accentuate the situation that was described at the beginning of this paper—namely, the inability of the social work profession to establish hegemony or even a dominant position in its field of service. To the extent that social workers were involved in the expanding programs, they were to be found primarily in supervisory and administrative positions rather than in line positions rendering direct service to clients.

These developments gave impetus to the awareness, noted in the task force report of 1965 and discussed for many years prior to that time, of the need to develop a hierarchy, or "ladder," of professional positions. The persistent discrepancy between the numbers of fully trained workers and the numbers of personnel in the mass service fields had made it necessary to think about alternatives to the rigid model of the master of social work (M.S.W.) degree as the sole echelon in the professional service. For years it has been said that several different levels of practice should be identified, with appropriate differentiations as to the level of education and training required for each. The implementation of this obviously necessary policy foundered, however, on the difficulty of clarifying the differential elements of knowledge and skill on which the policy would have to rest. The 1965 task force called for further study of these matters, as did other professional bodies before and since. In a situation in which both trained and untrained workers were frequently being called upon to do essentially the same tasks in many areas of direct client practice, this has proved, thus far, to be an impossible assignment. Differentials continue to be defined as they have in the past by "input" rather than "output" criteria—i.e., by level of educational requirements rather than by job content.

The realities of the pressures described above did, however, prevail and brought about a modification in the basic definition of professionalism. The major breakthrough came in 1970, when the National Association of Social Workers agreed to admit to full membership individuals who had obtained a bachelor's degree in an undergraduate program of social welfare, provided only that this program meet criteria established by the Council on Social Work Education, the accrediting body for graduate programs.

The change was by no means a casual one, nor had it been easily achieved. Indeed, proposals to relax the membership requirements in the professional association had been under discussion for at least 12 years before the new regulations were formally instituted in April 1970. The major significance of the change was that the M.S.W. was no longer the first professional degree, but its position in this respect was replaced by the baccalaureate degree. In addition, the NASW established, for the first time, an associate membership category that was made available to individuals who had a baccalaureate degree in a field other than social work or social welfare but who were employed in some social work capacity.[3]

[3] It was left to the board of the NASW to struggle with the very difficult issue of how to define a "social work" job.

Provision was made for the possibility of shifting members from associate to regular membership after at least two years of experience and some further education, still to be specified.

Although the change is significant in revealing a shift in concepts and an adaptation to the pressures of the times, it is much too early to determine what its full impact will be upon the profession. The vast majority of members of the NASW continue to be graduates of master's degree programs in social work, and it will be many years before there is a significant proportion of members without graduate education. The number of associate members is still negligible. It is not as yet clear whether those newly defined as having a place in the profession will in fact feel identified with it or will consider that membership in the NASW is of sufficient value to them to warrant the cost.[4]

While the relaxation of membership requirements was probably the most important single development in the changing position of the social work profession, other trends and crosscurrents merit at least a brief comment.

Perhaps the most important of all the trends in the past decade was the renewed emphasis on social action. Community action programs financed by the federal government provided the means, for a time, for the organization of citizen groups in low-income urban neighborhoods to engage in protest activity of varying degrees of militance. Professional social workers, among others, became involved in the organization and leadership of such groups as community organizers and consultants. Such activities called for new definitions of professional roles. The idea of "advocacy" as a professional responsibility became very popular not only for the social workers in neighborhood organization, but for those in service bureaucracies. The notion of the social worker as a change agent received widespread approval, but there were many different conceptions of how such a role was to be performed.

A radical position called for militant attacks upon the existing service systems, such as public welfare, education, and housing administration. The "welfare rights" movement was an effort to organize recipients of public assistance to bring pressure upon public welfare administrations to correct faulty implementation of the welfare laws and regulations or, more broadly, to bring about im-

---

[4] The cost of NAWS membership is not small. The board of directors proposed and the membership accepted, in April 1972, uniform national dues of $60 per year for all regular members regardless of position and earnings.

proved benefits. Some professional social workers were actively involved as organizers of this movement. Others were advocates and helpers of its cause, providing not only their expert knowledge of the welfare system but also guidance on the strategy and tactics of protest.

These trends were notable particularly in the area of social work practice known as community organization. Prior to the expansion of the 1960s, it had been customary to view social work as a single profession in which there were three discernible *methods* of practice—casework, group work, and community organization. All were conceptualized as a client-oriented, helping process directed toward the achievement of client-determined goals. There had always been a value framework that combined concern for the improvement of social conditions with help to the client in achieving better social functioning and self-realization. It is generally recognized that the drive for professionalization had the effect of stressing the individual adjustment elements in that value framework, while the social change commitment frequently received only lip service. It was always more prominent, however, in some segments of the field than in others, and the commitment to a reform ideology was never completely absent.

At the point when the profession began to feel the impact of new postwar demands stemming from the racial tensions and the renewed awareness of poverty and deprivation in the disadvantaged segments of the society, it was dominated overwhelmingly by casework practitioners. Community organization, planning, and policy making constituted a very small segment of the total professional personnel. These functions were performed for the most part by administrators, managers, or expert consultants in the public and voluntary service organizations. The community action programs opened up new types of positions in the area of community organization, quite different in context, style, and basic objective from those that had been previously characteristic of community organization practice. It became necessary to differentiate several different "models" of such practice, ranging from grass-roots organization of disadvantaged groups at the neighborhood level to broad policy-making functions in large-scale governmental bureaucracies (Rothman, 1968).

Simultaneously, there were parallel modifications in the conceptions of practice at the level of direct service to clients. Even before the expansion of programs in the 1960s, indeed during the entire post-World War II period, there had been a gradual broadening of the theoretical foundations of casework practice and the development of a wider range of intervention approaches than the traditional one-to-one therapeutic practice model based for the most part on psychoanalytic theory. Work with multiproblem families was receiving attention some years prior to the rediscovery of poverty, and agencies began to recognize an obligation to "reach out" to clients more aggressively so that those needing services would in fact receive them. Family treatment, group therapy, and crisis intervention were some of the newer modalities of treatment that were described and advocated. Such a modification in the casework model did, however, continue to rest on counseling as the major component of the professional service to be rendered by social workers. It was not until more recent years that the efficacy of counseling came sharply under question by those who advocated that social workers devote themselves to the effort to secure greater resources for people in need and to try to change the conditions under which the disadvantaged live.[5]

It is very difficult to state in any general way what professional social work practice comprises at this point in history (early 1972) after some two decades of ferment and adaptation. A systematic study (which has not been undertaken) would undoubtedly reveal that many agencies and practitioners are conducting their activity as they always have, despite some changes at the level of rhetoric. Equally certainly, however, such a study would reflect a very wide range of roles, functions, and tasks—and many differing views held by professional social workers as to the rationale for their activities.

If that description of the present situation is accurate, then any attempt to generalize would be an oversimplification. Nevertheless, it is possible to identify two major tendencies that exist simultaneously within the profession. One is the tendency for the profession to become divided on the issues of "practice" (which refers primarily to direct services to clients, i.e., casework) versus "social action" or "social policy." Sometimes this division may take a philosophical form, as in the arguments over whether the role of the professional should be to help individuals adjust to an unjust social system or

[5] Early in 1971, the Community Service Society of New York, one of the oldest and most traditional casework agencies in the country, decided to shift its program from casework counseling to rendering service to indigenous neighborhood organizations.

to help people to change that system. It also enters into disputes about where the professional association should place its efforts — in the improvement of professional standards of work and the protection of practitioners or in political and legislative activity (Richan, 1969).

The contradictory tendency is to attempt a redefinition of practice that would resolve the supposedly contradictory strains between practice and policy in a new integrated view of a broadened conception of the social worker's professional role and responsibility. Such a reconciliation is not too difficult to achieve at the level of broad ideological and value commitments. Thus, the National Association of Social Workers has committed itself to certain reformist policy objectives and has become more active constantly in pressing its views in legislative and administrative channels. Such positions have the broad support of its membership, regardless of their particular commitments to one or another professional method.

There is great conceptual difficulty, however, in the attempt to build action objectives into the actual *practice* of the professional. This is difficult to achieve even in the field of community organization, where problems have arisen in trying to distinguish between professional and strictly political types of activity. It is even less feasible at the level of direct client service. Recent attempts either to rethink the common professional base for all of social work practice (Bartlett) or to find a professional framework for a social change orientation in casework (Rein) are interesting but still very preliminary formulations. It is not at all clear that they set any direction for future work (Bartlett, 1971; Rein, 1970, pp. 13–28; Kraft, 1969, pp. 343–366).

The net result of all of this is that the profession of social work is extremely pluralistic at the present time and likely to remain so as long as can now be foreseen. Different elements within the field are closely related to medicine, others to psychology and psychotherapy, others to urban affairs. A broader field of human services at the level of public administration and public policy is emerging that incorporates many different disciplines, professions, and vocations, including some segments of social work. The professional social work establishment, as represented in the national association, necessarily attempts to keep all these elements together and to strengthen the unifying elements of the profession. As a result, multiple objectives are pursued simultaneously, some of which tend to work at contradictory purposes. One major development, as we have seen, was the opening of professional membership to people with less than graduate training. At the other pole, the association maintains an Academy of Certified Social Workers to give additional recognition to more highly trained and experienced social workers, and is now advocating that there be an examination for admission to the academy. It is also pursuing the attempt to have social workers licensed in the various states. These are continuing efforts to obtain greater professional control over the fields in which social workers are employed. To date, however, most of these efforts are subject to continuing frustration because the profession has not established this hegemony and most positions continue to be occupied by social workers without professional status.

It is obvious that the tasks of an educational system that is attempting to prepare people for practice are enormously difficult if the profession itself is in the state of ferment that has been described. Social work education today is faced with the task of preparing students for a rapidly changing, fluid, and ill-defined field of professional practice. There is in truth no single field of practice, but many. It is therefore to be expected, as the ensuing discussion will show, that social work education is similarly pluralistic, ill-defined, and subject to a great deal of instability and change. Within less than a decade, the educational system in social work has moved from a relatively uniform curricular format to a highly permissive and flexible set of options open to schools and to individual students within schools. Increasingly, the view is expressed that schools cannot prepare students for any specific roles in the future, since these are not possible to predict, but that they should try to help students to acquire some basic concepts and tools that will arm them for dealing with the major characteristics of future professional responsibilities—namely, change and uncertainty.

THE CHANGING SCHOOLS Social work education in the past decade and in the immediate present has been at least as volatile as has the professional practice of social work. Some of the salient aspects of the changing scene will be described under the following headings:

1   Statistical Trends
2   Student Characteristics
3   Curricular Developments

Statistical Trends One of the major characteristics of the recent past has been *growth*.[6] The number of accredited graduate schools of social work in the United States grew from 51 in 1952 to 56 in 1960 to 70 in 1970; and the number is continuing to grow rapidly. In 1970, 10 additional graduate schools were in operation and working toward accreditation and several others were planning to open in the near future (Pins, 1971, p. 9). The number of full-time students enrolled in master's degree programs rose from 3,944 in 1952 to 12,821 in 1970—more than a threefold increase. The number of master's degrees awarded also tripled, rising from 1,946 to 5,638 in the 18-year period.

The growth in social work graduate education was considerably higher proportionally than the overall increase in the total population graduating from college. The number of master's of social work (M.S.W.) degrees awarded for 10,000 of all bachelor's degrees obtained two years earlier rose from 45 in 1952 to 85 in 1969.[7]

Year-by-year rates of enrollment growth reached a peak in the mid-1960s, when many types of social service programs were expanding with enlarged support from the federal government. The figures in the accompanying table indicate the acceleration during that period as well as the tapering off in the rate of increase in enrollment in graduate schools of social work in more recent years.

Despite the tapering off of the rate of increase after the peak year 1965–66, the growth in enrollment in the last year on which information is available continued to be at a higher rate than the average of the period preceding 1963. Whether this rate of increase will continue is uncertain. There seems to be some lessening in demand for social workers due to retrenchment in a number of the programs of the 1960s. On the other hand, it is not yet clear that

---

[6] Except where specifically indicated, information in this section is based on annual publications of the Council on Social Work Education, New York, entitled *Statistics on Social Work Education*. The latest edition (1970) contains information as of November 1, 1970.

[7] Unpublished material of the Council on Social Work Education, based on its own statistical compilations, and the American Council on Education (1969, p. 9191).

Rate of enrollment increase for graduate schools of social work, 1962–1970	*Period*	*Percentage increase by years*
	1962–63	9.2
	1963–64	12.4
	1964–65	13.1
	1965–66	14.7
	1966–67	9.0
	1967–68	6.6
	1968–69	8.0
	1969–70	9.5

SOURCE: Council on Social Work Education (1969, table 200).

enrollment has been affected by that development or that the demand will continue to decline.

Growth was not restricted to the students at the master's level. There was at least comparable expansion of undergraduate education—a development of particular significance, as discussed in the previous section. Pins reported in 1971 that there were about 750 undergraduate programs in social welfare in the United States. Such programs are very diverse, ranging from a single course to a full major. They include, however, 184 programs that are structured to meet the membership requirements of the Council on Social Work Education. Such programs must have full-time faculty and sequences of courses and must provide field instruction. They are programs geared to preparing students for beginning levels of practice, in accordance with the newly adopted policy of recognizing a bachelor's degree instead of a master's degree as the permissible entry point into professional practice. In 1970, a total of 6,247 students were enrolled in the "approved" programs.

Not included in these figures are numerous courses, sequences, or programs in junior colleges and community colleges that attempt to prepare students for other positions in social service organizations that do not have professional status. Thus, social welfare is one of the fields in which students pursuing a two-year degree (associate in arts) may specialize. Because of the relative newness of these developments, there is as yet no body of systematic data to describe trends precisely, but it is known that the number of such programs is growing rapidly. As noted earlier, the growth in training is not necessarily reflected in the actual labor market since many of the positions in social service organization do not as yet require such specific background. That is part of the problem of professionalization of the field that was discussed earlier.

At the other end of the continuum — i.e., in education beyond the master's level — the same pattern of growth prevailed. In 1952, the total enrollment in post-master's programs of all types was 62. By 1970, the number had risen to 384, and in the same period the number of doctoral degrees awarded rose from 8 to 84. In 1970, 22 schools of social work were offering doctoral degrees. Of these, 12 offered a doctor of social work or social welfare (D.S.W.), 9 a Ph.D., and 1 both a D.S.W. and a Ph.D. Doctoral programs are designed to prepare people primarily for teaching and research and, to a lesser extent, for administrative positions in practice. Some post-master's programs are concerned with training for more advanced levels of clinical work, but they are the exception. In general, the great increase in doctoral programs was a response to the general expansion in social work education and the need generated by that expansion for a parallel expansion in teaching personnel. Increasingly, it became necessary for social work faculty to have doctorates if they were to participate fully in the universities of which they were a part.

In all the figures that have been cited, only full-time students were included. Many schools do offer opportunities for part-time work, and a growing number of them conduct programs of "continuing education" for the benefit of practitioners of various types. It is difficult to generalize about these activities except to indicate that they are another aspect of growth in the total field of social work education. It is estimated that about two-thirds of all schools now conduct some form of continuing education and that the number of such programs is growing. The growing importance of the area of continuing education is reflected in the fact that the Council on Social Work Education has recently established a national committee to deal with this subject and has allocated staff time to provide consultation to schools developing such programs. The changing demands of the field, involving new types of programs, new professional and nonprofessional roles, and new categories of personnel, generate needs for specialized short-term training of many types, including such diverse functions as management and administration, supervision, training of volunteers and/or nonprofessionals, community organization, and "advocacy" (Boehm, 1971, pp. 266–267).

Social work, perhaps earlier and more urgently than some other
professions, has been challenged to provide opportunities for minorities to enter higher levels of education and practice. It is, therefore, not surprising that the proportion of students who come from
economically disadvantaged minority groups has risen in the past
decade. In 1960, social work was already attracting a disproportionate share of black students. At that time, 10 percent of all graduate
students in social work were blacks, whereas blacks constituted
only 5 percent of the total graduate school population in all fields.
That proportion remained relatively stable for the first half of the
decade. During the latter half of the 1960s, however, there was a
substantial rise in the proportion of students from all minority
groups. In 1970, the breakdown of all first-year master's degree
students was as follows:

White	75.8%	*American Indian*	0.6%
Black	14.5%	*Asian American*	1.5%
Chicano	1.8%	*Other (including foreign)*	3.6%
Puerto Rican	2.5%		

The same trend is evident at the post-master's level. Similar proportions appear in post-M.S.W. programs in which, in 1970, 11.7
percent of the students were black and 3.9 percent were of other
minorities.

   In looking toward the future, it seems safe to predict continuing
pressure to increase the numbers of minority group students at all
levels of social work education. No information is available on the
numbers now enrolled in undergraduate baccalaureate and associate in arts programs, but these should reach very large proportions
in the immediate future. Governmental policy in the support of
educational programs in the human service fields is continuing to
emphasize priority for the education of members of minority
groups. That policy has its justification both in the need to find
fields of employment for minority groups that provide opportunities for upward mobility and in the fact that large numbers of the
clientele of the social services are themselves members of minority
groups.

   Other demographic characteristics of the social work student
body that have some significance in relation to the changing
character of the field are sex and age. Part of the historical problem

of the struggle of social work toward higher professional status has been its public image as a female profession. While the great majority of the master's degree students are still women (72 percent in 1970), the reverse is true at the post-master's level, where 70 percent of all enrolled students are men. Within the master's degree group, there are also variations in relation to particular specializations. Thus, among students specializing in community organization, administration, and planning in 1966, it was found that 60 percent were men.

The women students tend to enter graduate school earlier than the men. More than half (53 percent) of all master's degree women students were 25 years of age and under in 1970, compared with only 31 percent of the men students. The modal age group for men is 26 to 30 (41 percent of the total male student body), whereas less than one-fourth (24 percent) of women students are in this group. At the other end of the age spectrum, a somewhat larger proportion of women than of men students are over 40 years of age (9.3 percent compared with 6.1 percent).

Age distribution of social work graduate students as of November 1970

	Percent	
	Men	*Women*
25 and under	31.3	52.9
26–30	40.7	24.1
31–35	14.7	8.1
36–40	7.2	5.6
41–45	4.1	4.9
45 and over	2.0	4.4
TOTAL	100.0	100.0

SOURCE: Council on Social Work Education (1970, p. 24).

It is clear from the figures in the accompanying table that women are more likely than men to enter graduate school directly from college. In part, this may be attributable to the time spent by some men in military service between the point of graduation from college and entry into graduate school. In addition, however, it has been suggested that women tend to decide upon a social work career earlier in their educational career than men (Golden et al, 1972).

In general, it has been found that social work tends to be a "second choice" career for many who enter it (Pins, 1963, pp. 134–

135). Not as well known as other professions, such as teaching, law, business, or medicine, social work becomes visible as a career possibility for most students toward the latter part of their college experience or after graduation. A study of entering master's degree students in 1966 found, however, that they had entered at a somewhat earlier age than a comparable group some six years earlier. While the second-choice phenomenon was still evident, there was a slight change toward making the choice for social work somewhat earlier in life (Golden et al., 1972).

It has also been found that there are substantial socioeconomic differences between men and women who choose social work as a career. A national survey of college students and a survey of first-year social work graduate students both found that women choosing social work were higher on many measures of socioeconomic status than their men student counterparts (Golden, et al., 1972; and Gockel, 1966). The fathers of women students had better jobs, their parents were better educated, and they came from homes with larger family incomes than the men students. This difference was captured in the title of one of the studies, *Silk Stockings and Blue Collars.*

A number of other changes have been observed among students choosing social work as a career during the middle and late 1960s in regard to attitudes and motivations. These are, however, largely impressionistic and do not rest on firm statistical data. They are reported here on the basis of two sources: (1) the 1966 Golden-Pins-Jones study cited earlier and (2) interviews that were conducted with faculty during visits to several schools in different parts of the country.

The 1966 study found that social work graduate students entering in 1966 were somewhat stronger academically than those who had enrolled in 1960. They had better undergraduate grade-point averages and came more often from more "selective" institutions than did members of earlier classes. Many students made their decision about field of graduate study after actual post-B.A. work experience in social work–related fields and particularly over the last years in Great Society programs. By 1966, over 90 percent of incoming students had had preprofessional work experience of some type, either as undergraduates or between college and graduate school.

It is the impression of faculty informants whose views were

tapped for this paper that the social work graduate students have been more career-oriented and less militantly idealistic or cynical than their undergraduate counterparts. They are, however, "children of their decade." They seem to believe more firmly than did their predecessors that the most important changes in the condition of the poor, the sick, and the oppressed will come about as the result of societal and institutional restructuring rather than induced changes in the character, behavior, or feelings of the individual victims of the system. And they feel more strongly than have professionals in the past that the proper aim of their efforts must be a change in the condition imposed upon the poor and the disadvantaged.

One reflection of that shift in motivation was the relative decline in enrollment during the decade in casework concentrations and the parallel rise in community organization. Thus the number of students concentrating in community organization rose from 1 percent in 1960 to 9 percent in 1970, while those specializing only in casework declined from 74 percent to 36 percent of all students.[8]

It was the impression of many of those interviewed for this study that the students' pressure for change has been directed, however, less to the content of the social work program than to the *process* of education. Today's student seems much more oriented toward a pleasant and productive experience while still in school than was the student of the past, who expected pleasure and productivity to begin, more often, upon graduation. Today's graduate student has done considerable thinking about how he or she shall be taught and has had, in previous schooling, experience of innovative and engaging teaching. Such students demand that faculty be well-prepared, collectively wide-ranging, and individually committed to their subjects and to their roles as teachers.

Admissions officers and faculty members remark upon the decrease in the numbers of students pursuing degrees while on leave from employing agencies (such as the large public welfare bureaucracies) and the relative increase of students whose goal is the learning offered in the schools, with lessened emphasis upon grades

---

[8] Most of the decline in the casework enrollment was due to the broadening of the curriculum toward a more "generic" approach, which combines casework with group work or community organization, or eliminates such specializations althogether. This approach will be discussed later in reviewing curriculum developments.

and degrees. Students are aware of, and demand, a wide variety of teaching methods—direct experience, games, videotapes, etc.—and insist that the lecture method be used sparingly. Above all, they want involvement in the learning process. They are less willing to "endure" the present merely for the sake of the future.

Schools of social work have also been subject to student demands for greater participation in governance and have responded by developing faculty-student structures for policy making in all major areas of the educational program.

Curricular Developments Both student demands and the rapidly changing demands of the field of practice combined to bring about major modifications in the curriculum. The one major characteristic of this change is a constantly broadening diversity. That diversity is apparent at all levels. Schools differed more from one another in 1970 than they did in 1960, and students within given schools had available to them a much greater number of options and differed more from one another in their programs of study than was true of their counterparts 10 years earlier.

At the national level, these trends may be traced through a series of curricular policy statements adopted by the Council on Social Work Education as guidelines for its accreditation function in relation to graduate social work education. The first such statement was adopted in 1952. It was modified in 1962 and then revised much more radically in 1969. In 1952, the curriculum clearly called for a strong base in a psychological or psychotherapeutic frame of reference and in "person-to-person" practice. This was broadened in 1962, when the theoretical base was defined as "Human Behavior and the Social Environment" instead of "Human Growth and Behavior," and parity was accorded to casework, group work, and community organization as equally legitimate concentrations in learning a systematic "method" of social work practice.

By 1969, the national policy statement abandoned all requirements that a school structure its curriculum in any prescribed sequences or that it offer any specified areas of concentration. It stated the general goals of social work education in terms of social work professional values and commitments to service of people, social change, etc., and outlined areas of knowledge that were to be reflected in a curriculum. It left schools great flexibility, however, in the way they could organize these elements. Subsequently, in 1971, the format of social work education was modified further through adoption by the council of a policy permitting schools to decrease the residence requirement for students who had completed undergraduate studies in social welfare, thus opening the way to the five-year undergraduate-graduate continuum as against the four-year bachelor's plus the two-year master's program which had been an almost universal requirement, except for special programs approved by the council as experiments for a limited time.

The field visits to schools that one of us made in 1971 found the schools operating under the new conditions of flexibility made possible by the council's relaxed requirements. The following observations are indicative of current curricular trends.

In the schools visited for this study, the curriculum built on a single method (casework) or even a choice among three methods (casework, group work, or community organization) is no longer the dominant model as it was less than 10 years ago. Some groups of students still get a rather traditional educational experience, and for this group, the program is largely prescribed—i.e., all students take the same set of courses in the same sequence and cover the same material in about the same depth. But for an increasing number of students who may, by now, be a majority, the curriculum operates much more as a market or grab bag from which they may select a unique combination of courses taken in a unique sequence.

Many mechanisms have been developed by faculties to provide such individualization. Some of the more important ones are:

Proliferation of courses
Particularly in those schools which see themselves as "problem" rather than "method" oriented, many subjects are broken down into highly specialized one-semester courses, including courses dealing with such provocative topics as social action and community action programs, drug use and abuse, belief and value systems in social work, crisis intervention in social work practice, government and health services, metropolitan problems and urban change, racism in American society, gerontology, and housing problems. Alongside this growth in number and diversity of formal courses, we see a rise in common use of readings courses and tutorials to provide independent investigation in highly specialized areas.

Variety in field placements
Concomitant with the increase in breadth and depth of offerings in classroom courses has been the proliferation of varied settings and

experiences in field instruction available to the student today. Placements outside traditional social work settings are now commonplace; housing authorities, mayors' offices, congressional offices, labor unions, county agricultural extension offices, international exchange bureaus, and other nontraditional organizations not only have provided new settings, but require (because these settings do not have M.S.W.'s on the payroll) new fieldwork supervisory arrangements. Students placed in nontraditional fieldwork settings must seek supervision from classroom faculty. Such supervision frequently takes the form of consultations or seminars rather than the familiar form of immediate work direction. Equally important is the development of field settings organized and operated by the schools themselves. In such arrangements, generally known as "training centers," faculty members take some responsibility for the actual work of the organization or agency as well as supervise student work. Training centers are somewhat analogous to the teaching hospital in medical education (Jones, 1969).

Modular units

One school in particular is experimenting with the idea that the subject content of courses does not lend itself to completion within either semesters or quarters, but, instead, should be taught in discrete modular units which might be covered in one session or in many weeks and which could be shuffled in a variety of combinations to form several types of courses.

Avoidance of redundancy

Much of this flowering of courses, subjects, and content is in answer to the plea of students for greater breadth and depth in social work education, but it is also a reflection of the better undergraduate preparation of the incoming student. In particular, the advent in large numbers of students holding bachelor's degrees in social work has forced the schools to avoid repetition of materials which these students are likely to have covered in their undergraduate study. One mechanism used by schools to avoid redundant education is the institution of the "challenge." If the student believes that he already has an adequate knowledge of the subject matter of a course, he can "challenge" that course and either be peremptorily excused upon examination of his academic record or take a preprepared test on the subject matter. With the use of discrete modular units, the student may do the same thing in relation to any one of the units.

Loss of orthodoxy

In the early 1960s it was possible for an entire school of social work to have a reputation for being a "Freudian" or a "Rankian" school, etc. By 1969, such a designation could not cover a third of the teaching and learning foundations of a school of social work. In part, this is true simply because of the acceptance by social workers of a wide variety of theoretical approaches leading to a similar variety of practice methodologies, ranging from the renewed popularity of learning and behavior theories to radical socialist critiques and social action methodologies.

The more diversified curriculum mentioned above is both cause and effect of the new heterodoxy. It is also the result of the wider range of student undergraduate preparation and work experience and of the growing tendency of faculty to treat the master's program more and more as if it were doctoral study. The questions raised by the difficulties experienced by the profession in trying to make its contribution to the eradication of poverty, injustice, and illness during the past decade have added impetus to the search for new theories and methods.

The development of a career continuum of paraprofessionals, A.B.'s, M.S.W.'s, and Ph.D.'s, which tends to remove the advanced degree graduates from direct service giving and creates administrative and planning roles for these personnel (frequently outside the traditional social work agencies), has operated to further underscore the need for variety in preparation and knowledge.

Social science disciplines

One of the major changes in the curriculum has been the extension of the range of social science disciplines that it incorporates. Two studies made at different points in time (1958 and 1965) provide an opportunity to examine this change in some detail.

In 1958, Grace Coyle examined the curricula of 52 accredited schools of social work. She found that most of the curricula were directed to the preparation of workers who would deal with the psychosocial relations of the clientele of social agencies and that personality theory as derived from Freud and Rank and their followers and developed in the fields of psychiatry and psychoanalysis was seen as the basic theoretical knowledge to be communicated. Schools to varying degrees also included the following "core" areas in descending order of frequency: (1) small-group process and structure—the individual and his relation to a group; the philosophy, goals, and techniques of the group worker; group formation; group goals; roles; and the relation of the group to the surrounding society; (2) culture as a behavioral determinant—the most widespread anthropological and sociological theory current in social work at that time; (3) family structure—age and sex roles in the family and developmental stages; (4) social ecology—the significance of the physical "layout" of communities; (5) social norms and values—ethnic, racial, religious, and socioeconomic class patterns and social differentiation.

Schools included in the 1958 study also offered from one to five courses drawn from economics and political science and dealing with subjects traditionally linked to social work. These courses were variously called Social Insurance, Income Maintenance Programs, Public and Private Services, and The Law and Social Welfare. Many, but not all, schools offered courses that would help to prepare their graduates to assume roles as public administrators, and some course content in these schools generally dealt with the functions of government, the institutions of the state and political democracy, personnel administration, budgeting, and the relations of public and private organizations. Several schools offered information about income distribution in our society, characteristics of the economic system (wages, profits), and theories of taxation. Perhaps the most important point to be made about these courses in political science and economics is that they were almost entirely *descriptive* in character. They were not seen as an integral element of practice and, therefore, did not concentrate on the development of analytic skills, but were largely limited to explicating the context of social welfare programs and activities. Offerings in sociology, except as they related to the small group or the neighborhood, were few. However, the introduction into the curriculum of a new content area was already beginning to emerge. Small in size and available at only four or five large schools, this content area centered on the process of social change, social reform, and social planning and included material on social movements, the power structure of American communities, civil rights, housing, neighborhoods, war, and "social normalcy."

As part of a general study of the community organization curriculum of graduate schools of social work in 1965, Armand Lauffer surveyed the course content of 20 schools, including all but one of the graduate schools which then offered a two-year curriculum in community organization (Gurin, 1970, Chap. 2). The schools included were primarily concentrated in the Northern and Eastern quarter of the United States, but there was some representation of schools from the South and the Far West.

Lauffer makes a distinction between "basic" social science courses and "social science–related" courses. Basic courses were those judged equivalent to others that might be taught in an academic department. Related courses were those dealing with social science content from the point of view of a social welfare practitioner. Any course in which concentration on social work practice, values, ethics, and role predominated over social science content was omitted from the study.

Most schools required for graduation from 36 to 44 units, in addition to fieldwork for graduation. Of these, 10.8 units, on the average, were required in basic social science courses, while 9.5 units were required in social science–related course work. Thus, students were taking one-half or more of their work in the social sciences in addition to social work methods and courses dealing with social welfare institutions.

Lauffer calculated that about 40 percent of the social science courses dealt with psychological and social-psychological content, primarily individual and small-group behavior, as well as personality and culture; about 35 percent of the courses were primarily sociological; about 25 percent were devoted to the teaching of research and statistics; and a small fraction of the courses fell into the categories of political science and economics.

The major shift in the seven years between the two studies was from a psychological to a sociological emphasis. In addition, the range of social science theory drawn upon by social work education has been considerably expanded. The courses of the late 1960s dealt with the broad sociological, economic, and political science areas which have played important parts in these disciplines within the academic departments: community analysis, power and decision making, theories of social change, macroeconomic analysis, urban economics, manpower, learning theory, general systems theory, complex organizations, etc. Furthermore, this content is now presented in separate, discrete courses rather than as mere segments of an omnibus "foundations" course as was common a few years ago. Thus, social science theory is now wider-ranging and, at the same time, presented more "purely"; i.e., subjects are covered in depth for their intrinsic theoretical importance rather than solely for their direct connection with social welfare practice and institutions.

The shift to analysis

Both in social science and in other curricular areas, the focus of much of the curriculum has become less descriptive and more analytic. Thus, earlier courses in social policy or administration, for example, consisted of extensive lists of governmental programs and their characteristics, frequently presented in chronological order, detailing the history of these programs and their successive modifications. The achievement demanded of the learner in such courses was that of increased familiarity with the resources which could be brought to bear in the service of a client or an agency.

In contrast, the schools of the late 1960s approached frequently similar content with the demand that the learner develop *analytic* skills which can be used to evaluate, recommend, or initiate both new programs and changes in ongoing policies or programs. Use is being made of the case study method that proved so valuable to casework, critiques of programs, and simulations involving real or projected programs, operations, and results.

The following is a representative statement of current approaches to the knowledge base of the social work curriculum:

Progress in the development of professional knowledge is marked by progress in conceptualization, in the development of theoretical constructs on which practice is based. As professional knowledge develops it removes itself from empiricism. I do not say that it removes itself from practice, much less from reality, but that professional constructs become more theoretical. "Probably the most important distinguishing characteristic of a science-based practice is that the practitioner is guided by generalizations of a relatively high order of abstraction and coherence, rather than by rules of thumb based on his own experience or that of his elders." As the saying has it, "nothing is as practical as a good theory" (Coughlin, 1970 p. 60).

In summary, the intellectual climate of the schools is changing, and these changes can be attributed to several influences. First, they reflect the widening mandate imposed upon the profession during the decade. Social workers have been made to feel responsible for the continuing existence of poverty, hunger, and poor housing and for the heightening of intergroup conflict; and the profession has been made to feel acutely the necessity to respond with theories, programs, evaluations, recommendations, and action with regard to a very broad construction of the nature of these problems.

Secondly, both students and faculty members brought with them to the schools in the late 1960s a wide variety of unorthodox experience in the civil rights and war-on-poverty movements which created a new urgency for both broader and more sociopolitical understandings of causation and action strategies.

Thirdly, the schools came under the influence of the universities of which they are a part as a result of:

1 The greater readiness of faculty to participate reciprocally with other parts of the university community in their intellectual concerns.

2 The expectation in many universities that the school of social work could be an important vehicle in dealing with the demands of the local community and in utilizing the opportunities offered by the new federal programs.

3 The sheer increase in the size of the schools (particularly of their doctoral programs), which made them a more salient part of the overall university operation. This new prominence and attention brought with it the expectation that the school would conform to a greater degree than in the past to the theoretical and research commitments of the dominant academic sector of the university.

University Relationships Schools of social work and universities have become more and more compatible since the Chicago Extension School moved onto the University of Chicago campus in the early years of the century. Two major periods stand out in the history of this complex relationship: that of the early 1950s, when the last of the nonuniversity-, noncollege-connected schools disappeared, and that of the middle-to-late sixties, when the phenomenal growth of the schools and vastly increased federal support altered the ties between the schools of social work and the rest of the campus.

Several changes which have operated to strengthen the school-university relationship are growth related to the availability of federal support, an increasingly well-prepared faculty, the creation of interdisciplinary research institutes, the creation and expansion of doctoral programs, increasing areas of common interest between academic and professional curricula, the encouragement of student exchange between courses in the professional school and those in the academic schools, and the growth of undergraduate programs. Some of these points have already been discussed.

Size alone has been an important factor in gaining the attention of the rest of the university. Growth in student body was accompanied by increases in the number of faculty members. Many schools that began the decade as a division or department headed by a director were later advanced in status to an autonomous school headed by a dean. Since growth was due in large measure to the increase in outside support, universities had an obvious incentive to support the development and expansion of the social work schools.

The creation or expansion of doctoral programs is linked to the emergence of research institutes as instruments of interdisciplinary cooperation. The growing size of both student body and faculty makes the doctoral programs easier to build because of the ready availability of both staff and students and because of the expanded job market in teaching which the new and bigger schools have created. The hiring of teachers from outside the profession and the cross-registration of doctoral students in courses offered by other departments were both interdisciplinary acts in and of themselves and an encouragement to interdisciplinary cooperation at the lower rungs of the graduate school ladder.

Interdisciplinary research institutes (covering such areas as poverty, urban problems, and gerontology), were created to facilitate dissertation research and to channel federal grants through an easily administered entity. The involvement of scholars from other disciplines with social work scholars in the administration or activities of these institutes appears to have helped to gain acceptance for social work's intellectual, action, and status goals in other sectors of the university. These interdisciplinary research and action efforts proved so attractive to the social work faculty that one dean informed us that he encountered difficulty in holding social work scholars to their original teaching commitments.

Some doctoral programs have as their central characteristic an interdisciplinary focus including, in one case, the awarding of a joint degree in social work and one of several social sciences. Several patterns of interdisciplinary cooperation can be found. Perhaps the most successful is the inclusion on the faculty of the school of social work of full-time teachers from other disciplines. These faculty members can be found offering specialized courses in sociology, economics, political science, or research and statistics. Joint appointments with other departments are also utilized, but this procedure is sometimes only peripheral. With increasing frequency, social work-trained faculty are requested to fill joint appointments in other professional schools or other academic departments of the university.

At the time of this writing, a reduction in federal grant support for schools of social work is widely anticipated. It is expected by the deans interviewed for this report that the increased integration of the school of social work with the rest of the university will result in an increase in financial support by the universities and state governments as federal funds grow more scarce; in fact, this replacement of some federal funds by university funds is already in process in several schools.

Despite these positive indications of closer integration of schools of social work within the universities, it would be misleading to assume that problems in this area have been overcome. Schools vary widely in the degree to which they have achieved such integration. In addition to the general problems of ineffective communication and coordination among departments that pervade all aspects of university life, the schools of social work typically have special problems stemming from the generally poor academic image that social work as a profession has inherited from the past. At the master's level (in contrast with doctoral work), the operation of the school does not easily lend itself to frequent close contact between the social work student and students on other parts of the campus. The classroom work of the student takes place within the self-contained school, both physically and intellectually. Despite the recent encouragement by the schools to take classes on other parts of the campus, only a small minority of the students are actually able to so arrange their schedules to accommodate such an interdisciplinary exchange. Several factors make such cross-fertilization difficult: the schedules of the schools of social work and those of the other departments of any university do not necessarily coincide, and in addition, fieldwork commitments make doubly difficult the scheduling and logistics problems of those students who might be interested in such an exchange. Also, students are aware and wary of the possibly differing standards and expectations of faculty and students in other disciplines. Social life, too, is generally quite contained within the school.

Community Relationships

The school of social work, the local community, and the profession are very much intertwined. For most schools, the service aspect of their mandate is expressed predominantly through services rendered to local professional and social work agencies. In state land-grant universities, schools of social work participate in university extension programs directed toward the upgrading of social service employees of state health and welfare departments and educational institutions. Frequently, the social work extension offers the only training available to paraprofessionals. More often, extension provides an opportunity for the school to influence directly the attitudes and competence of the bachelor's degree personnel or to introduce social work concepts and perspectives to school teachers and other non-social work employees.

Sometimes the school, as an institution, contracts to perform research or to provide consultation services to the highest levels of state government or to federal agencies. The University of Chicago participates in a unique arrangement in which it staffs and provides consultation and services to the "in-house" Institute for Social Welfare Policy within the Illinois Department of Public Welfare. More often, individual faculty members are called upon to provide ongoing or specific consultation to public and private social welfare agencies in the fields of health, mental health, housing, manpower and employment, and public welfare. A good many faculty members provide paid or free advice and support to "people's" organizations and movements and to funded organizations connected with the war on poverty, model cities programs, and similar undertakings. Faculty members also sit on local, state, or national boards or commissions.

Institutionally sanctioned and managed efforts by schools to provide direct service to local communities have taken two forms. An overwhelming percentage of these efforts is channeled through the fieldwork experience of students operating out of established social work and non-social work agencies in the community. Particularly in the non-social work agencies, students may provide almost the entire direct service field staff of the agency as in housing authorities, neighborhood organizations, storefront drug centers, and the like. The other type of effort is mounted when the school itself undertakes to operate community services directed and staffed by faculty and students. Though this means has been widely discussed, it has not been so widely implemented. One notable example is the University of Wisconsin's effort to send a team of faculty and students to a rural county where, after surveying the need, they developed a community-based service to the retarded persons of the county. In the end, the team served as midwife to the birth of a new agency which took over and expanded its efforts.

The schools which have attempted to operate combined teaching and service centers report several problems. A perceived conflict between the roles of student as learner and student as service giver, scheduling and staffing problems, and the possibilities of increased vulnerability of the schools' image in the community have combined to dim the enthusiasm of some administrators for such projects. Yet attempts to make the model work are increasing among faculty and students who hold that practicing is a crucial part of education and who wish to certify that the school's graduates have satisfactorily performed a certain range of activities not always available in established agencies. An ideology of service to many populations previously unserved or poorly served also strongly influences the experimenters in this activity. In some cases, these direct service operations have drawn the schools into a new dialogue with the local community which have aided both the image and the educational mission of the school.

Because of the expansion of faculty-supervised field placements, the schools are less dependent upon agencies to provide field placement settings and supervision, while at the same time the expansion of the federal stipend has reduced the importance of agency-furnished stipends. Some segments of the agency-professional community have expressed concern that the skills of the new graduates do not match the types of activities that have been traditionally carried on in the agency and that the schools are, therefore, not meeting their needs adequately. At the same time, agencies are looking to the schools to prepare students for new types of responsibility, particularly in such areas as planning and administration.

A word should be said about differences between "national" schools of social work and "local" schools. Although the differences between schools may not be as marked as between national and local schools of law, it is apparent that there exist within social work education several schools of high national reputation whose student bodies are drawn to a greater extent than others from a national pool, which have close contacts with decision makers in the federal government, and which easily attract scholars of national and international reputation from social work and from other disciplines. Other schools located in smaller colleges or in state universities that are strongly committed to state constituencies make do with well-qualified but less illustrious professors, a student body drawn more from local and less prestigious undergraduate colleges and universities, and fewer contacts with national and international institutions. The large established national schools can obtain the freedom to lead and to experiment with social work practice (although they may not make full use of this freedom), while the local schools must be much more responsive to pressures from traditional practitioners. This picture may change, however, as new schools are created, unhampered as well as unaided by long-term traditions and commitments.

SOME EMERGING MODELS For the well-established school, size and drawing power may create opportunities for diversity and innovation both in the content and in the process of education. The result may be interesting and thoughtful new programs which come by accretion to be added to a shrinking but prominent core of traditional teaching and traditional content. In such situations it sometimes seems that there are two or more educational institutions occupying the same ground under the same administrative umbrella but with quite different methods, goals, and resources. Such a division creates obvious tensions.

The newly created school of social work, on the other hand, may feel itself to be more vulnerable to traditional professional pressures, since it must undergo a "guilty until proven innocent" period of candidacy for accreditation, but also freer to establish a school with a more homogeneous viewpoint. Starting from scratch, the new school has an opportunity to hire a complete faculty having congenial ideology and experience, to identify and cultivate its own constituency, and to develop new types of programs. One might view the new schools, therefore, as a "purer" example of emerging models of social work education.

The new School of Social Welfare at the State University of New York (SUNY) at Stony Brook, the School of Social Administration at Temple University in Philadelphia, and the School of Social Work at San Diego State College, California, are three new schools that were visited in the course of preparing this paper. Their programs and approaches represent an accentuation of trends we have already noted as not uncommon in social work education elsewhere. In the new schools, these trends become the standard practice and develop a coherence not easily obtainable in the older schools.

Prevalent in these new schools is the emphasis on the *social* causation of social problems. Thus, Stony Brook uses the following formulation to describe its underlying assumptions:

... contemporary human problems—poverty, poor housing, environmental pollution, unmet health needs, alienation, inadequate education, racism, coercion, exploitation, and unrealized human potential—are conditions of society that can be explained by the structure of existing institutional arrangements and patterns of relationships that are sustained by certain values and beliefs (School of Social Welfare, 1970).

The language used at Temple is very similar:

This School does not view problems of coping as rooted primarily in the self, as illness, as negative, and as requiring "rehabilitation" and therapy. There are more positive and productive approaches which are *facilitative* in that they enable people to become increasingly more responsible on their own behalf, and to move on to engagement with the institutional issues affecting their lives.

Intervention with individuals, families and groups which neglects as its ultimate goal the need for social, economic, and political change, which does not make a case for intervention in the larger sense out of the intra-inter-personal situations with which it has dealt, leads nowhere and has no lasting effect (*School of Social Administration . . . Vol. I*, 1970).

While the schools are similar in their underlying assumptions, they differ in the way in which they organize curricular content. Stony Brook attempts to use *social change* as an organizing concept, as the following statement indicates:

Each of the content areas is organized from the perspective of usefulness in social change.

1. Critiques of Contemporary Society

Students are provided with comparisons of socio-political and economic systems and their consequences with respect to the centralization of power and equitable distribution of resources.

2. Organizational Analysis

This involves examination of formal organizations both as systems and as subsystems within society. The policies, programs, and structures of organizations are studies in relation to establishment of goals and practices.

3. Research: Modes and Functions

A wide variety of methods ranging from muck-raking investigational reporting to experimental research is used to confirm or to challenge definitions of social reality. These methods and their structure and process are analyzed to determine the underlying value judgments or theoretical premises which influence their outcome.

4. Development and Analysis of Social Policy and Service Delivery Systems

Analysis is made of those societal and organizational decisions that determine the distribution of resources, power, social position, and human rights, and how these decisions are transformed into social policies, services, and programs through a variety of organizational structures, or service systems, in fields such as education, health, welfare, housing.

5. Theories and Analyses of Social Change

Specific change theories are related directly to the students' problem areas of concern. The student is exposed to the range of social action programming in his area of concern, but he brings to the information a critical analysis of the theoretical assumptions about the change process.

6. The Self and Society

An examination is made of various concepts and perspectives regarding personality development and its relationship to social structure; the implications of these concepts for social organization and social change; the interaction of cultural, ethnic, social class, and familial forces in human development and its implications for social change.

7. Communication: Modes and Functions

Analysis is undertaken of how the social order is maintained (or changed) through the process of interpersonal, intergroup, and mass communication and interaction around different perceptions of reality; how the form and content of reality—defining media (ranging from non-verbal communication to electronic communications) affect the development and implementation of social policy . . . (School of Social Welfare, 1970, pp. 38–41).

At Stony Brook, these modes of analysis are applied to specific social problems. Students are expected to select one problem area each year and to demonstrate through class assignments and field-work their ability to apply the analytic and interactive skills that are communicated by the curriculum. It is obvious that this school makes explicit and central the "social criticism" function that has always been an important but often merely implicit part of social work education. Course descriptions, as the following excerpts illustrate, are permeated by this critical stance.

SOCIETAL CONTEXT OF SOCIAL POLICY

Social Welfare and the Social Order—An historical analysis of the field of social welfare and its response to political and economic development in America. The emphasis is on the manifest and latent functions of social welfare institutions and intervention approaches as they have related to the stages of economic expansion and urbanization which have taken place in this country.

Power Conceptions and Policy-Making Process—Three different perceptions of the structure of power in this country are examined: The elitist or ruling class theory, pluralist theory, and the recent theoretical material on the role of the technological or managerial class. Controversial matters of current public policy, e.g., ecological or consumer protection issues, provide case materials for examination. . . .

IDEOLOGY AND SOCIAL RESEARCH . . .

Reality Construction and Social Consciousness—An examination of the process through which a prevailing definition of reality is communicated to individuals and of the social construction of that definition. Consciousness as a reflection of the dominant value matrix and form of social organization within society is explored. . . . Particular emphasis is placed on how social welfare workers come to understand and define the problems which they confront in their daily roles. . . .

Explanation in Social Science—This seminar examines the conditions which influence acceptability of explanations of social phenomena as well as the temporal and spatial context within which any claimed explanation is held to be valid. Central to this seminar is a study, Thomas Kuhn's *The Structure of Scientific Revolutions,* and its application to social research. . . .

Research Methods in Social Science—This course examines the reality constructions serving as the premises for social science research methodology. . . . An analysis is made of different research strategies in the academic disciplines in terms of their premises, contextual assumptions, and relationship to the "normal science" model.

HUMAN SERVICE SYSTEMS

Comparative Approaches to the Analysis of Human Service Systems—The use of organizational theories and interorganizational theories to analyze the functioning of formal organizations is related to case material on human service systems. . . . Emphasis is given to the location of policy decisions, problem definitions, and program construction. . . .

The Administration of Human Service Systems—An analysis of the various forces which influence the direction and operation of human service organizations functioning at the community level. The relationship between the agency and external forces such as funding agencies at the state and federal levels, professional associations, and local and national political decisions is compared to the influence exerted by clientele.

THE SELF AND SOCIETY . . .

The Self and the Social Order—Comparative study of theoretical perspectives on the relationship between the nature of man and the purposes of a society. Emphasis is given to contrasting priorities placed on individual freedom from social order versus freedom within an organized social structure. . . .

Institutional Responses to Deviance—An examination of institutions which function in the area of serving or controlling deviance (penal system, court systems, mental hospitals and mental health centers). Labelling theory and social interaction theory are utilized to examine the nature of the relationship between institutional employees and their clients. . . .

Theories of Personality—Study of differing theories of personality development, with emphasis on the assumptions made about the nature of man and the process of identity formation. Assumptions about normality and explanations of deviance are related to the position of each theorist on the effectiveness and desirability of the political and economic structures in society.

STRATEGIES OF SOCIAL CHANGE . . .

Theories of Social Change—A Comparative Analysis—This course attempts to create a typology of change theories based on ideological stance, target of change efforts, and suggested actions or tactics.

Historical Analysis of Social Movements—The social forces and conditions which gave rise to large-scale social movements are examined in relation to the selection of the social movement as a change strategy.

Change Strategies Within the Public Policy Arena—This course addresses itself to the question, how is public social policy changed? The historical development of policy decisions and programs in such areas as welfare, health care, housing, education and transportation are explored (*The Undergraduate Program. . .* , 1971).

Temple, although sharing many of the same assumptions and goals as Stony Brook, is somewhat more traditional in its conceptualization of social work practice:

All students should gain a basic understanding of alternative modes of direct intervention with individuals, families, groups, community organizations and formal institutions. While each student will have an opportunity to develop specific practice skill on only some of these levels, he should understand the basic conceptual framework of all of them. . . . At the outset, the student chooses to specialize in either (1) Social Planning, Policy, and Community Organization, or (2) Social Service Delivery. Beyond this, the student is encouraged to further special interests. These may be more intensive work on a particular level of intervention (e.g., group counseling);

work with a selected population (e.g., low-income blacks); work in a field of service (e.g., corrections); or focusing on a social problem area (e.g., drug addiction) (*School of Social Administration . . . , Vol. II,* 1970).

At Temple, the course titles are those used by most social work schools and are prescribed in detail (until recently by the Council on Social Work Education). The basic core courses and some of the electives fall into two general categories: (1) methods courses for dealing with individuals, groups, or communities and (2) omnibus social science courses designed to present background knowledge in sociology, psychology, or political science, to be integrated with methods courses or courses taken elsewhere in the university. Course descriptions demonstrate the ways in which these traditional categories are modified by the basic philosophic orientation of the school. They emphasize, as do the courses at Stony Brook, a critical analysis of social institutions and the probing of opportunities for social change. The teaching of social work practice at Temple is, however, closer to older professional models than seems to be the case at Stony Brook:

Social Service Delivery
All students take a sequence entitled "Social Service Delivery". . . . Students are expected to:
1. Gain experience in the analysis of problems in social functioning of individuals, families, and group; goal formulation; selection and application of social work interventions sufficiently comprehensive to resolve problems and effect change.
2. Gain understanding of choices which have to be made, of the variety of interventions both in and outside of social work.
3. Understand the concepts, principles and procedures basic to social work and their application to preventive, curative and rehabilitative work with individuals or groups. To learn to apply these with flexibility, creativity, and a commitment to rendering such services as flow from the nature of the client's need(s).
4. Develop an understanding of the functions of the social worker as advocate, broker, and helper.
5. Understand the nature of the helping process itself in its many dynamic facets . . . (*School of Social Administration . . . , vol. II, Appendix,* 1970, pp. 10, 12, 13).

These contrasting structures for organizing the *content* of social work education reflect differing degrees of innovation in the process of education as well. In a "market" curriculum of discrete courses, considerable decision making must be done by both students and faculty in designing an individualized educational plan.

The curriculum of "omnibus social science" courses and methods courses combined with electives precludes such extensive individualization and assumes a bimodal set of experiences for the student body. Stony Brook views the student as a consumer:

> The School provides a setting and range of resources for the exploration and development of new ideas and patterns of action that are prerequisites to addressing social problems. . . .
>
> In the School there is purposeful structure and conscious effort to facilitate an individualized approach to learning, recognizing the primacy of self-determination over predefined or imposed roles and statuses among the members of the learning-teaching community. . . . Each student with the help of other members of the learning-teaching-action community is expected to develop his own coherent explanatory system appropriate to the identification and analysis of those particular areas of society which are perceived as requiring intervention (*The Undergraduate Program* . . . . 1971, pp. 31–32).

The student is also seen as "co-learner," "co-investigator," and "responsible adult decision-maker" along with the faculty.

> . . . real learning both for students and faculty comes from an inner-directed need rather than from "measuring up" to a reward system which elicits "correct" responses. The School proposes to maximize inner-directed learning by placing in students and faculty the responsibility for developing a collegial relationship in thought and practice (ibid.).

Even in the more structured curriculum at Temple there has been an increase in student participation and choice. The entire last semester at Temple is given over to elective courses. Student participation has increased in other ways as well, particularly within the classroom. A good example is the Interaction Workshop course at Temple:

> . . . the Interaction Workshop places central importance upon the verbalizing/experiencing/verbalizing sequence as the core of the teaching/learning situation. A deliberate attempt is made to avoid a lecture format as the central teaching modality and even the use of flexible group discussion with the teacher in control of the flow of the process is sparingly used. Instead, a wide range of teaching/learning modalities are deliberately introduced.

. . . Buzz groups, tasks groups, leaderless groups, audiotapes, video-tapes, slides and pictures as stimuli, observer reports, instrumentation (check list, observation guides, evaluation forms), etc. Modalities of interaction have included: Games, drama, role play, simulations, puzzles, quizzes, crafts, music, and silence. Furthermore, spatial arrangements are deliberately varied and brought to conscious awareness as well as a valuation placed upon movement and the use of the total self in interaction as part of the emphasis upon *experiencing* and *working.*

Teaching methodology consists of creating situations illustrative of various social work concepts and socio-behavioral principles. Students explore the situation observing, analyzing, experimenting with their own actions and assessing the outcomes (*School of Social Administration . . . , vol. I,* 1970, p. 63).

Another example from Temple is Community Encounter:

We believe the initial experiences of the student are vital in setting the tone and expectations of his total learning experience. Were our students to enter immediately into standard field work placements in social agencies, there would be a tendency for them quickly to become socialized to the agency's perception of the community and its problems. Often, we believe, this would present a one-sided and even distorted view of the people the student would be trying to help. The Community Encounter is intended to help deal with this problem by presenting the student with a number of different perspectives on the urban community. Thus, we see the Encounter, coming as it does in the initial month of the first year, as an important opportunity to grapple with the realities of community life, unencumbered by the field agency's function, organizational pressures and the staff role and orientation.

We employ residents of the respective areas as "Community Representatives" to act as field teachers. The student team accompanies the Community Representative as the latter goes about his or her daily work. The Community Representative may arrange for students to visit in homes in the neighborhood. We try to make sure that all student teams attend at least one community meeting. Students visit and observe community action and service programs in which community residents are involved. And all students visit a large institution (e.g., a court, police, hospital, community mental health facility, etc.). In this last-mentioned encounter, the focus is on the institution as the client-population views it. We encourage the Community Representative to give the students specific tasks to do; thus, the visit to a hospital emergency room may be as an escort for an elderly person or the mother of a sick child (*School of Social Administration . . . , Vol. I,* 1970, pp. 67–69).

Social work, of course, has always devoted a very large part of the educational process to experiential learning through fieldwork, but as these few illustrations show, the dichotomous organization of education into classwork and fieldwork is breaking down, and experiential learning is becoming interlaced through the classroom experience. Both schools have plans to accelerate this process.

Since these new schools are more homogeneous in philosophy and educational policies than the older institutions, it might be expected that they would attract a less diverse and more specialized student body. In our conversations with both deans and admissions officers of these schools, it was more than once asserted that they were attracting some students who would not have entered social work except through a school of their philosophic and pedagogical commitment. Stony Brook as a matter of policy admits to its master's program students with outstanding careers in their community who have little or no prior college experience. At Temple there is a vision of a complete continuum of social work education, beginning (for some people) with the New Careers program, through the B.A., and continuing to advanced degrees. Both schools aim to attract students from a wide range of cultural and academic backgrounds, including both community leaders and the academically oriented undergraduates who would otherwise have pursued careers in sociology, political science, or economics.

Our concern in all of these distributions is not with quotas but rather with diversity per se. If our student body were to gravitate toward being all-white or all-Black, all-male or all-female, etc., we would be concerned to restore a balance. We believe the diversity greatly enriches the experience for all students and the total educational program itself. . . . The "Main Line" housewife with a degree from a high prestige institution, the person who grew up in the ghetto and has acquired substantial "street wisdom," the young dedicated person who has been involved in radical change-oriented movements, and the career social worker all add enrichment to the educational process; any of them alone would yield a less satisfactory result (*School of Social Administration . . . , Vol. I,* 1970, p. 96).

The School of Social Work at San Diego State College, although still relatively new, was established a few years before either Temple or Stony Brook and has thus had time to test out some of its original assumptions and to modify its initial decisions in the light of experience.

Two aspects of San Diego's experience are of interest to our discussion. The first is its position as part of a large state system of higher education in which it has responsibilities for the training of different levels of professional personnel. As a result, San Diego experimented with one of the first combined undergraduate-graduate programs of social work education. This was a three-year program including a major in the junior and senior years of college and 12 months in graduate school, culminating in a master's degree. In addition, the school offers a terminal bachelor's degree (B.S.W.) and is expanding its responsibility for serving community colleges and for providing opportunities for part-time study to employees of state social service agencies.

The other noteworthy aspect of San Diego's development has been its attempt to work out a holistic and integrated model of social work practice as a basis for its curriculum. Faced with the multiple demands of changing social work roles discussed at various points in this paper, San Diego's response was not to increase the number of varieties of specializations but rather to help students to form a cohesive view of those roles and their respective place in an overall frame of reference.

Experience has revealed the great difficulties of achieving such integration. Over a period of years, several theoretical approaches have been attempted and quickly modified. Thus, an effort was made at one time to cast the curriculum into a mold of social problem entities, within each of which there would be an integration of theoretical material and training in modes of intervention. That proved inadequate to provide the scope of training the faculty considered necessary. The search continues for a holistic social science approach that will provide a coherent theoretical base. As at Stony Brook and Temple, the emphasis is on social change, and particularly on how to change organizations, from both within and without.

On the practice side, the San Diego program attempts to achieve both integration and specialization. It offers two "tracks" of specialization: (1) social treatment and (2) social policy-planning-action. Great emphasis is placed, however, on the interrelationship between the two and on the need for all students to become acquainted with both. The spirit of the program's orientation is captured in the following statements by its faculty:

We aim to teach eventually a holistic practice that equips the social worker to start with whatever complex social reality he professionally confronts and to proceed responsibly to analyze, plan, and implement with and for the relevant individuals, families, groups, organizations, and communities for an improved social reality. Problem reduction usually requires both individual change and social change or conservation, and what the social worker does to facilitate and influence those changes or conservations constitutes social work practice (Stumpf, 1970, p. 6).

We do not intend that our graduates be equally capable of both social treatment and social policy-planning-action practice orientations. Each is allowed to *concentrate* his learnings on one or the other in his second year, while also having class and field requirements for learning in the "other" orientation. The interdependence of the two orientations is emphasized with appropriate skill learnings. And in the second year, in class and field there are learnings and assignments related to administration, consultation and staff development or education (Stumpf, 1970, p. 7).

San Diego reports some shifts in the distribution of students between the two major areas of specialization that may have significance in pointing to possible reversals in major trends that were noted earlier in this paper. In the first year of the school (late 1960s), some 40 percent of the students were concentrated in the community organization–planning area. In 1970, this number had fallen to 20 percent. The San Diego faculty attributed the shift to several factors. One was the change in the market—the cutbacks in governmental programs that had called for large numbers of community organizers. Another, they thought, was a sense of disillusionment on the part of students who had been through the community organization experience with its failure to achieve significant social change. Students also seemed to have some feeling that they would be able to achieve more tangible and reliable skills through clinical training than in the less structured areas of planning and community organization.

This is not to say, however, that there has been a shift in basic social attitudes of the student body. The students continue to be oriented toward social change. If they shift to clinical training, they continue to be interested in helping individuals and groups to achieve changes in their environment. They still hold to the concept of "advocacy" as a central responsibility of the social worker rendering direct client service. This orientation is expressed, among other ways, in extensive faculty-student collaboration in the field. One of the features of San Diego's development is its use of field training to develop new (generally small) agencies and services in fields not served by established agencies.

The model that emerges from these descriptions of new schools reflects the broadening mandate that characterizes the social work profession today. While the majority of students are still being prepared for roles involving the rendering of direct service to individuals, families, or small groups, great emphasis is placed on orienting them to the social context of those responsibilities and to the social causation of the problems with which they will be expected to deal. Attempts are being made to prepare them for a great diversity of roles, and there are still many unresolved problems in attempting to combine holistic and specialized approaches. All three schools emphasize a critical approach to the analysis of society, and all attempt to inculcate analytical skills. Close working collaboration between faculty and students is a goal of all these programs, expressed in a variety of ways, and all seek a very diversified student body that includes members of disadvantaged minorities who have minimal educational background. They therefore have responsibilities not only for graduate education but for undergraduate education and for certain types of nonprofessional training.

OUTLOOK FOR THE FUTURE At the present (the beginning of 1972) it is difficult to predict which of the elements of change that characterize social work education can be relied upon as indicators of future directions. For the first time in over a decade, there is no clearly accelerating demand for social workers of all levels of training or of no training whatsoever. The vast expansion in social work education that has been described in this paper was a partial and inadequate response to a very high level of demand that continued to increase throughout the decade of the 1960s. While there are no hard data on current demand, it seems evident that there is a change in the current labor market. Members of faculties of schools of social work, as well as practitioners, have been commenting widely during the very recent period on the increased difficulty in finding suitable positions for trained workers. A recent report that deals only with the employment of social workers in the public services indicates that the supply of social workers with master's degrees seems, at least for the moment, to be adequate to the demands of such agencies (National Association of Social Workers, 1971, p. 15). This is in sudden contrast to the predictions made a few years ago that demand would continue to outrun supply almost indefinitely.

Because this reversal of the trends of a decade is so recent, we cannot reasonably predict a continuing decline in demand for social workers with the possibility of an oversupply in the near future. An alternative interpretation and one to which we are inclined to give greater credence is that these are short-term phenomena rather than a permanent reversal of the previous expansion. There are, in fact, many indications that there will be continuing growth in what has been described loosely as the "human service" occupations.

Even under present conditions, encouragement is being given through federal programs (under somewhat different categories than those in the past) to employment and training of human services personnel. The fact that there is still considerable unemployment in the country means that there is continuing pressure to find ways whereby people marginal to the labor market can be absorbed. Human service occupations provide the most feasible mechanism for achieving that objective. It is noteworthy that a number of programs have been started very recently to help engineers displaced from reduced aerospace programs to become retrained as managers in human service organizations. If those organizations become the channel for absorbing highly trained personnel who cannot find employment in their normal occupations, then it seems even more certain that they will continue to play the role that they have assumed in the past decade of offering channels for employment to those with the least developed skills. In economic terms, the continuation of large public expenditures is necessary to maintain high levels of economic activity and to overcome unemployment. Given the nature of the industrial economy those expenditures must be made largely in the service fields.

While there is thus reason to believe that the trend of expansion which characterized the decades of the sixties will probably be continued into the future, it seems abundantly evident that the character of the demand and, therefore, the nature of both professional practice and education for practice will be very different in 1980 from what they were in 1960. The major transition has already taken place with the establishment of the bachelor's degree as the first professional degree instead of the M.S.W. Although the profession has not yet absorbed all the implications of this change, any predictions for the next decade must start with the recognition that professional education for social work is no longer the monopoly of graduate schools.

It has now been accepted, at least as a general proposition, that social work education will cover a wide continuum ranging from the preparation of subprofessionals at levels below the baccalaureate degree to the baccalaureate and master's degree levels of professional education and to the post-master's programs for the preparation of teachers, researchers, and certain types of "advanced practice." The latter term at this time encompasses both advanced clinical work and administration. In addition to all of this, there is a growing commitment within the schools to programs of continuing education that will offer diverse forms of non-degree training to many different kinds of practitioners at various levels of practice.

As these commitments of the field of social work education become more and more diverse, it becomes increasingly difficult to say just what social work education is, or, more significantly, what social work practice is and will be. This basic lack of clarity concerning the nature of professional practice is the most significant emerging issue with which the entire field will have to grapple in the coming period; and the outlook on this issue is cloudy indeed at the present time.

At the risk of oversimplification, the issue confronting social work may be described as a choice between defining the essential professional contribution and competence either in *clinical* or in *administrative* terms. The diversification that has taken place in social work education at the graduate level during the past decade was in many respects an attempt to move away from a clinical model that had developed largely within the framework of psychotherapy toward an emphasis on such matters as organization, planning, policy, and administration. Whatever uncertainties exist about the clinical model, it is even more difficult to define exactly what the alternative approach really means. Within the organization-planning-policy areas, there are also several approaches, ranging from a quasi-clinical therapeutic orientation (e.g., in such fields as community mental health) to a concern with very broad aspects of social and economic policy at the national level.

In attempting to deal with these confusions, the field of social work education, taken as an entity, has attempted to meet various demands and to avoid a monolithic choice. This is the inevitable tendency of any organized field of activity that is concerned with problems of domain. To make a choice at the present time among the various demands would mean a delimitation of the areas in which the social work profession might have a claim to render service.

The situation is, however, highly volatile, and it is by no means assured that the social work profession will be able to establish a central place for itself in the many diverse areas of human service occupations where social work professionals have had historic claims for participation; nor that social work as a profession can successfully encompass the various levels of practice that are emerging. In all these matters, there are growing numbers of occupations with various degrees of professionalization that represent competition for domination of the field.

Both at the undergraduate and at the graduate levels, tendencies are emerging toward the development of more integrated educational programs that can cut across traditional lines of existing service occupations. For example, undergraduate programs having such titles as Human Services are appearing at an apparently rapid rate in a number of universities—particularly the publicly financed universities that have always made a significant contribution to undergraduate training for service professions. In these emerging programs, there are various combinations of such fields as nursing, social work, rehabilitation, and corrections, as well as paramedical specialties. Such programs offer educational opportunities to people with various degrees of academic background, paralleling the beginning efforts in social work to develop a continuum from subprofessional toward professional positions.

At the graduate level, there is a similar proliferation of professional and academic disciplines around such concepts as "policy sciences," "public policy," and "urban affairs," as well as previously existing titles such as Urban Planning and Public Administration. There is no single pattern to such programs. Most of them developed out of a base in one or another of the established professions or disciplines, such as urban (physical) planning or public administration. The trend in social work education that has been discussed in this paper—namely, toward a greater emphasis on policy planning and administration—has made it possible for social work to also claim a role in training for policy fields, but it is one among many professions now attempting to prepare people for leadership at the policy level in dealing with social problems.

At this stage in its development, social work education continues to have a very large commitment to clinical types of practice. Indeed, even though (as described above) the number of students who are now enrolled exclusively in casework concentrations has reached a remarkably low point, closer analysis indicates that the majority of social work students are still being trained for individualized direct service to the clientele who come to the attention of social agencies. Only a minority, even at the graduate level, are being trained specifically for positions as the organizers and managers of those services.

With the rapid pace of development of many alternative forms of training for the rendering of direct service and with the parallel development in other fields of training programs for people who will aspire to be managers and directors of such services, it is questionable whether the field of social work can maintain its position in both areas without making a more definitive choice about where its essential responsibilities will lie. One possible alternative will be to hold fast to the historic commitment of social work to skilled individualized treatment of people in trouble in relation to their social environment. This would call for social work to have a specialized role within broad human service structures, providing the highly skilled clinical services where needed and perhaps also training people with lesser professional preparation. The other alternative would be for the profession of social work to reassert its earlier commitment to the effective organization and provision of services for people in need and to define professional practice in relation to the management of such services at various degrees of skill and responsibility.

It is difficult to say whether the field of social work education will or can make such a choice or, if the choice were made, what the eventual position of social work would be in the human service fields and in relation to other professions and disciplines. In view of these uncertainties, the prospect for the immediate future would seem to be a continuing development of all aspects of social work education as it is presently organized. Within each subarea and at every level of the undergraduate-graduate continuum, it does seem likely that social work will find itself in ever-closer contact with other professions and academic disciplines that share its aspirations to contribute to the personnel needs of the human service fields.

References

Abrams, Herbert K., and R. R. Byrd III: "Survey of Grading Procedures of American Associated Medical Colleges," *Journal of Medical Education*, vol. 46, pp. 316–319, April 1971.

Accrediting Association of Bible Colleges: *Pastoral-Theological Programs in the Bible College*, Wheaton, Ill., 1968.

Allied Health Professions Education Subcommittee of the National Advisory Health Council: *Education for the Allied Health Professions and Services*, U.S. Public Health Service Publication 1600, 1967.

American Association of Theological Schools: *Bulletin 28: The Handbook*, Dayton, Ohio, 1968a.

American Association of Theological Schools: *Report of a Resources Planning Commission*, Dayton, Ohio, 1968b.

American Association of Theological Schools: *Fact Book on Theological Education, 1969–1970; 1970–1971*, Dayton, Ohio, 1971.

American Bar Association Section of Legal Education: *Admissions to the Bar*, Chicago, 1944, 1960, 1970, 1971.

American Medical Association and Association of American Medical Colleges: "Joint Statement of Health Manpower," *Journal of Medical Education*, vol. 43, p. 1009, September 1968.

American Priests, National Opinion Research Center, Chicago, 1971.

Annual Review of Legal Education, Carnegie Foundation for the Advancement of Teaching, New York, 1926; 1928; 1930: 1944; 1960; 1961; 1970; 1971.

Association of American Law Schools: *Pre-Law Handbook*, Washington, D.C., 1968.

Bartlett, Harriet M.: "Social Work Fields of Practice," *Encyclopedia of Social Work*, National Association of Social Workers, New York, 1971.

Bartlett, James W.: "Changes in Entering Medical Students," in Robert G. Page and Mary H. Littlemeyer (eds.), *Conference on the Optimal Preparation for the Study of Medicine,* The University of Chicago Press, Chicago, 1969.

Becker, Howard S.: "Notes on the Concept of Commitment," *American Journal of Sociology,* vol. 67, pp. 32–45, 1960.

Becker, Howard S., and Blanche Geer: "Latent Culture: A Note on the Theory of Latent Social Roles," *Administrative Science Quarterly,* vol. 5, pp. 304–313, September 1960.

Becker, Howard S., Blanche Geer, Everett C. Hughes, and Anselm L. Strauss: *Boys in White: Student Culture in Medical School,* The University of Chicago Press, Chicago, 1961.

Bellow, Gary: "The Extension of Legal Services to the Poor: New Approaches to the Bar's Responsibility," in A. Sutherland (ed.), *The Path of the Law from 1967,* Harvard University Press, Cambridge, Mass., 1968.

Bloom, Samuel W.: "The Sociology of Medical Education: Some Comments on the State of a Field," *The Milbank Memorial Fund Quarterly,* vol. 43, pp. 143–184, April 1965.

Bloom, Samuel W.: "The Medical School as a Social System: A Case Study of Faculty-Student Relations," *The Milbank Memorial Fund Quarterly,* vol. 49, part 2, April 1971.

Blumberg, Mark S., and Eve C. Clark: *Major Locational Factors: U.S. Medical Schools,* University of California, Berkeley, May 1967. (Mimeographed.)

Boehm, Werner W.: "Education for Social Work," *Encyclopedia of Social Work,* National Association of Social Workers, vol. 16, New York, 1971.

Bojar, S.: "Psychiatric Problems of Medical Students," in G. B. Blaine, Jr., et al. (eds.), *Emotional Problems of the Students,* Appleton-Century-Crofts, Inc., New York, 1961.

Bok, Derek: "A Different Way of Looking at the World," *Harvard Law School Bulletin,* vol. 20, pp. 2–4, March–April 1969.

Bosch, Samuel J., and H. David Banta: "Medical Education in Prepaid Group Practice," *Journal of the American Medical Association,* vol. 212, pp. 2101–2104, June 22, 1970.

The Boston Globe, p. 20, Feb. 4, 1971.

Boston Herald Traveler, Jan. 18, 1970.

Bucher, Rue: "Social Process and Power in a Medical School," in Mayer N. Zald (ed.), *Power in Organizations,* Vanderbilt University Press, Nashville, Tenn., 1970.

Bucher, Rue, and Anselm Strauss: "Professions in Process," *The American Journal of Sociology,* vol. 66, pp. 325–334, January 1961.

Cahn, Edgar S., and Jean Camper Cahn: "Power to the People or the Profession?—The Public Interest in Public Interest Law," *The Yale Law Journal,* vol. 79, pp. 1005–1048, May 1970.

Carlin, Jerome E.: *Lawyers on Their Own,* Rutgers University Press, New Brunswick, N.J., 1962.

Carlin, Jerome E.: *Lawyers' Ethics: A Survey of the New York City Bar,* Russell Sage Foundation, New York, 1966.

Carlin, Jerome E.: "Store Front Lawyers in San Francisco," *Transaction,* vol. 7, pp. 64–74, April 1970*a.*

Carlin, Jerome E.: "Will Clinical Education Make It?" *CLEPR Newsletter,* vol. 3, no. 1, pp. 1–4, September 1970*b.*

Carlin, Jerome E., Jan Howard, and Sheldon L. Messinger: *Civil Justice and the Poor: Issues for Sociological Research,* Russell Sage Foundation, New York, 1967.

Carnegie Commission on Higher Education: *Higher Education and the Nation's Health,* McGraw-Hill Book Company, New York, 1970.

"The Case for First Year Summer Clerkships," *Yale Medicine,* Yale University, New Haven, Conn., Winter 1970.

Cavers, David F.: "Lawyers in the Making," *University of Chicago Law Review,* vol. 33, pp. 898–906, 1966.

Cavers, David F.: "Legal Education in Forward-looking Perspective," in Geoffrey C. Hazard, Jr. (ed.), *Law in a Changing America,* Prentice-Hall, Inc., Englewood Cliffs, N.J., 1968.

Cavers, David F.: "Law School Enrollments Boom, Applications Increase throughout Country," *Harvard Law Record,* vol. 52, pp. 8–9, Apr. 23, 1971.

Center for Applied Research in the Apostolate (CARA): *U.S. Catholic Institutions for the Training of Candidates for the Priesthood,* Washington, D.C., 1969.

Charlton, K.: *Education in Renaissance England,* Routledge and Kegan Paul, Ltd., London, 1965.

Chrisite, Richard, and Robert K. Merton: "Procedures for the Sociological Study of the Value Climate in Medical Schools," in Helen H. Gee and

Robert J. Glaser (eds.), *The Ecology of the Medical Student,* Association of American Medical Colleges, Evanston, Ill., 1958.

Chronicle of Higher Education, National League for Nursing, Annual Survey for 1968–1969, Mar. 16, 1970.

Chronicle of Higher Education, Apr. 20, 1970.

The Citizens Commission on Graduate Medical Education: *The Report of The Commission on Graduate Medical Education,* Chicago, 1966.

CLEPR Newsletter: vol. 1, no. 1, January 1969; vol. 1, no. 3, April 1969; vol. 2, no. 6, January 1970; vol. 3, no. 4, January 1971; vol. 3, no. 7, March 1971; vol. 4, no. 6, November 1971.

Cohen, Morton P.: "The Law Office as a Law School: Two Experiments in New York City," in Edmund W. Kitch (ed.), *Clinical Education and the Law School of the Future,* The University of Chicago Law School, Chicago, 1970.

Committee on Specialization of the State Bar of California: "The 1968 Survey on Specialization in the Practice of Law of the State Bar of California," *California Bar Journal,* vol. 44, March–April 1969.

Conference of California Law Schools on Minority Students and the Law Schools, University of California, Los Angeles Law School, Nov. 8–10, 1968. (Mimeographed.)

Cope, Oliver: "The Endicott House Conference on Medical Education," in John H. Knowles (ed.), *Views of Medical Education and Medical Care,* Harvard University Press, Cambridge, Mass., 1965.

Cornely, P. B.: "Distribution of Negro Physicians in the United States in 1942," *Journal of the American Medical Association,* vol. 124, 1944.

Coughlin, Bernard J.: "Reconceptualizing the Theoretical Base of Social Work Practice," in Lilian Ripple (ed.), *Innovations in Teaching Social Work Practice,* Council on Social Work Education, New York, 1970.

Council on Legal Education for Professional Responsibility: *First Biennial Report,* New York, 1970.

Coyle, Grace: *Social Science in the Professional Education of Social Workers,* Council on Social Work Education, New York, 1958.

Cray, Ed: *In Failing Health,* The Bobbs-Merrill Company, Inc., Indianapolis and New York, 1971.

Crocker, Ann R., and Louis C. Remund Smith: *How Medical Students Finance Their Education: Results of a Survey of Medical and Osteopathic Students, 1967–1968,* U.S. Department of Health, Education and Welfare, National Institutes of Health, Washington, D.C., 1970.

Crowley, Anne E., and Hayden C. Nicholson: "Negro Enrollment in Medical Schools," *Journal of the American Medical Association,* vol. 210, pp. 96–100, Oct. 6, 1969.

Curtis, James L.: *Black Medical Schools, and Society,* The University of Michigan Press, Ann Arbor, 1971.

"Datagrams: U.S. Medical Student Enrollments, 1968–69 through 1970–71," *Journal of Medical Education,* vol. 46, pp. 96–97, January 1971.

"Dead End Found in 'New Careers,'" *The New York Times,* Feb. 27, 1971.

DeMuth, George R., and John A. Gronvall: "The Questionnaire and Its Analysis," in William N. Hubbard, Jr., John A. Gronvall, and George R. DeMuth (eds.), *The Medical School Curriculum: Journal of Medical Education,* part 2, November 1970.

Dinerman, Beatrice: "Sex Discrimination in the Legal Profession," *American Bar Association Journal,* vol. 55, pp. 951–954, October 1969.

Dolan, Andrew: "Lawyers and the Class Struggle," *Juris Doctor,* vol. 1, pp. 32–34, April 1971.

Dove, Dennis B.: "Minority Admissions: The Medical Educational Establishment Called to Task," *The New Physician,* vol. 19, pp. 903–907, November 1970.

Duff, Raymond S., and August B. Hollingshead: *Sickness and Society,* Harper & Row, Publishers, Inc. New York, 1968.

Ehrenreich, Barbara and John Ehrenreich: *The American Health Empire: Power, Profits, and Politics,* A Report from the Health Policy Advisory Center, Vintage Books, Random House, Inc., New York, 1971.

Ehrlich, Thomas, and Bayless A. Manning: "Programs in Law at the University of Hawaii," *Journal of Legal Education,* vol. 24, no. 1, pp. 3–41, 1971.

Eichenberger, Ralph W., and Robert F. Gloor: "A Team Approach to Learning Community Health," *Journal of Medical Education,* vol. 44, pp. 655–662, August 1969.

Elam, Lloyd C.: "Problems of the Predominantly Negro Medical School," *Journal of the American Medical Association,* vol. 209, pp. 1070–1072, Aug. 18, 1969.

Epstein, Cynthia: "Encountering the Male Establishment: Sex-Status Limits on Women's Careers in the Professions," *The American Journal of Sociology,* vol. 75, pp. 965–982, May 1970a.

Epstein, Cynthia: *Woman's Place: Options and Limits in Professional Careers,* University of California Press, Berkeley, 1970b.

A Fact Book on Higher Education, unpublished material of the Council on Social Work Education, based on their statistical compilations plus The American Council on Education, 1969.

Fein, Rashi, and Gerald I. Weber: *Financing Medical Education,* McGraw-Hill Book Company, New York, 1971.

Ferren, John M.: "Goals, Models and Prospects for Clinical-Legal Education," in Edmund W. Kitch (ed.), *Clinical Education and the Law School of the Future,* The University of Chicago Law School, Chicago, 1970.

Fichter, Joseph H.: *Religion as an Occupation,* University of Notre Dame Press, Notre Dame, Ind., 1961.

Fichter, Joseph H.: *Priest and People,* Sheed and Ward, Inc., New York, 1965.

Fichter, Joseph H.: *America's Forgotten Priests — What They Are Saying,* Harper & Row, Publishers, Inc., New York, 1968.

Field, John: "Medical Education in the United States: Late Nineteenth and Twentieth Centuries," in C. D. O'Malley (ed.), *The History of Medical Education,* University of California Press, Berkeley, 1970.

"Financial Cutbacks in Medical Schools," *Chronicle of Higher Education,* vol. 5, no. 6, p. 1, Nov. 2, 1970.

"Flexible New Careers Programs at University of Minnesota," *New Careers Newsletter,* vol. 2, p. 9, Spring 1968.

Flexner, Abraham: *Medical Education in the United Sates and Canada,* A Report of the Carnegie Foundation for the Advancement of Teaching, Bulletin 4, The Merrymount Press, Boston, 1910.

Flexner, Abraham: "Is Social Work a Profession?" *Proceedings of the National Conference of Charities and Correction,* Chicago, 1915.

Flexner, Abraham: *Medical Education: A Comparative Study,* The Macmillan Company, New York, 1925.

Freedman, Monroe: "Solicitation of Clients: For the Poor, Not the Privileged," *Juris Doctor,* vol. 1, pp. 10–12, April 1971.

Freidson, Eliot: "Paramedical Personnel," *International Encyclopedia of the Social Science,* vol. 10, The Macmillan Company and The Free Press, New York, 1968.

Freidson, Eliot: *Profession of Medicine,* Dodd, Mead & Company, Inc., New York, 1970*a*.

Freidson, Eliot: *Professional Dominance: The Social Structure of Medical Care,* Aldine-Atherton Press, New York, 1970*b*.

Funkenstein, Daniel H.: "Our Obsolete Residencies," *Archives of Internal Medicine,* vol. 122, pp. 279–280, September 1968.

Funkenstein, Daniel H.: "Medical Education for Social Responsibility," *The New Physician,* vol. 18, pp. 883–897, September 1969*a.*

Funkenstein, Daniel H.: "Medical Students, Medical Schools, and Society during Three Eras," paper presented at the Conference on Medical Students at the Bowman Gray School of Medicine, Winston-Salem, N.C., June 25, 1969*b* (unpublished manuscript).

Funkenstein, Daniel H.: "The Learning and Personal Development of Medical Students: Reconsidered," *The New Physician,* vol. 19, pp. 740–755, September 1970.

Gambrell, Mary L.: *Ministerial Training in 18th Century New England,* Columbia University Press, New York, 1937.

Geer, Blanche, Jack Haas, Charles ViVona, Stephen J. Miller, Clyde Woods, and Howard S. Becker: "Learning the Ropes: Situational Learning in Four Occupational Training Programs," in Irwin Deutscher and Elizabeth J. Thompson (eds.), *Among the People: Encounters with the Poor,* Basic Books, Inc., Publishers, New York, 1968.

Gockel, Galen L.: *Silk Stockings and Blue Collars,* National Opinion Research Center, Report 114, University of Chicago, 1966.

Golden, Deborah, Arnulf Pins, and Wyatt Jones: *Students in Schools of Social Work: A Study of Characteristics and Factors Affecting Career Choice and Practice Concentration,* Council on Social Work Education, New York, 1972.

Goldstein, Abraham S.: "The Unfulfilled Promise of Legal Education," in Geoffrey C. Hazard, Jr. (ed.), *Law in a Changing America,* Prentice-Hall, Inc., Englewood Cliffs, N.J., 1968.

Golton, Margaret A.: "Private Practice in Social Work," *Encyclopedia of Social Work,* vol. 2, pp. 949–955, 1971.

The Graduate Education of Physicians: *Report of the Citizens Commission on Graduate Medical Education,* commissioned by the American Medical Association, Chicago, 1966.

Griswold, Erwin: "Intellect and Spirit," in A. Sutherland (ed.), *The Path of the Law from 1967,* Harvard University Press, Cambridge, Mass., 1968.

Gurin, Arnold: *Community Organization Curriculum in Graduate Social Work Education: Report and Recommendations,* Council on Social Work Education, New York, 1970.

Gustafson, James M.: "Theological Education and Professional Education," *Theological Education,* vol. 5, no. 3, pp. 243–261, Spring 1969.

Halpern, Charles: *Washington Post,* p. A–18. Oct. 14, 1970.

Hankin, F., and K. Drohnke: *The American Lawyer, 1964 Statistical Report,* no. 29, American Bar Association, Chicago, 1965.

Harden, K. Albert: "The Black Medical School: Its Problems and Its Opportunities," in *The Impact of Cultural and Economic Background on Programs to Recruit Negroes for Medicine,* Macy Conference, Princeton, N.J., Apr. 13–16. (Mimeographed.)

Harrington, William J., William J. Whelan, B. J. Fogel, and E. J. Papper: "Alleviating the Shortage of Physicians," *Science,* vol. 172, June 11, 1971.

Harris, Seymour E.: *A Statistical Portrait of Higher Education,* McGraw-Hill Book Company, New York, 1972.

Harvard Law Record: vol. 29, Nov. 29, 1969; vol. 51, no. 5, Oct. 29, 1970; vol. 53, no. 5, Oct. 29, 1971.

Herberg, W.: *Protestant-Catholic-Jew,* Anchor Books, Doubleday & Company, Inc., rev. ed., Garden City, N.Y., 1960.

Hiltner, Seward: "From the Obvious to the Significant," *Journal of Higher Education,* vol. 25, no. 5, pp. 245–255, May 1954.

Hinds, Lennox: "Background to the Rutgers Report: The White Law School and the Black Liberation Struggle," in Robert Lefcourt (ed.), *Law against the People,* Vintage Books, Random House, Inc., New York, 1971.

Hubbard, William N., Jr, John A. Gronvall, and George R. DeMuth (eds.): *The Medical School Curriculum: The Journal of Medical Education,* part 2, November 1970.

Hughes, Everett C.: "Dilemmas and Contradictions of Status," *The American Journal of Sociology,* vol. 50, pp. 353–359, March 1945.

Hughes, Everett C.: "The Study of Occupations," in Merton and Broom (eds.), *Sociology Today,* Basic Books, Inc., Publishers, New York, 1959.

Hughes, Everett C.: "Going Concerns: The Study of American Institutions," presented at American Sociological Association, Washington, 1957, and *The Sociological Eye,* Aldine Publishing Company, Chicago, 1971a.

Hughes, Everett C.: "Psychology: Science and/or Profession," *The American Psychologist,* vol. 7, 1952, and *The Sociological Eye,* Aldine Publishing Company, Chicago, 1971b.

The Impact of Cultural and Economic Background on Programs to Recruit Negroes for Medicine, Macy Conference, Princeton, N.J., Apr. 13–16, 1969. (Mimeographed.)

James, George: "Medical Education: Medical Technique or Disease Control?" in Hans Popper (ed.), *Trends in New Medical Schools,* Grune & Stratton, Inc., New York, 1967.

Jason, Hilliard: "The Relevance of Medical Education to Medical Practice," *Journal of the American Medical Association,* vol. 212, pp. 2092–2095, June 22, 1970.

Jencks, Christopher, and David Riesman: *The Academic Revolution,* Anchor Books, Doubleday & Company, Inc., Garden City, N.Y., 1969.

Johnson, C. Dale: "Priest, Prophet, Professional Man: A Typology of Contemporary Religious Leadership," paper read at The Annual Meeting of American Sociological Association, St. Louis, Sept. 2, 1961.

Johnstone, Quentin, and Dan Hopson, Jr.: *Lawyers and Their Work: An Analysis of the Legal Profession in the United States and England,* The Bobbs-Merrill Company, Inc., Indianapolis, 1967.

Jones, Betty Lacy (ed.): *Current Patterns in Field Instruction in Graduate Social Work Education,* Council on Social Work Education, New York, 1969.

Journal of the American Medical Association, vol. 37, Sept. 21, 1901; Aug. 21, 1915; vol. 144, Sept. 9, 1950; vol. 202, Nov. 20, 1967; vol. 206, Nov. 25, 1968; vol. 214, Nov. 23, 1970; vol. 46, Jan. 1971; vol. 218, Nov. 22, 1971.

Journal of Medical Education, Jan. 1971, p. 96.

Kahn, Alfred J. (ed.): *Issues in American Social Work,* Columbia University Press, New York, 1959.

Kaplan, Harold I.: "Women Physicians: The More Effective Recruitment and Utilization of Their Talents and the Resistance to It—The Final Conclusions of a Seven-Year Study," *The Woman Physician,* vol. 25, pp. 561–570, September 1970.

Kelley, Robert L.: *Theological Education in America: A Study of One Hundred Sixty One Theological Schools in the United States and Canada,* Doubleday & Company, Inc., Garden City, N.Y., 1924.

Kendall, Patricia L.: "The Relationships between Medical Educators and Medical Practitioners," in S. G. Wolf, Jr., and W. Darley (eds.), *Medical Education and Practices: Relationships and Responsibilities in a Changing Society, Journal of Medical Education,* vol. 40, part 2, pp. 137–245, January 1965.

Kennedy, Duncan: "How the Law School Fails: A Polemic," *Yale Review of Law and Social Action,* vol. 1, Spring 1970.

Kitch, Edmund W. (ed.): *Clinical Education and the Law School of the Future,* The University of Chicago Law School, Chicago, 1970.

Kraft, Ivor: "The State of the Social Work Profession," in Willard Richan (ed.), *Human Services and Social Work Responsibility,* National Association of Social Workers, New York, 1969.

Langer, Elinor: "Inside the Hospital Workers' Union," *New York Review of Books,* pp. 25–33, May 20, 1971.

"Law, Lawyers and the System" *The Washington Post,* Oct. 14, 1970.

Lee, Philip R.: "Role of the Federal Government in Health and Medical Affairs," *The New England Journal of Medicine,* vol. 279, pp. 1139–1147, Nov. 21, 1968.

Lerner, Monroe, and Odin W. Anderson: *Health Progress in the United States: 1900–1960,* The University of Chicago Press, Chicago, 1963.

Letwin, Leon: "Some Perspectives on Minority Access to Legal Education," *Experiment and Innovation: New Directions in Education at the University of California,* vol. 2, pp. 1–24, May 1969.

Levi-Strauss, Claude: *The Savage Mind,* The University of Chicago Press, Chicago, 1966.

Lipset, Seymour M.: *The First New Nation: The United States in Historical and Comparative Perspective,* Basic Books, Inc., Publishers, New York, 1963.

Littlemeyer, Mary H.: "Medical School Admissions Requirements and Curricula," app. 5, in Robert G. Page, and Mary H. Littlemeyer (eds.), *Preparation for the Study of Medicine,* The University of Chicago Press, Chicago, 1969.

Lopate, Carol: *Women in Medicine,* The Johns Hopkins Press, Baltimore, 1968.

Lortie, Dan C.: "Layman to Lawman: Law School Careers and Professional Socialization," *Harvard Educational Review,* vol. 29, no. 4, pp. 363–367, Fall 1959.

Lyden, Fremont J., H. Jack Geiger, and Osler L. Peterson: *The Training of Good Physicians: Critical Factors in Career Choices,* Harvard University Press, Cambridge, Mass., 1968.

Lynn, Kenneth (ed.): *The Professions in America,* Beacon Press, Boston, 1967.

Manning, Bayless: "Introduction: New Tasks for Lawyers," in Geoffrey C. Hazard, Jr. (ed.), *Law in a Changing America,* Prentice-Hall, Inc., Englewood Cliffs, N.J., 1968.

Manning, Bayless: "American Legal Education: Evolution and Mutation — Three Models," address to the Western Assembly on Law and the Changing Society, June 12–15, 1969 (private reprint).

"Marquette School of Medicine: State Aid and Self Improvement," *Science,* vol. 166, pp. 1491–1493, Dec. 19, 1969.

Marshall, T. H.: "The Recent History of Professionalism in Relation to Social Structure and Social Policy," *The Canadian Journal of Economics and Political Science,* vol. 5, pp. 325–340, August 1939.

Mayer, Martin: *The Lawyers,* Harper & Row, Publishers, Inc., New York, 1966.

Mayhew, Lewis B.: *Graduate and Professional Education, 1980,* McGraw-Hill Book Company, New York, 1970.

Merton, Robert K., George G. Reader, and Patricia L. Kendall (eds.): *The Student Physician,* Harvard University Press, Cambridge, Mass., 1957.

Meyer, Henry J.: "Profession of Social Work: Contemporary Characteristics," *Encyclopedia of Social Work,* vol. 16, National Association of Social Workers, New York, 1971.

Meyers, Charles J.: "Report of the Chairman of the A.A.L.S. Committee on Curriculum," *Proceedings, A.A.L.S. 1968 Annual Meeting,* part 1.

Michaelson, Michael G.: "Medical Students: Healers Become Activists," *Saturday Review,* vol. 52, pp. 41–43, 53–54, Aug. 16, 1969.

Michaelson, Michael G.: "The Coming Medical War," *New York Review of Books,* pp. 32–38, July 1, 1971.

Miller, George E.: "Medicine," in Nelson B. Henry (ed.), *Education for the Professions,* 61st Yearbook of the National Society for the Study of Education, The University of Chicago Press, Chicago, 1962.

Miller, Stephen J.: *Prescription for Leadership: Training for the Medical Elite,* Aldine-Atherton Publishing Co., New York, 1969.

Millis, John S.: *A National Policy for Medical Education and Its Financing,* The National Fund for Medical Education, New York, 1971.

Moore, Wilbert E.: *The Professions: Roles and Rules,* Russell Sage Foundation, New York, 1970.

Mumford, Emily: *Interns: From Students to Physicians,* Harvard University Press, Cambridge, Mass., 1970.

Nader, Ralph: "Crumbling of the Old Order: Law Schools and Law Firms," *The New Republic,* vol. 161, pp. 20–23, Oct. 11, 1969.

"Nader Urges Student Investigations," *Harvard Law Record,* vol. 49, pp. 1, 7, 10, Oct. 2, 1969.

National Association of Social Workers: *NASW News,* vol. 16, no. 6, October 1971.

National Council of Churches: *Survey of Clergy Support,* New York, 1964.

National League for Nursing: *Report of the National League for Nursing,* New York, 1970.

"The New Public Interest Lawyer," *The Yale Law Journal,* vol. 79, pp. 1069–1157, May, 1970.

The New York Times, p. 16, May 18, 1966; pp. 37, 39, Nov. 19, 1969; March 1, 1970; Nov. 29, 1970; Dec. 15, 1970; p. 25, March 10, 1971; March 11, 1971; May 16, 1971; July 16, 1971; July 19, 1971; p. 10, Nov. 14, 1971; Dec. 5, 1971; March 14, 1972.

Niebuhr, H. Richard, and Daniel B. Williams (eds.): *The Ministry in Historical Perspectives,* Harper & Row, Publishers, Inc., New York, 1956.

Norwood, William F.: *Medical Education in the United States before the Civil War,* University of Pennsylvania Press, Philadelphia, 1941.

Norwood, William F.: "Medical Education in the United States before 1900," in C. D. O'Malley (ed.), *The History of Medical Education,* University of California Press, Berkeley, 1970.

O'Dea, Thomas F.: "The Intellectual in the Catholic Tradition," *Daedalus,* vol. 101, pp. 151–189, Spring 1972.

Oliphant, Robert E.: "Clinical Education at the University of Minnesota," in Edmund W. Kitch (ed.), *Clinical Education and the Law School of the Future,* The University of Chicago Law School, Chicago, 1970.

Olmsted, Ann G., and Marianne A. Paget: "Some Theoretical Issues in Professional Socialization," *Journal of Medical Education,* vol. 44, pp. 663–669, August 1969.

O'Neil, Robert M.: "Preferential Admissions Equalizing Access to Legal Education," *The University of Toledo Law Review,* vol. 1970, nos. 2–3, pp. 281–320, Spring–Summer 1970.

"On the Rise," *Juris Doctor,* vol. 1, p. 44, April 1971.

Page, Robert G.: "The Different Applicant to Medical School," in Robert G. Page and Mary H. Littlemeyer (eds.), *Preparation for the Study of Medicine,* The University of Chicago Press, Chicago, 1969.

Page, Robert G.: "The Three-Year-Medical Curriculum," *Journal of the American Medical Association,* vol. 213, pp. 1012–1015, Aug. 10, 1970.

Patton, Michael J.: "The Student, the Situation and Performance during the First Year of Law School," *Journal of Legal Education,* vol. 21, no. 1, pp. 10–51, 1968.

Pincus, William: "The Lawyer's Professional Responsibility," *Journal of Legal Education,* vol. 22, no. 1, pp. 1–21, 1969.

Pincus, William: "Changing Today's Law Schools," *CLEPR Newsletter,* vol. 4, no. 4, pp. 1–7, September 1971.

Pins, Arnulf M.: *Who Chooses Social Work, When, and Why?* Council of Social Work Education, New York, 1963.

Pins, Arnulf M.: "Changes in Social Work Education and Their Implications for Practice," *Social Work,* vol. 16, no. 2, pp. 5–15, April 1971.

Poole, Stafford, C. M.: *Seminary in Crisis,* Herder and Herder, Inc. New York, 1965.

"A Preliminary Report of the Committee on Specialization," *Journal of the State Bar of California,* 1969, pp. 140–187.

Pusey, Nathan, M., and Charles L. Taylor: *Ministry for Tomorrow: Report of the Special Committee on Theological Education,* Seabury Press, Inc., New York, 1967.

Reader, W. J.: *Professional Men: The Rise of the Professional Classes in Nineteenth-Century England,* Basic Books, Inc., Publishers, New York, 1966.

"A Record Number of Minority Group Members Are Admitted to Medical Schools, But Many Drop Out," *The New York Times,* p. 4, Nov. 21, 1971.

Reed, Alfred Z.: *Training for the Public Profession of the Law,* Carnegie Foundation Bulletin, New York, Nov. 15, 1921.

Reich, Charles: "Toward the Humanistic Study of Law," *Yale Law Journal,* vol. 74, pp. 1402–1408, July 1965.

Reichert, Irving F., Jr.: "The Future of Continuing Legal Education," in Geoffrey C. Hazard, Jr. (ed.), *Law in a Changing America,* Prentice-Hall, Inc., Englewood Cliffs, N.J., 1968.

Rein, Martin: "Social Work in Search of a Radical Profession," *Social Work,* vol. 15, no. 2, pp. 13–28, April 1970.

Report of the Association of American Medical Colleges Task Force to the Inter-Association Commission on Expanding Educational Opportunities in Medicine for Blacks and Other Minority Students, Stanford, Calif., Apr. 22, 1970.

Richan, Willard C. (ed.): *Human Services and Social Work Responsibility,* National Association of Social Workers, 1969.

Ridberg, Michael D.: "Student Practice Rules and Statutes," in Edmund W. Kitch (ed.), *Clinical Education and the Law School of the Future,* The University of Chicago Law School, Chicago, 1970.

Riesman, David: "Law and Sociology: Recruitment, Training and Colleagueship," in William M. Evan (ed.), *Law and Sociology,* The Free Press of Glencoe, Division of Macmillan Company, New York, 1962.

Riesman, David: "Some Observations on Legal Education," *Wisconsin Law Review,* vol. 63, no. 1, pp. 63–82, University of Wisconsin Law School, Madison, 1968.

Rockwell, David N.: "The Education of the Capitalist Lawyer: The Law School," in Robert Lefcourt (ed.), *Law Against the People,* Vintage Books, Random House, Inc., New York, 1971.

Rosen, Sumner M.: "Upgrading and New Careers in Health," *Social Policy,* vol. 1, pp. 15–24, January–February 1971.

Rothman, Jack: "Three Models of Community Organization Practice," *Social Work Practice, 1968: National Conference on Social Welfare,* Columbia University Press, New York, 1968.

"Salaries Paid by Public Health Nursing Services—1967," *Nursing Outlook,* vol. 15, pp. 46–49, December 1967.

Sanazaro, Paul J.: "The Response of Medical Schools," in Robert G. Page and Mary H. Littlemeyer (eds.), *Preparation for the Study of Medicine,* The University of Chicago Press, Chicago, 1969.

Savoy, Paul: "Today a New Politics of Legal Education," *The Yale Law Journal,* vol. 70, no. 3, pp. 444–504, January 1970.

Scherer, Ross P., and Theodore Wedel (eds.): *The Church and Its Manpower Management: A Report of the First National Consultation on Church Personnel, Policies, and Practices,* Department of Publication Services, National Council of the Churches of Christ in the U.S.A., New York, 1966.

School of Social Administration, Self Study Report, Vol. 1, Description of the Program; Vol. 11, Appendix, Temple University, Philadelphia, November 1970.

School of Social Welfare: *Social Welfare at Stony Brook: A Self Study,* State University of New York at Stony Brook, Stony Brook, 1970.

Schreckenberger, Paul C.: "Playing for the Health Team," *Journal of the American Medical Association,* vol. 213, pp. 279–281, July 13, 1970.

Seldin, Donald W.: "Some Reflections on the Role of Basic Research and Service in Clinical Departments," *Journal of Clinical Investigation,* vol. 45, pp. 976–979, June 1966.

Selinger, Carl M.: "Functional Division of the American Legal Profession: The Legal Paraprofessional," *Journal of Legal Education,* vol. 22, pp. 22–36, 1969.

Shanahan, Eileen: "President Bypasses Women for Court," *The New York Times,* p. 68, October 3, 1971.

Shanahan, Eileen: "Women Lawyer Pool Rising," *The New York Times,* October 22, 1971, p. 10.

Sheps, Cecil G.: "The Medical School—Community Expectations," in Hans Popper (ed.), *Trends in New Medical Schools,* Grune & Stratton, Inc., New York and London, 1967.

The Shorter Oxford English Dictionary on Historical Principles, 2d ed., Clarendon Press, Oxford, 1936.

Shryock, Richard Harrison: *Medicine and Society in America: 1960,* New York University Press, New York, 1960.

Smigel, Erwin O.: *The Wall Street Lawyer,* Indiana University Press, Bloomington, 1969.

Souter, Lamar: "The Wedding of an Off-Campus Medical School with a Community of Moderate Size," in Hans Popper (ed.), *Trends in New Medical Schools,* Grune & Stratton, Inc., New York and London, 1967.

Statistics on Social Work Education, Council on Social Work Education, New York, Nov. 1, 1970.

Stevens, Robert: "Aging Mistress: The Law School in America," *Change,* vol. 2, pp. 32–42, January–February 1970.

Stolz, Preble: "Clinical Experience in American Legal Education: Why Has It Failed?" in Edmund W. Kitch (ed.), *Clinical Education and the Law School of the Future,* The University of Chicago Law School, Chicago, 1970.

Stolz, Preble: "Training for the Public Profession of the Law, 1921: A Contemporary Review," unpublished (mimeographed) memorandum included as an appendix to the *Report of the American Association of Law Schools Curriculum Committee,* May 1971.

"Strategy for Change by the Tripartite Commission of the Rutgers Law School, May 6, 1970," in Robert Lefcourt (ed.), *Law against the People,* Vintage Books, Random House, Inc., New York, 1971.

Strauss, Anselm, L.: "Medical Ghettos," *Transaction,* vol. 4, no. 6, pp. 7–15, 62, May 1967.

Stumpf, Jack: "Developing the Social Work Practice Curriculum at San Diego State College," Dec. 31, 1970. (Mimeographed.)

Thielens, Wagner, Jr.: "Some Comparisons of Entrants to Medical and Law Schools," in Robert K. Merton, George Reader, and Patricia L. Kendall (eds.), *The Student Physician,* Harvard University Press, Cambridge, Mass., 1957.

The Undergraduate Program in Social Welfare at Stony Brook, State University of New York at Stony Brook, March 1971.

U.S. Bureau of the Census: *Statistical Abstract of the United States: 1970,* 1970.

U.S. Catholic Conference: *The Catholic Priest in the United States: Sociological Investigation,* Publishing Office, Washington, D.C., 1972.

U.S. Department of Health, Education and Welfare: *Closing the Gap . . . in Social Work Manpower,* Report of the Departmental Task Force on Social Education and Manpower, November 1965.

U.S. Department of Health, Education and Welfare Social and Rehabilitation Service: *National Study of Social Welfare and Rehabilitation Workers, Work, and Organization Contexts,* SRS-ORDO177, April 1971.

Van Loon, Eric E.: "The Law School Response: How to Make Students Sharp by Making Them Narrow," in Bruce Wasserstein and Mark J. Green (eds.), *With Justice for Some: An Indictment of the Law by Young Advocates,* Beacon Press, Boston, 1970.

Vargas, Philip: "Some Observations on the 'Professionalization' of Law Students," Harvard Law School, 1969 (unpublished paper).

Wagoner, Walter D.: *The Seminary: Protestant and Catholic,* Sheed and Ward, Inc., New York, 1966.

Walsh, John: "Stanford School of Medicine (III): Varieties of Medical Experience," *Science,* vol. 171, no. 3974, pp. 785–787, Feb. 26, 1971.

Warkov, Seymour, and Joseph Zelan: *Lawyers in the Making,* Aldine-Atherton Publishing Co., New York, 1965.

Weber, Max: *Economy and Society,* Bedminster Press, Totowa, N.J., 1968.

Weiskotten, Herman G., Alphonse M. Schwitalia, William D. Cutter, and Hamilton H. Anderson: *Medical Education in the United States, 1934–1939,* prepared for the Council on Medical Education and Hospitals of the American Medical Association, Chicago, 1940.

Wexler, Stephen, "Practicing Law for Poor People," *The Yale Law Journal,* vol. 79, pp. 1049–1067, May 1970.

White, A. Sandri: *Guide to Religious Education, Directory of Seminaries, Bible Colleges, and Theology Schools, Covering USA and Canada,* Aurea Publishers, Allenhurst, N.J., 1965.

White, James J.: "Women in the Law," *Michigan Law Review,* vol. 65, pp. 1051–1122, 1967.

Wilensky, Harold L., and Charles N. Lebaux: *Industrial Society and Social Welfare,* The Free Press, New York, 1965.

Wilson, B. R.: "Pentecostal Ministers: Role Conflict and Status Contradiction," *American Journal of Sociology,* vol. 64, pp. 494–504, March 1959.

Wilson, John P.: "Clinical Programs at Boston University School of Law," in Edmund W. Kitch (ed.), *Clinical Education at the Law School of the Future,* The University of Chicago Law School, Chicago, 1970.

Wise, Harold: "Training for Social Medicine with Emphasis on Internal Medicine and Pediatrics," *Postgraduate Medicine,* vol. 48, pp. 183–187 August 1970.

Wolfbein, S.: *Work in American Society,* Scott, Foresman & Co., Glenview, Ill., 1971.

Wolfft, Robert Paul: *The Ideal of the University,* Beacon Press, Boston, 1969.

Yegge, Robert B., Wilbert E. Moore, and Howard Holme: "New Careers in Law," 1969, in *Report of the A.A.L.S. Curriculum Committee,* May 1971.

Index

This book was set in Vladimir by University Graphics, Inc.
It was printed on acid-free, long-life paper and bound by
The Maple Press Company. The designers were Elliot Epstein
and Edward Butler. The editors were Nancy Tressel and
Terry Y. Allen for McGraw-Hill Book Company and Verne A.
Stadtman and Sidney J. P. Hollister for the Carnegie Commission
on Higher Education. Bill Greenwood supervised the production.